More Effective Resources for Able & Talented Children

Barry Teare

Published by Network Educational Press Ltd.
PO Box 635
Stafford
ST16 1BF

© Barry Teare 2001

ISBN 1 85539 063 9

Barry Teare asserts his moral right to be
identified as the author of this work.

All rights reserved. No part of this publication may be reproduced,
stored in a retrieval system or reproduced or transmitted in any form or
by any means, electronic, mechanical, photocopying (with the exception of the
following pages, which may be copied for use in the purchasing institution: 16–41, 45–79,
83–102, 106–156, 159–171, 175–189, 194–218, 221–244, 247–256, 259–268),
recording or otherwise, without the prior written permission of the publishers.
This book may not be lent, resold, hired out or otherwise disposed of by way of
trade in any form of binding or cover other than that in which it is published
without the prior consent of the Publishers.

Every effort has been made to contact copyright holders
of materials reproduced in this book.
The Publishers apologise for any omissions and will be
pleased to rectify them at the earliest opportunity.

Edited by Gina Walker
Design & layout by
Neil Hawkins, Network Educational Press Ltd.
Illustrations by Barking Dog Art, Stroud, Glos.

Printed in Great Britain by
MPG Books Ltd., Bodmin, Cornwall.

Contents

Introduction		5
Theme One:	English, Literacy	13
Theme Two:	Mathematics, Numeracy	42
Theme Three:	Science	80
Theme Four:	Humanities, Citizenship, Problem Solving, Decision Making, Information Processing	103
Theme Five:	Modern Foreign Languages	157
Theme Six:	Young Children	172
Theme Seven:	Logical Thought	190
Theme Eight:	Detective Work, Codes	219
Theme Nine:	Lateral Thinking	245
Theme Ten:	Competitions	257

Special Acknowledgement

This book is dedicated to Christina Teare in grateful thanks for her
encouragement, patience and tireless efforts in the production of not only this book
but also the two earlier publications by the author for
Network Educational Press – *Effective Provision For Able And Talented Children* (1997)
and *Effective Resources For Able And Talented Children* (1999).

Introduction

On The Menu ... 'Cream Of Curriculum'

Many areas of prescribed content can be delivered in a challenging and entertaining way. In this book there are lots of examples of work that does exactly that. This is one of the key messages of this book and its two predecessors for Network Educational Press – *Effective Provision For Able And Talented Children* (1997) and *Effective Resources For Able And Talented Children* (1999).

Such a method of working is one way to solve another of the current concerns, that of time. The other is to recognise that most able children complete standard tasks quickly and well. (A minority do not because they are both able and idle and this presents other problems to be solved.) Consequently, these children make time that can be used for more challenging work, as long as that time is not wasted by doing more of the same. The time problem is that of the teacher and, again, the hope is that books like this one and its predecessor will provide hard-pressed teachers with material that they can use immediately.

There are, then, positive ways forward to deal with a climate in which many teachers are worried that they are not able to challenge able pupils due to curriculum guidelines that they see as both prescriptive and time-consuming. They also feel that their creativity has been shackled and, as a result, they are not able to employ methods that they would want to use for excitement, enrichment and enjoyment.

Professor Ken Robinson's committee – the National Advisory Committee on Creative and Cultural Education – produced its report in 1999, entitled *All Our Futures: Creativity, Culture and Education* (DfEE Publications). A telling passage in the introduction states:

> *'The curriculum is already over-full and we think it should be thinned out. We want teachers to have more freedom to use their own creative and professional skills. Greater freedom for teachers in the classroom will help to promote creative teaching and this is essential to promote creative learning.'*

In *More Effective Resources For Able And Talented Children*, the author has endeavoured to provide resources within this spirit, which do work in schools to provide challenge, enjoyment and good results.

The Balance Of The Menu

It is physically impossible for any teacher to use exciting, challenging methods for every lesson of every day of every week. Some standard tasks have to be covered and human energy is not inexhaustible. However it is very important that 'cream of curriculum' is on offer for a reasonable percentage of the time. Able pupils need enrichment even if that is not feasible for the whole of the time.

It is also necessary to realise that the menu covers many other types of provision. Undoubtedly, normal classroom lessons are the highest priority by far. Even so, teachers need tasks and resources for differentiated homework, enrichment days, weekends, summer schools, cluster activities, clubs, societies and competitions. The author has borne this in mind in writing this book, with various contexts suggested for many pieces of work.

The 'Curriculum Code'

When using particular items of work in this book, it is important to understand why they are there, how they fit the theory about able children and how they deliver curriculum guidelines. These points are covered in the commentaries for each Theme and the teaching notes for pieces of work.

Many aspects of life lead participants to develop a list of principles to be followed – The Country Code, for instance. Below is a suggested Curriculum Code to keep in mind while using items from the book.

The Curriculum Code

- Do not underestimate what able pupils can do, including young able children.
- Make every effort to regard curriculum guidelines as building bricks from which to explore rather than straitjackets to restrict.
- Use enjoyable methods and tasks to deliver even the most serious of purposes.
- Encourage alternative approaches and answers and make space for them.
- Use the time that able children create to enrich, to expand and to extend, not to repeat.
- Give space and encouragement for able children to develop work along their own lines.
- See all children, including the most able, as individuals in terms of starting-point, number of steps needed to accomplish the task and preferred learning styles.
- Plan to increase the proportion of higher order thinking skills within schemes of work, question-and-answer sessions and individual tasks.
- Use a judicious mix of the various types of differentiation – outcome, resource, task, dialogue, support, pace, content and responsibility.
- Do not clutter able children with too much instruction – let them think for themselves.
- Give able children their fair share of the teacher's time and attention but in appropriate ways.
- Use the characteristics of ability in an area of the curriculum to help inform provision in that same area.
- Build a rich provision for able children from a programme involving the classroom, extra-curricular activities, cluster activities and opportunities within the community but recognise that normal lessons are substantially more important than anything else.

Using This Book

The resources are set out in ten Themes, some of which combine elements together. The commentary at the beginning of each Theme introduces relevant theory, links the items to curriculum guidelines in both England and Scotland and describes the contents of that section. The teaching notes that follow each piece of work give solutions where appropriate but they also discuss why the piece is suitable for able children and the various ways in which the work can be used.

The resources have been grouped in Themes but this is sometimes a somewhat arbitrary process as they are linked to other Themes and areas of the curriculum. Do not let Theme titles put you off from using pieces in other ways. Theme Six, for instance, is entitled 'Young Children', but it includes items that could be used profitably with older children. The suggestions in *Twice Upon A Time* (page 182) have been employed with great success with sixth-formers.

At the end of each commentary you will see:

ATTENTION

This is to draw your attention to other pieces of work in other Themes of this book and in the author's two previous books for Network Educational Press – *Effective Provision For Able And Talented Children* (1997) and *Effective Resources For Able And Talented Children* (1999). Those two books also contain theory on all aspects of providing for able children and most especially on curriculum principles. They do, therefore, expand the ideas expressed in this introduction.

To assist readers further in seeing the various possibilities of individual resources, there follows a summary guide to all the resources in book order.

Summary Guide To The Resources In This Book

KEY TO SYMBOLS

Theme	Symbol
Theme One: English, Literacy	
Theme Two: Mathematics, Numeracy	
Theme Three: Science	
Theme Four: Humanities, Citizenship, Problem Solving, Decision Making, Information Processing	
Theme Five: Modern Foreign Languages	
Theme Six: Young Children	
Theme Seven: Logical Thought	
Theme Eight: Detective Work, Codes	
Theme Nine: Lateral Thinking	
Theme Ten: Competitions	
Older Children	

THEME ONE: ENGLISH, LITERACY

Title	Brief description	Other applicable areas
Ten To Net	word play	
Tin Can	word play	
Bitter Sweet	oxymorons	
Nuts And Bolts	pairs	
A School Of Whales	collective nouns	
Achilles Heel	reviving classical references	
Tempting Titles	reading, writing, deduction	
The Mystery Unfolds	collaborative writing	
Every Picture Tells A Story	writing from picture and written clues	

THEME TWO: MATHEMATICS, NUMERACY

Title	Brief description	Other applicable areas
Fox, Rabbit, Rat	hilarious game	
Crossnumbers	the mathematics equivalent of crosswords, mathematical language	
Single Surprise	calculation, problem solving	
Ancient Romans	puzzle using Roman numerals, palindromes	
Professor Remains	puzzle using equations	
Watch Carefully	time, problem solving	
Running Total	patterns, real-life mathematics from cross-country running	
And That Leaves One!	patterns in mathematics via a fancy dress competition	
Par For The Course	the mathematics of golf	
Canny Crag	the mathematics from a game of dice	
Aerial Noughts And Crosses	mental agility, co-ordinates, spatial	
Make A Date	problem solving, deduction, spatial	

THEME THREE: SCIENCE

Title	Brief description	Other applicable areas
Thanks To Science	a look at moral, social and ethical issues	
Talking Science	cryptic paragraphs to science content	
The Spider That Loves Mozart	explanation of animal behaviour	
Carol Catalyst, The Cryptic Chemist	a code in chemistry	
Running Rings Round Saturn	astronomy, physical processes, logic	

THEME FOUR: HUMANITIES, CITIZENSHIP, PROBLEM SOLVING, DECISION MAKING, INFORMATION PROCESSING

Title	Brief description	Other applicable areas
Shipping Forecast	geographical concepts and language, maps	
Anachorisms	classification, concepts, word play	
Finders Keepers ... Sometimes	documentary evidence, deduction	
Groundwork	archaeology, creativity	
Peace Treaty	citizenship, role play, problems of peacemaking	
Silence In Court	citizenship, role play, murder trial	
Tournament	organisation of games event, information processing	

THEME FIVE: MODERN FOREIGN LANGUAGES

Title	Brief description	Other applicable areas
Playing With Language	word games in the target language	
Hier sind	vocabulary work in German through a picture	
Adjectifs	a code based upon correct and incorrect use of adjectives in French	
J'Habite	a logical thought problem using French vocabulary	
Daylight Robbery	a detective exercise in German	

THEME SIX: YOUNG CHILDREN

Title	Brief description	Other Applicable Area
The Bear's Name	short logic problem on a teddy bear	
A Is For Apple, Or Is It?	code on picture book format	
Wondrous Words In The Woods	made-up words, imagination	
Twice Upon A Time	humorous creative writing, word humour	
One Thing Leads To Another	classification, sequencing	
The Terrific Toyshop	mathematics and toys	

THEME SEVEN: LOGICAL THOUGHT

Title	Brief description	Other applicable areas
The Votewell Election	logic through true and false statements	
First Past The Post	synthesis to get finishing positions in a horserace	
Take Any Five From Fifty Two	number in a problem on playing cards	
Just The Job	a short problem that could use a matrix	
Case Histories	two variables in a detective context, could use a matrix	
Detective Case Clues	three variable extension from above	
Birds Of A Feather	long logical thought exercise, mathematics, word play, content, span of concentration	

THEME EIGHT: DETECTIVE WORK, CODES

Title	Brief description	Other applicable areas
Critical Clues	five varied detective cases, logical and lateral thinking	
Cliffhanger	analysis, synthesis, map work, use of the protractor	
Mrs Pascal's Proposition	mathematical code, equations	
The Shapes	number code, use of child's comic, rhyme	
The Hidden Will Of Gresham Grange	a positioning code, map, cryptic clues, synthesis	
Searching For Words	a language code, synthesis, wordsearch	

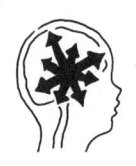

THEME NINE: LATERAL THINKING

Title	Brief description	Other applicable areas
One Question, Many Answers	twelve contrasting situations for alternative answers	
Eureka	mathematics, science, history, imagination	
Classified Information	classification, exceptions, connections	

THEME TEN: COMPETITIONS

Title	Brief description	Other applicable areas
Games Teasers	light interpretation of numbers and initials	
The People Of Britain	place names from people, geography, word play	
Snakes and Races, Squares And Quotients	mathematical language and operations	
The Millennium Sampler Competition	the most significant events of the last millennium	
Horse Sense	the word play behind the naming of horses	

Theme One: English, Literacy

As literacy schemes have become more familiar and teachers have become used to dealing with the 'mechanics', more attention has turned to the most effective way of dealing with particular groups of children, including those who are more able.

Identifying the characteristics of the most able pupils in English is one clue to providing effectively for them in curriculum planning. In both England and Scotland, major documents have listed such characteristics including the following:

> *'a cognitive grasp of quite sophisticated ideas and linguistic concepts'*
>
> *'linguistic resourcefulness'*
>
> *'imaginative versatility'*

Scottish 5–14 Guidelines on English language

> *'manipulate language, sentence structure and punctuation'*
>
> *'use apt terminology and varied vocabulary'*

National Literacy and Numeracy Strategies: Guidance on
Teaching Able Children (DfEE, January 2000)

Nor do we have to go outside mainstream advice in curriculum guidelines to find suitable themes to challenge able pupils. The Literacy Framework contains a detailed theme of vocabulary extension that allows 'pure magic' in terms of word games, the origins of words, word humour and the joy of language.

The revised National Curriculum in operation from September 2000 contains a number of exciting extracts including the following:

> *'look for meaning beyond the literal'*
>
> *'engage with challenging and demanding subject matter'*
>
> *'exploring, hypothesising, debating, analysing'*
>
> *'to analyse and discuss alternative interpretations, ambiguity and allusion'*
>
> *'how language is used in imaginative, original and diverse ways'*

Word games and word exercises set in a cryptic format are profitable methods of extending vocabulary in an enjoyable and challenging way. ***Ten To Net*** (page 16) and ***Tin Can*** (page 18) are such pieces of work. Dealing with various literary terms in an accessible way is represented in ***Bitter Sweet*** (page 20) on oxymorons. This also involves word humour and one of the characteristics of many able pupils in English is their love of puns, nuances, double meanings, and so on.

Many years ago a blue book called First Aid In English was used extensively in schools. Some of the areas covered seem to have fallen into disuse. Two of them – pairs and collective nouns – are the focus of ***Nuts And Bolts*** (page 22) and ***A School Of Whales*** (page 25) respectively. The former uses a cryptic format whereas the latter allows considerable opportunity for imaginative and creative responses that are likely to include features such as onomatopoeia and alliteration as well as word humour.

As curriculum guidelines point out, language changes. Pupils should be aware of the changes and the reasons for them. Working on the origins of new words that have come perhaps from computers or the environmental movement encourages challenging tasks. However, there have also been casualties. Classical references are little known, which is a pity as we should try to preserve richness and diversity of language. ***Achilles' Heel*** (page 30) has been written for that very purpose. Used in enrichment sessions, it has provoked considerable interest, for children still find the background stories fascinating.

Reading is represented through ***Tempting Titles*** (page 33), allowing analysis and synthesis to be combined with creativity. The effective use of a very limited number of words is also involved – a key feature of many poems.

The Mystery Unfolds (page 36) involves a particular genre but it has some unusual demands. Pupils write a chapter as part of a team. Collaborative writing is very challenging because you have to pick up clues from before and make an appropriate contribution, given your particular place in the complete story. *Improving Writing 5–14* (Scottish Executive Education Department, 1999) commented:

> '... the value of knowing the qualities of type of writing (genre, characteristics) is that they provide strategies for addressing the particular problem faced in the task.'

A different stimulus for writing is used in ***Every Picture Tells A Story*** (page 39). This uses the very productive combination of open-endedness but within some parameters – in this case the title, the picture and the accompanying paragraph.

ATTENTION

See also the resources suggested below.

Book	Theme or Section	Activity
Elsewhere in this book	Theme Three: Science	Thanks To Science
	Theme Four: Humanities, Citizenship ...	Silence In Court
		Anachorisms
		Peace Treaty
	Theme Five: Modern Foreign Languages	Playing With Language
	Theme Six: Young Children (but relevant for older pupils)	Twice Upon A Time
		Wondrous Words In The Woods
	Theme Eight: Detective Work, Codes	Searching For Words
	Theme Nine: Lateral Thinking	One Question, Many Answers
		Classified Information
	Theme Ten: Competitions	The People Of Britain
		Games Teasers
		Horse Sense
Effective Provision For Able And Talented Children, Network Educational Press, 1997	Section Six	A Capital Idea
	Section Seven	Words Are Magic, Words Are Fun
		The Geography Person
		Goldilocks
Effective Resources For Able And Talented Children, Network Educational Press, 1999	Theme One: Literacy	Carp
		Ant
		Lemon Sole
		The Missing Letter
		Doing The Proverbial
		The Full Monty
		Poetic Licence
	Theme Two: Language Across The Curriculum	Depict
		Quintessential Qualities
		Four
	Theme Three: Reading	Mole, Rat, Badger, Toad And ... Who?
		The Bare Bones
		Tangled Tales
	Theme Four: Writing	... And That Is The End Of The Story
		Straight From The Horse's Mouth
		The Man In The Van
		Mouthwatering
		Opening Up A New Chapter
	Theme Six: Science	Property To Let
		Professor Malaprop
	Theme Seven: Logical Thought	According To The Book
	Theme Eight: Codes	Crossedwords
		The Way The Wind Blows
	Theme Ten: Detective Work	Vital Evidence
	Theme Eleven: Alternative Answers, Imagination ...	The Question Is

Ten To Net

Some words make other words when spelt backwards. The title is an example: ten, net. A cryptic clue to the pair of words could be:

> More than a single figure in the back of the goal (3).

where (3) denotes the number of letters.

Your tasks

Now identify the following pairs of words, which are constructed in the same way.

1   Plural rodents feature prominently in the performance (4).
2   A restraining belt over the various components (5).
3   Succeeded in the present (3).
4   Illustrate a section of a hospital (4).
5   A curved figure makes an area of water (4).
6   Beat a game of greens (4).
7   Cooking containers break (4).
8   Strike gently the control of water (3).
9   Cut the pointed pieces of metal (4).
10 Water plant houses the hoofed animals (4).
11 A superhuman being leads to a quadruped (3).
12 Send in payment for egg measurer (5).
13 Part of a building in the upland heather (4).
14 On the contrary a bath (3).
15 Well-groomed passenger vehicles (5).

Ten To Net

Teaching notes

Solution

1. rats, star
2. strap, parts
3. won, now
4. draw, ward
5. loop, pool
6. flog, golf
7. pans, snap
8. pat, tap
9. snip, pins
10. reed, deer
11. god, dog
12. remit, timer
13. room, moor
14. but, tub
15. smart, trams

TIN CAN

Your Task

Can you identify the 20 words described below? Each contains 'tin' at the start of the word or in the middle or at the end. A clue is given together with the number of letters in the word. For example:

> Making a loud noise (8) = shou<u>tin</u>g

1. Dry wood (6).
2. Silvery-white metallic element (8).
3. A classical language (5).
4. Slight tint (5).
5. A medicinal extract in a solution of alcohol (8).
6. Part of the eye (6).
7. A small musical instrument (10).
8. A bird (6).
9. A person keeping guard (8).
10. Relating to the matter in hand (9).
11. A stinging sensation of the flesh (6).
12. An allotted or fixed amount of work (5).
13. A citrus fruit (10).
14. A smooth, glossy fabric (5).
15. Christmas decoration (6).
16. A grille of metal bars (7).
17. Route (9).
18. End of a journey (11).
19. A time for prayer (6).
20. Takes place on election days (6).

TIN CAN
Teaching Notes

Solution

1	tinder
2	platinum
3	Latin
4	tinge
5	tincture
6	retina
7	concertina
8	martin
9	sentinel
10	pertinent
11	tingle
12	stint
13	clementine
14	satin
15	tinsel
16	grating
17	itinerary
18	destination
19	matins
20	voting

Bitter Sweet

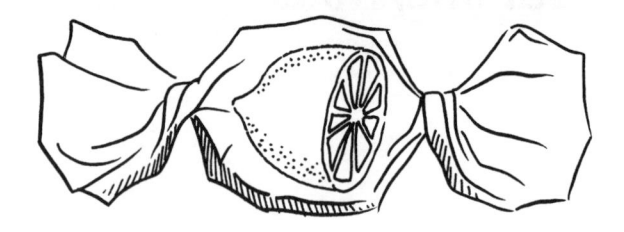

'Bitter Sweet', which gives its name to this work, is an example of a phrase that is contradictory, where opposites are brought together.

Your Task

Below are two columns, each containing 20 words. The order has been confused. You are asked to match the appropriate words as pairs to make phrases such as 'bitter sweet'.

Column one		Column two	
1	pointless	A	perfect
2	act	B	memory
3	virtual	C	natural
4	uneasy	D	ugly
5	nearly	E	doubt
6	common	F	resistance
7	forgotten	G	ruin
8	similar	H	together
9	pretty	I	silence
10	individual	J	particulars
11	well-preserved	K	absence
12	passive	L	direction
13	thunderous	M	collection
14	almost	N	awful
15	clear	O	calm
16	general	P	distinction
17	ill	Q	reality
18	perfectly	R	totally
19	conspicuous	S	health
20	alone	T	differences

Extension Tasks

1 Find out the official term for these phrases and its origin.
2 Explain the meaning of each phrase.
3 Compile some additional examples, especially those regarded as sarcastic.

Bitter Sweet

Teaching Notes

Each of these phrases is an oxymoron, from the Greek 'oxys' meaning sharp and 'moros' meaning foolish. Literally therefore oxymoron means pointedly foolish. The phrases thus bring opposites together in a paradoxical manner.

Some people delight in using oxymorons in an ironic way, such as 'military intelligence'. Oxymorons are part of the richness of our language that is promoted by references to word play in curriculum guidelines in both England and Scotland.

Solution

1–L   pointless direction

2–C   act natural

3–Q   virtual reality

4–O   uneasy calm

5–A   nearly perfect

6–P   common distinction

7–B   forgotten memory

8–T   similar differences

9–D   pretty ugly

10–M   individual collection

11–G   well-preserved ruin

12–F   passive resistance

13–I   thunderous silence

14–R   almost totally

15–E   clear doubt

16–J   general particulars

17–S   ill health

18–N   perfectly awful

19–K   conspicuous absence

20–H   alone together

Nuts And Bolts

Pairs of words are often used together to describe a situation or an object or objects. 'Fish and chips' rolls off the tongue in more than one sense! 'Nuts and bolts' is another example. A clue could be:

> The essential or practical (4 and 5).

The numbers indicate how many letters there are in the two linked words.

Your Task

Can you identify the 20 pairs of words described by clues below?

1. Invalid (4 and 4).
2. Stranded (4 and 3).
3. Disgusted or weary (4 and 5).
4. Obvious, especially in a case (4 and 4).
5. Livelihood, perhaps in the kitchen (5 and 6).
6. Contrasting fortunes (3 and 5).
7. Search out a popular game for children (4 and 4).
8. The 'ordinary' members (4 and 4).
9. Very neat and clean (5 and 4).
10. Make a rapid escape or exit from a situation (3 and 3).
11. Putting everything you have got into something (5 and 4).
12. In a very low state (4 and 3).
13. Tides and situations change (3 and 4).
14. A firm or inflexible rule or situation (4 and 4).
15. Methods of dealing with a problem (4 and 5).
16. Detailed information in written and numerical form (5 and 7).
17. Exciting action at a great pace (4 and 7).
18. Dismissing an argument as having no merit nor reason (5 and 8).
19. A crude and elementary way of dealing with a situation (5 and 5).
20. The misdemeanour is followed by the penalty (5 and 10).

Nuts And Bolts

Optional Sheet Of Mixed Up Answers

This sheet can be used in conjunction with the title sheet as an aid to reaching the answers. This can be used at the start or after an attempt has been made using the initial clues only.

The correct 20 answers follow, but not in the correct order. Match them with the clues.

- **A** stuff and nonsense
- **B** bread and butter
- **C** rank and file
- **D** crime and punishment
- **E** null and void
- **F** cut and run
- **G** rough and ready
- **H** fast and furious
- **I** heart and soul
- **J** ups and downs
- **K** high and dry
- **L** sick and tired
- **M** spick and span
- **N** hide and seek
- **O** open and shut
- **P** down and out
- **Q** hard and fast
- **R** ebb and flow
- **S** ways and means
- **T** facts and figures

Nuts And Bolts
Teaching Notes

Nuts And Bolts is a demanding piece and some pupils find it difficult. The optional sheet of mixed-up answers (page 23) has been provided to allow an alternative method; that is, matching two lists. A compromise solution is to get children to work on the initial sheet first and see how far they get. If they are in difficulty or at the end of what will be achieved, the extra sheet can then be used.

Solution

1. null and void
2. high and dry
3. sick and tired
4. open and shut
5. bread and butter
6. ups and downs
7. hide and seek
8. rank and file
9. spick and span
10. cut and run
11. heart and soul
12. down and out
13. ebb and flow
14. hard and fast
15. ways and means
16. facts and figures
17. fast and furious
18. stuff and nonsense
19. rough and ready
20. crime and punishment

A School Of Whales

A 'school of whales' is an example of a collective noun or name. Such phrases add colour to our language and, often, they convey a humorous image.

Part One

Your Task

Below there are two columns of words – the first refers to collective nouns, the second to the group they describe. The lists are out of order. Your task is to sort them out correctly.

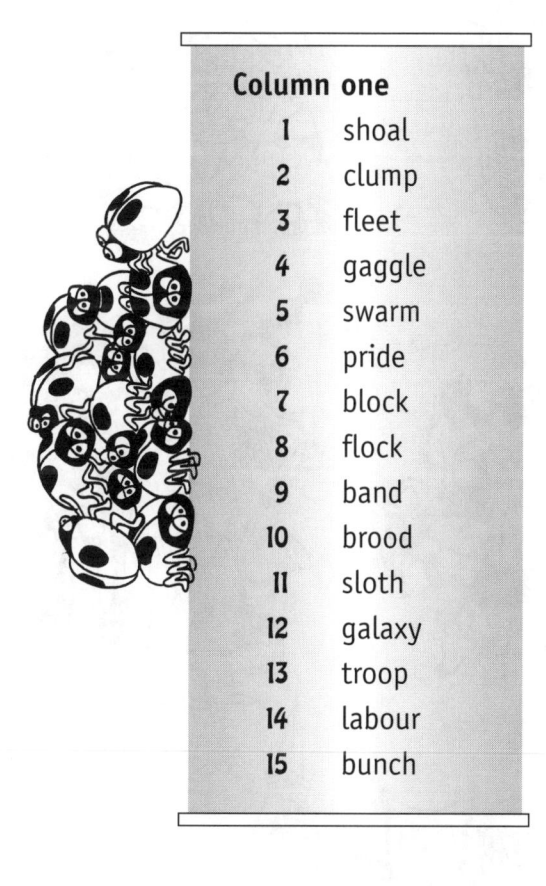

Column one		Column two	
1	shoal	A	sheep
2	clump	B	moles
3	fleet	C	flowers
4	gaggle	D	fish
5	swarm	E	gorillas
6	pride	F	trees
7	block	G	chickens
8	flock	H	bears
9	band	I	geese
10	brood	J	ships
11	sloth	K	bees
12	galaxy	L	baboons
13	troop	M	flats
14	labour	N	lions
15	bunch	O	stars

2/4 A School Of Whales

Part Two

Your Task

Below are phrases involving ten collective nouns or names in pictorial form. See if you can work out what the pictures represent.

A School Of Whales

Part Three

Steve Palin, in his wonderful book *A Dissimulation Of Birds* (Minerva Press, 1998), has produced a catalogue of collective nouns of birds. For example:

A Chime Of Wrens

A Siege Of Herons

For each bird, Steve Palin has illustrated the initial letter of the collective noun, written about the bird and commented upon the origins of the phrase.

Your Task

Your task is to follow Steve Palin's example but under the title:

A Kennel Of Dogs

For each dog, create an appropriate collective name and write a sentence or two to explain its supposed origin.

Start with these particular dogs:

- labradors
- poodles
- alsatians
- spaniels
- boxers

Then carry out the same exercise with dogs of your choice.

If you enjoy drawing you may also wish to produce an illustrated initial letter of the collective name.

A School Of Whales

Part Four

Some phrases have been in use for a considerable period of time. The joy of language, however, is that it is always changing and additions appear. Now is the chance for you to create some collective names of your own.

Your Task

What collective names would you use to describe the following?

A   referees
B   judges
C   traffic wardens
D   hedgehogs
E   disc jockeys
F   robots
G   vultures
H   skateboarders
I   computer fanatics
J   surfers

Add others of your own choosing.

Part Five

Now let us reverse the process. Below there are collective names but without the group that they describe.

Your Task

Complete the following:

1   a crunch of ...
2   a relaxation of ...
3   a cool of ...
4   a grace of ...
5   a mock of ...
6   a clutter of ...
7   a danger of ...
8   an explosion of ...
9   a celebration of ...
10   a snap of ...

Again, add others of your own choice.

A School Of Whales
Teaching Notes

Curriculum guidelines on English encourage the varied use of language. Collective nouns are a rich source of colour and interest. They used to be very much in fashion in terms of classwork but in recent years less attention has been paid to them. Some parts of the work here are concerned with existing collective nouns – some well known, others not so well known. Part two involves pictorial representation, which is helpful for those who have a visual preferred learning style.

Parts three, four and five move into a different context, allowing pupils to use their imagination and creativity to come up with some examples of their own. Made-up words based upon linguistic principles are featured in the National Curriculum for English and in the Literacy Framework. This creative use of language is a joy to many able pupils as is the opportunity to explore word humour.

Contexts

A **School of Whales** can be used for a variety of purposes:

- as extension material to other work on vocabulary and literary terms
- as an enrichment activity for those well ahead in their normal work
- as differentiated homework
- as an activity within a word-based enrichment session, summer school or cluster day
- as an open-access competition
- as an activity for the English Club.

Answers

PART ONE

1–D	a shoal of fish	2–F	a clump of trees	3–J	a fleet of ships
4–I	a gaggle of geese	5–K	a swarm of bees	6–N	a pride of lions
7–M	a block of flats	8–A	a flock of sheep	9–E	a band of gorillas
10–G	a brood of chickens	11–H	a sloth of bears	12–O	a galaxy of stars
13–L	a troop of baboons	14–B	a labour of moles	15–C	a bunch of flowers

PART TWO

1	a cloud of flies	2	a parcel of penguins	3	a sea of faces
4	a litter of cubs	5	a carpet of flowers	6	a bank of clouds
7	a herd of cows	8	a band of musicians	9	an army of ants
10	a parliament of owls				

NOTE

- Answers for parts three, four and five will include a number of possibilities. Quality depends upon suitability and creativity. Onomatopoeia and alliteration are also likely to figure.

ACHILLES' HEEL

You and your friends will know a number of words and expressions that have come into our language in recent years through developing areas of life. Computer terms and language linked to the environmental movement are good examples. In addition, you use existing words in new ways from past generations, such as 'cool' and 'wicked'.

However, you may not be so familiar with equally exciting and rich words and expressions that originate in mythology and classical literature. The stories behind them are fascinating.

THE TEN WORDS AND PHRASES

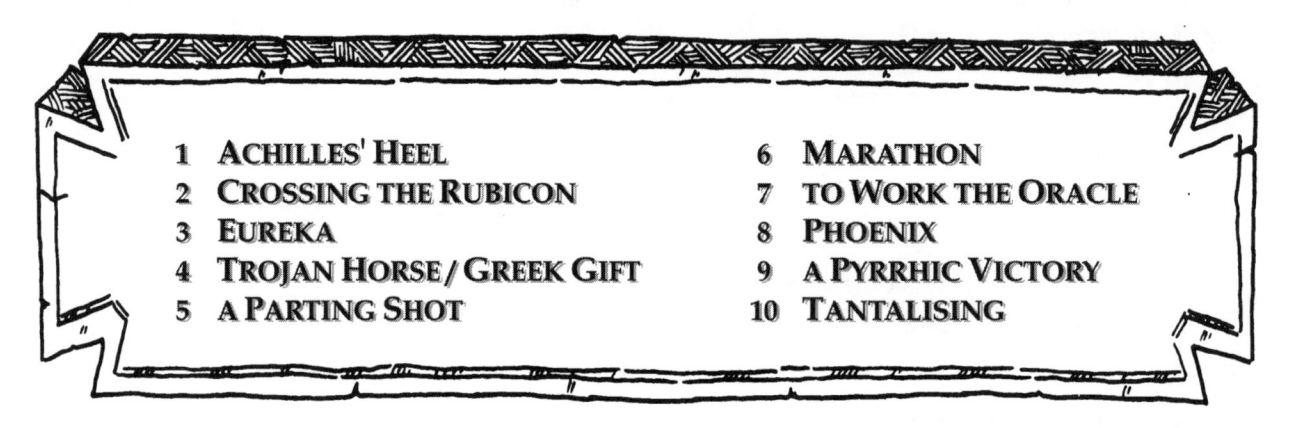

1. ACHILLES' HEEL
2. CROSSING THE RUBICON
3. EUREKA
4. TROJAN HORSE / GREEK GIFT
5. A PARTING SHOT
6. MARATHON
7. TO WORK THE ORACLE
8. PHOENIX
9. A PYRRHIC VICTORY
10. TANTALISING

Your Tasks

For each of the ten words or phrases:
1. Explain the meaning when used in everyday language.
2. Describe the origin of the word or phrase.
3. Explain how the original situation has led to the current meaning and usage.

Extension Task

Write a paragraph for some or all of the ten words and phrases so that the current meaning is clearly demonstrated by your passage.

Further Reading

There are many enthralling stories to read concerning folktales, mythology and ancient civilisations, including:

Anancy And Mr Drybone, Fiona French (Frances Lincoln)
Black Ships Before Troy, Rosemary Sutcliffe (Frances Lincoln)
Book Of Creation Stories, Margaret Mayo (Orchard)
Greek Myths For Young Children, Marcia Williams (Walker)
Orchard Book Of Greek Myths, Geraldine McCaughrean (Orchard)
Seasons Of Splendour, Madhur Jaffrey (Puffin)
The Puffin Classics Myths And Legends, Roger Lancelyn Green (Puffin)
The Story Of King Arthur, Robin Lister (Kingfisher)
The Wanderings Of Odysseus, Rosemary Sutcliffe (Frances Lincoln)

ACHILLES' HEEL

Teaching Notes

Language is always changing. Our vocabulary has been enriched in recent years by the addition of new words coming from developing areas such as computers and growing environmental awareness. Unfortunately there have also been some losses. Classical literature is no longer as well known, with the result that children have lost the use of many rich words and expressions. Achilles' Heel looks to renew interest in those words and expressions.

Contexts

Achilles' Heel can be used in the following ways:

- as differentiated homework
- as an enrichment activity for pupils ahead with their normal work
- as extension material to work on word origins
- as an activity within an enrichment session, summer school or cluster day.

The Ten Words And Phrases

ACHILLES' HEEL
Thetis took her son Achilles by the heel, and dipped him in the River Styx to make him invulnerable, but the heel in her hand remained dry. Achilles was killed by an arrow wound in the heel, his only weak spot.

As a result 'Achilles' Heel' is an expression used to refer to a small weakness, but one that can be very damaging to a person, and that can be exploited.

CROSSING THE RUBICON
The Rubicon was a small river between ancient Italy and Cisalpine Gaul, the province allotted to Julius Caesar. When Caesar crossed this stream in 49 BC he became an invader into Italy. This led to war.

'Crossing the Rubicon' means to take an irrevocable step.

EUREKA
Archimedes wanted to test the purity of Hiero's crown but at first did not know how. In getting into a full bath he saw that some of the water ran over. Archimedes realised that a body must displace its own bulk of water when immersed. He also found that the crown was deficient in gold and contained some silver by using the same experiment – pure gold of a certain mass displaces less water than 'contaminated' gold of the same mass, because it has a greater density.

The Greek word 'heureka', meaning 'I have found out', is therefore a phrase used when somebody finds a solution or way forward (most often in the form 'eureka').

TROJAN HORSE/GREEK GIFT
After the death of Hector, during the siege of Troy by the Greeks, Odysseus had a large wooden horse made and said that it was an offering to the gods to secure a prosperous voyage back to Greece. The Trojans, thinking the Greeks were defeated and had left, dragged the horse within

Achilles' Heel

their city. It was full of Grecian soldiers who stole out at night, killed the guards, opened the city gates and set fire to the city.

A 'Trojan horse' is therefore something that seems good but turns out to be a problem, and a 'Greek gift' is a treacherous gift ('Beware of Greeks bearing gifts'). A Trojan horse is an enemy within. In computing, this term is used to refer to a programme that is supposed to be carrying out some routine function but which breaches the security of the computer system.

A PARTING SHOT

This is a corruption of 'a Parthian shot', referring to the practice of Parthian horsemen of firing arrows at their pursuers as they rode away.

A 'parting shot' is a telling remark made while leaving that gives little chance of reply.

MARATHON

After the battle of Marathon (490 BC) a runner went to Athens to announce the result, having run 23 miles.

A 'marathon' is a long-distance run but the word is also used for a long-lasting event or effort.

TO WORK THE ORACLE

In Ancient Greece, oracles gave answers to questions about the future. Often an ambiguous response was given. For example, Pyrrhus – being about to make war against Rome – was told by the oracle, *'I believe, Pyrrhus, that you the Romans can conquer'*. Another prince was told, *'You shall go you shall return never you shall perish by the war'* (where are the commas?!).

'To work the oracle' means to persuade somebody to support a plan or project even when the chance of success is slight.

PHOENIX

This was an Arabian bird that, according to Greek legend, lived a certain number of years before burning itself to ashes. It then came to life again.

'Phoenix' refers to anything that comes back to life or existence after destruction, 'rising from the ashes'.

A PYRRHIC VICTORY

Pyrrhus, king of Epirus, won a battle in 279 BC but at a very heavy cost – he lost all his best officers and many men.

'A pyrrhic victory' is a victory won at too heavy a price.

TANTALISING

In Greek mythology, Tantalus offended the gods. He was plunged up to the chin in a river in Hades, a tree hung with clusters of fruit being just above his head. Every time he tried to drink, the waters receded from him and the fruit was always just out of reach. So he kept expecting his hunger and thirst to be satisfied but they never were.

'Tantalising' means tormenting or teasing by the sight or promise of what is unobtainable. (Also note that a tantalus is a chest containing bottles of spirit that can be seen but not reached without a key.)

Tempting Titles

It is said that you should never judge a book by its cover. However, it is undoubtedly true that certain features do help to sell a book. One of the features is an intriguing or tempting title – something that fits the novel and that captures the reader's interest.

Your Task

Below there is a synopsis for each of ten different novels. You are asked to make up a tempting title for each, which is appropriate for the story and entices the reader or customer. Explain your choice of title.

BOOK ONE
This book has a historical setting – France at the time of Napoleon. The heroine, Catherine Dumas, is from an English family but now lives near Paris. She risks her own safety to gain valuable information for her home country by taking advantage of her connections in French society gained when she married Paul Dumas.

BOOK TWO
A property tycoon, Keith Rendell, is anxious to acquire a piece of countryside near Northampton to complete his ownership of a sizeable area that he intends to turn into executive homes and exclusive leisure facilities. The local environmental group, led by Barbara Turner, has to use every available means to protect Worsley Woods from the rich developer.

BOOK THREE
A fantasy story aimed at 8–11 year old children, this book is very much about the age-long struggle between good and evil. The brother and sisters, Amy, Larry and Tanya Smithers, find themselves in the magical land of Gracia where the peace and happiness of the inhabitants is being threatened by the power of Eil Brovis and her followers. The story ends with a titanic battle to determine the fate of Gracia.

BOOK FOUR
This is a 'whodunnit' in the classical style of English village murders. The body of local celebrity actress Vivienne Mackay is found behind the fortune teller's tent during the fete at Lower Stonebarrow in the Cotswolds. Chief Inspector Roger Fernley and Sergeant Mary Wilde uncover a number of motives for the murder before the truth is finally revealed.

Tempting Titles

BOOK FIVE
Here we have a tragic love story with a not-so-happy ending. Jason Jackson overcomes social disadvantage, ill fortune and prejudice to win the love of Joyce Denby, daughter of wealthy barrister Lionel Denby, only to find that his happiness is short-lived.

BOOK SIX
Jill Brownsley is modelled upon the character of real North Country vet Susan Grant in this entertaining tale of life among the farmers and their animals in Cumbria. Jill wrestles not only with a variety of animal illnesses and injuries but also the prejudice of a male-dominated country society. Episodes of great humour are punctuated with moments of sadness and despair.

BOOK SEVEN
This is a detective story but with a difference for the 'sleuth' is not a modern day policeman but rather a merchant in the reign of Elizabeth I. The merchant, Walter Effingham, wins the favours of his queen by solving an unpleasant murder that occurs at court.

BOOK EIGHT
Based upon the exploits of the SAS during the Gulf War, this is a fast-moving thriller. Gordon Lightfoot, aptly named, is involved in a dangerous mission behind enemy lines to secure information about mobile missile-launchers that are threatening neighbouring countries.

BOOK NINE
The friendship between local teenager Brian Andrews and political refugee Ruela Zvarbo is the focal point in this powerful novel about racial prejudice and intolerance. Set against the rise of a small but extremely unpleasant and violent neo-Nazi group, the story highlights the power of determination.

BOOK TEN
The hilarious story of an outwardly staid and ultra-respectable bank manager who decides that she has had enough of rules, regulations and paperwork and instead joins an environmental protest group. The exploits of Carole Yorke as she grapples with a new life in the trees and in underground tunnels are full of humour but they are also thought-provoking and challenging.

Tempting Titles

Teaching Notes

Curriculum guidelines for English include phrases such as:

> *'... use inference and deduction.'*
> *'... how language is used in imaginative, original and diverse ways.'*
> *'... identifying the genre of a text.'*

All three areas are involved in **Tempting Titles** which, like poetry and mini-sagas, puts a premium on the choice of each word.

The ten books reflect some of the various genres that pupils are likely to encounter. They have been given enough data to inform their choice of title, without overloading them with too much detail, which might begin to narrow down the range.

Contexts

Tempting Titles could be used in a number of ways:

- as normal classwork linked to reading and writing activities
- as normal homework linked to reading and writing activities
- as differentiated homework
- as a competition piece for teams
- for individuals as a piece of extension or enrichment work when they have finished ahead of the class
- as part of an enrichment activity
- as an English or Reading Club activity.

Success Criteria

The quality of response is likely to be judged by the following criteria:

- the appreciation of the genre
- the originality, creativity and imagination displayed
- the suitability for the likely target audience
- the skills of inference and deduction shown by using the 'clues' in the synopsis
- the choice of words, given how few can be used.

The Mystery Unfolds

You write for a variety of purposes but have you tried to write collaboratively before?

In 1931, a detective novel called *The Floating Admiral* was published. It was written by members of the Detection Club – members were writers of detective stories, some of them with extremely well-known names, such as Dorothy Sayers, G. K. Chesterton and Agatha Christie. Each of the contributors wrote one chapter and it was their task in turn to continue the story and to develop clues already included. At the end of the book the authors each gave the solution that they would have written. It is fascinating to see how different those solutions were.

Here is a chance for you to try something similar.

Your Task

Provided on a separate sheet is the start of a detective story that has been written for you (unlike the Detection Club scenario, where one of the members started off the story with Chapter One). You should work in small groups of perhaps four or five. Decide among yourselves the order in which you are going to write. The last person must of course end the story with a 'solution'. The number of chapters will depend upon the number of people in the group (plus your 'starter' of course). Make sure that your chapter continues the story and that it makes use of the clues already given. Add an appropriate title.

You may like to adopt one of the ideas used for *The Floating Admiral* project by having each member of the group write briefly about the development plan and a solution that would follow logically from the end of their own particular chapter. When the story is complete, compare the various developments and solutions that have been suggested.

Chapter One

Detective Inspector Little rang the door bell and waited. After a short delay, the door was opened by an anxious-looking woman in her thirties.

'Mrs Adams?' asked the detective.

'Yes, I'm Judy Adams,' she replied.

'Detective Inspector Little, Brantley CID,' the man said, holding up his identification card. He then followed Judy Adams into the luxurious lounge of the smart, detached house that was typical of the prosperous suburb.

Judy Adams beckoned for the inspector to sit down and, after he had refused politely the offer of a cup of tea, she explained why she had telephoned the police station.

'I just do not know what to do. My husband, Bernard, has just disappeared into thin air without any warning or explanation. It doesn't make any sense. What is going on?'

'Keep as calm as you can, Mrs Adams, and tell me, in as much detail as possible, the events leading to your husband's disappearance,' responded the detective.

'My husband works for a firm of solicitors in town – indeed he is one of the partners. He is good at his job and he has made good progress. As you can see from the house, we are comfortably off. However, recently, Bernard has been very touchy about money. He has questioned me about items of expenditure that normally he would ignore. Bernard is usually easy-going but in the last two or three months he has been irritable and on edge as though something is worrying him. When I asked him if there was a problem he dismissed my enquiry in a very off-hand way.

'Things have got worse in the past few days. As I was tidying up last week, I picked up a piece of paper with the title 'Contingency Plan' on the top. Bernard snatched it from me and told me to leave his possessions alone. The night before last he did not notice me passing by his study door while he was on the telephone. He sounded both frightened and angry. I do not know who he was talking to but I caught some of his comments – "I told you that I would not be party to violence" and "The signature would not fool an expert".

'Within minutes he went out carrying a briefcase that I have not seen previously. Bernard muttered something about important business that would not wait and that he would not be long.

'Inspector Little, that was eight o'clock on Wednesday evening and it is now Friday morning. I have not heard from Bernard since. Whatever can have happened?'

The Mystery Unfolds
Teaching Notes

The Mystery Unfolds uses the vehicle of a detective story. Creative writing combines with logical thought and the deductive process, thus developing a requirement stated in the new National Curriculum for English document, to:

> '... develop logical arguments and cite evidence.'

The first chapter given allows various possibilities but it does lay down a number of important points that should not be ignored. The 'crime' itself is as yet unspecified and pupils can take a number of routes.

Challenge

Participants have to take a number of factors into account:

- the genre
- the opening chapter with its pointers and suggestions
- writing as a team or group to complete the story.

Each writer has to give consideration to the stage reached, what has gone before and how much 'space' needs to be left.

It is this element that makes **The Mystery Unfolds** a very challenging piece of writing.

Context

There is a strong practical consideration to think through – that is, when the work should be done, as only one person in each group can write at any one time. In class another activity would need to be set against this work. An alternative is to fit the individual chapters into the homework schedule.

Extension Task

The detective genre has been used here but clearly the same process can be employed for any type of story. If the teacher prefers a different genre, he or she needs to create an appropriate opening chapter in the required style.

Every Picture Tells A Story

Ideas for writing come from many sources. In this piece of work the stimulus is a picture – four pictures, in fact, linked to titles and background information.

Your Task

Choose one or more of the following titles to write a story based on the picture and information given:

- Sensation
- The Scene Of The Crime
- Dig A Little Deeper
- Christmas Comes But Once A Year

Success Criteria

For any piece of work you should know in advance how it will be judged. The success criteria for *Every Picture Tells A Story* are as follows:

- ✔ The story fits the title.
- ✔ The details in the picture are used to inform the writing.
- ✔ The 'pointers' in the paragraph of information are noted and included.
- ✔ Imagination and creativity are displayed.
- ✔ An appropriate genre is adopted.

Sensation

This picture shows the scene of a mysterious episode that captured the imagination of people far and near. Of great significance in those happenings were the tree on the viewer's right and the stretch of water shown. The families who lived in the cottages, just out of the picture to the viewer's left, never forgot those incredible days.

Your Task

Write a story based upon the information given above to fit the title *Sensation*.

Every Picture Tells A Story

The Scene Of The Crime

This picturesque country setting, not far from the coast in East Anglia, was the scene of a crime that became one of the most celebrated cases in police records. Normally attention is drawn towards brutal events but this was not so in this case. Perhaps what intrigued the public was the brilliant detective work by the officer-in-charge.

Your Task
Write the story of a case set in the location shown in the picture, which fits its claims to be fascinating but not brutal.

Dig A Little Deeper

The house and garden had been left derelict and neglected for many years. It was only when new owners took over the property that the fantastic discovery was made. It started as an ordinary afternoon's gardening but nobody could have predicted the course of events that followed.

Your Task
Dig A Little Deeper into your imagination and write a story originating from the scenario above.

Christmas Comes But Once A Year

'Christmas comes but once a year, And when it does it brings good cheer.'

This is a well-known saying. However, for one particular family in 1999 it certainly did not apply. As you can see from the picture, all the preparations were in place but the very objects that normally bring pleasure and joy, on this occasion brought quite opposite results.

Your Task
Write a story explaining why this particular family were very relieved in 1999 that Christmas Comes But Once A Year.

Every Picture Tells A Story

Teaching Notes

The four picture-based scenarios are examples of material that allows pupils to use their imagination in what is an open-ended situation but with some parameters. It is this combination that many educationalists believe provides the most creative opportunities.

There are a large number of interpretations. For instance, these particular pictures, and the accompanying information, could lead to stories on:

- *Sensation* – fantasy, ghosts, unnatural happenings
- *The Scene Of The Crime* – a detailed police investigation full of forensic evidence used in a clever way
- *Dig A Little Deeper* – an incredible archaeological discovery
- *Christmas Comes But Once A Year* – a disaster resulting from unsafe presents.

The pupil instruction has been left in a general form deliberately so as not to restrict thinking through too much detail.

Success Criteria

These are as described on the initial pupil sheet (page 39) and should be made known ahead of the writing.

Further Examples

Many other pictures or photographs could be used in a similar way.
For wonderfully drawn pictures, see *The Mysteries of Harris Burdick*, by Chris Van Allsburg, (Andersen Press, reprinted 1999).

Contexts

Every Picture Tells A Story can be used:

- as a normal classroom activity
- for homework
- as an enrichment item when a child has completed set work ahead of others
- as an English competition
- as part of an enrichment session in one school or in a cluster.

Theme Two: **Mathematics, Numeracy**

Creating a good ethos is essential in any area of the curriculum. It is particularly important in mathematics, where some children feel that the work is not only hard but, at times, dull. The great majority of able mathematicians love the subject but sometimes find themselves faced with too many routine tasks, insufficient challenge and 'more of the same' when finishing tasks quickly and well. Homework also presents opportunities for a differentiated challenge but that possibility is not exploited as much as it might be.

There are important pointers in official documents:

> '… it is vitally important that teaching remains lively and stimulating.'
>
> '… non-routine problems which require pupils to think for themselves.'
>
> 'The widespread good practice in Scotland of emphasising problem solving and using appropriate real-life contexts promotes pupils' interest.'

Improving Mathematics Education 5–14 (Scottish Office Education and Industry Department, 1999)

> '… problem solving, through selecting and using methods and techniques, developing strategic thinking and reflecting on whether the approach taken to a problem was appropriate.'
>
> '… improving own learning and performance, through developing logical thinking, powers of concentration, analytical skills and reviewing approaches to solving problems.'

The National Curriculum (DfEE/QCA, 1999)

Able mathematicians make time by completing tasks quickly and well – unless they are highly able but idle, which poses a different set of problems. The key question is how this time is to be utilised. 'More of the same' is illogical, as those who need least practice do more than anybody else. It is also damaging, as some able pupils fail to see the point of finishing quickly if all they do is to continue with similar examples. There are many schemes taking place to promote five-year acceleration so that Year Six pupils take GCSE courses. If this approach is taken, it is vital that the partners in the child's education make sure that there is no repetition of material, especially at the transfer to secondary school. Consideration should be given to using the time produced to explore exciting and challenging areas of mathematics that are not normally fitted into the curriculum for reasons of time.

Mathematical language, and its use through specially designed tasks and activities, remains a priority for curriculum guidelines and rightly so. The following extracts are typical:

> '... communication, through learning to express ideas and methods, precisely, unambiguously and concisely.'
>
> '... use the correct language, symbols and vocabulary associated with number and data.'

The National Curriculum (DfEE/QCA, 1999)

Fox, Rabbit, Rat (page 45) is a very enjoyable way of exploring mathematics language and operations. This is particularly true of the extension work suggested, with its links to *Acute* in *Effective Resources For Able And Talented Children* (Network Educational Press, 1999). *Crossnumbers* (page 47) covers a large number of terms and operations within a puzzle format.

Ability at computation and calculation is a fascinating topic in that it is sometimes used overwhelmingly to identify able mathematicians when in fact it is only one of several relevant factors. Indeed, there are many able pupils who are not particularly good at calculation.

> '... may not be exceptional in carrying out calculations, but may see calculations as detail and less important than the problem as a whole.'

National Literacy and Numeracy Strategies: Guidance on Teaching Able Children (DfEE, 2000)

Single Surprise (page 50) has calculation as a strong element but within an information processing context and also involving synthesis of data.

Tackling mathematics in a wide variety of settings is valuable. *Ancient Romans* (page 54) and *Professor Remains* (page 56) use a puzzle format to deliver Roman numerals and equations respectively. They show content being handled in an unusual way and the latter poses pupils the problem of how to work mathematically from the information given.

Problem solving situations are promoted strongly in both England and Scotland. *Watch Carefully* (page 58) deals with the calendar and leap years and there are a number of potential slips to be avoided.

Solving real-life problems is another theme that is stressed. *Running Total* (page 60) is based upon mathematics in the outside world although some of the details have been altered. The piece also involves selecting the appropriate mathematics (see National Curriculum extract, above). Patterns of numbers give a pointer to the solution. Seeing a mathematical pattern, and the reason for it, is at the heart of *And That Leaves One!* (page 62), which uses the strange vehicle of a children's fancy dress competition at the seaside.

Sometimes the actual mathematics in a situation is not that difficult but it has to be used in an unfamiliar context. That is certainly true of *Par For The Course* (page 65) where a range of simple calculations like fractions have to be dealt with but are hidden within substantial text and systems relating to golf. Considerable synthesis is required. The same is true for *Canny Crag* (page 73) but the game this time is dice. Emphasis is placed upon logical thinking and extraction of information.

Spatial mathematics makes different demands to other branches of mathematics. *Aerial Noughts And Crosses* (page 75) is very demanding and it requires concentration, spatial awareness, visualisation and mental agility. It can be used either for individuals or for teams. It gives practice with co-ordinates. *Make A Date* (page 77) does have a spatial component but it also involves deduction, synthesis, problem solving and a little practical activity.

As is appropriate for a book written during the Year Of Mathematics (2000), this Theme includes twelve very varied items that aim to give enjoyment and challenge and to support an exciting subject ethos based upon the joys inherent in mathematics.

ATTENTION

See also the resources suggested below.

Book	Theme or Section	Activity
Elsewhere in this book	Theme Six: Young Children	The Terrific Toyshop
	Theme Seven: Logical Thought	Take Any Five From Fifty Two
		Birds Of A Feather
	Theme Eight: Detective Work, Codes	Cliffhanger
		Mrs Pascal's Proposition
		The Shapes
	Theme Nine: Lateral Thinking	Eureka
		Classified Information
	Theme Ten: Competitions	Snakes And Races,
		Squares And Quotients
Effective Resources For Able And Talented Children, Network Educational Press, 1999	Theme Two: Language Across The Curriculum	Four
	Theme Five: Numeracy, Mathematics	Acute
		Board With Numbers?
		In The Balance
		The Year Of The Dragon
		Lucky Programme
	Theme Eight: Codes	Lucky the Cat
		Mosaic
	Theme Ten: Detective Work	An Arresting Problem
	Theme Eleven: Alternative Answers, Imagination …	The Question Is

Fox, Rabbit, Rat

Here is your chance to play a fast-moving mathematical game where you really do have to have all your 'animal senses' about you. The games are fun but they are also challenging and utilise a number of important skills.

Instructions For The Game Of 'FOX'

1. Get into groups of 5, 6 or 7.
2. Nominate a person to start, who says '1'. The next person in a clockwise direction says '2', the next '3' and so on.
3. In the game of 'FOX' you are not allowed to say a number that is a multiple of 6 (for example, 18, 30) or a number that contains the number 6 (for example, 16, 26). For those numbers you say 'FOX' instead.
4. When 'FOX' is said the order of play changes direction; that is, clockwise to anticlockwise or vice-versa, depending upon the direction you have reached at the time.

Instructions For The Game Of 'FOX, RABBIT'

1. The rules are the same except for the fact that, in addition to the 'FOX' numbers, players are not allowed to say multiples of 7 (for example, 21, 28) nor numbers containing the number 7 (for example, 17, 27). For those numbers 'RABBIT' is said.
2. Some numbers need the call 'FOX, RABBIT' as they are multiples of both 6 and 7 (for example, 42) or contain both numbers (for example, 76).
3. Direction of play changes whenever 'FOX', 'RABBIT' or 'FOX, RABBIT' is called.

Instructions For 'FOX, RABBIT, RAT'

1. The rules are the same as for the previous two games except for the fact that, in addition to 'FOX', 'RABBIT' and 'FOX, RABBIT' numbers, players are not allowed to say multiples of 8 (for example, 32, 40) nor numbers containing 8 (for example, 38). For these numbers 'RAT' is called.
2. Some numbers need a combination of 'FOX', 'RABBIT' and 'RAT' to be called if more than one prohibition applies (for example, 24 is 'FOX, RAT' and 56 is 'FOX, RABBIT, RAT').
3. Direction of play changes whenever any single animal or a combination of animals is called.

More Effective Resources for Able and Talented Children © Barry Teare (Network Educational Press, 2001)

Fox, Rabbit, Rat

Teaching Notes

These games are variations upon others in use. The animal names add an extra dimension as does the combination of the numbers 6, 7, 8. It is a good idea to make a different person in the group start with the number 1 so that the players do not get used to their particular calls.

Features Of The Game

Clearly a major feature is that of fun and enjoyment – a commodity in short supply in some learning situations.

There are other, very real skills, involved:

1. listening skills – part of the National Curriculum
2. concentration – an important element in our 'ten second soundbite society'
3. following instructions – a generic feature
4. group dynamics – are members of the group pleasant to each other or do they make fun of those who make mistakes?
5. number work of two types – memory work and use of multiplication tables to avoid numbers like 24 and 32, but also visualisation to avoid numbers such as 17, 26 and so on. This involves a very simple contrast of preferred learning styles.

Variations

1. The games can be played collaboratively. If a mistake is made the group starts again. Able children are likely to try to set an unofficial world record!
2. The game can be played competitively so that when a player makes a mistake he or she drops out.
3. For younger or less able children the numbers can be amended.

Extensions

1. Participants can make up their own games based upon similar principles. This allows anybody up to professors of mathematics to devise and play their own versions.
2. Some of these versions can involve considerable mathematical language.
3. This piece is designed to be linked with **Acute** in *Effective Resources For Able And Talented Children* (Network Educational Press, 1999).
4. It would be interesting to set up a mathematics investigation into the consequences of having different sized groups for the games and therefore how much work each player has. Some games almost become 'table tennis' in sections as the calling falls upon certain players with many changes of direction.

Crossnumbers

You are familiar with crosswords and their play on language. Now try your hand at 'crossnumbers' with two important differences – numbers are placed, not letters, and the emphasis is upon mathematical language and operations. A rectangle has been used for the grid rather than a square.

Crossnumbers

Across

1. The lowest four-digit palindromic number.
3. 45 in base 7.
5. 5^4
8. 7!
9. A baker's dozen of baker's dozens.
11. 21 squared.
14. The sum of two angles in a triangle where the third angle is 110°.
15. The hypotenuse of a right-angled triangle where the other two sides are 9 and 12 units.
17. A traditional emergency call to ten centuries minus one.
18. The first three odd numbers in reverse order.
19. Apart from 1 and itself, the only factor is 7.
20. The perimeter of a rectangle where the length is 400 units and the width is 182 units.
23. The ninth triangular number.
24. Three-quarters of 52.
25. 2^5
26. You have one in ____ chance of drawing the nine of clubs from a pack of cards that includes two jokers.
29. A two-digit number where both digits are odd and the second digit is the square root of the first.
30. The numbers of ways in which the letters of the word PARTY can be arranged.
33. A three-digit number where the first digit is the sum of the other two.
35. The product of mean and median from the numbers 33, 22, 25, 33, 23, 24, 29.
36. Four different even digits.
37. This number can be represented as *xyx* where $y = 2x$.
38. The number of faces on a dodecahedron.

Down

1. Is the sixth prime number unlucky for some?
2. Three less than James Bond.
3. One of the angles of an equilateral triangle.
4. Comes before '6 down' in the clues but one after it in the sequence.
6. The eighth Fibonacci number.
7. The square root of 321,489.
8. One more than a half century.
10. Degrees in a right angle.
12. 17 cubed.
13. In Roman terms, M more than '12 down'.
16. A four-digit number consisting of the same odd number repeated four times.
17. The much greater probability left from one chance in a million
19. The mode of 40, 43, 47, 39, 43, 47, 43, 40.
21. A palindromic square of a palindrome.
22. Four centuries.
27. The cubic units of a box measuring 22 by 18 by 12 units.
28. This number is < the previous down clue by six score.
31. The radius of a circle where the diameter is 5126 units.
32. The number of degrees in a circle.
34. The number of days in the first six months of a leap year.

Crossnumbers

Teaching Notes

Like some pieces in *Effective Resources For Able And Talented Children* (Network Educational Press, 1999), **Crossnumbers** plays to mathematical language and to versatility and agility as so many different operations and terms are covered, one after the other.

Areas Covered

- angles in a triangle
- baker's dozen
- base 7
- calendar
- century
- cubes
- degrees in a circle
- diameter
- dodecahedron
- equations
- equilateral triangles
- even
- factor
- factorial
- Fibonacci sequence
- fractions
- leap years
- less than
- mean
- median
- mode
- odd
- palindromic numbers
- perimeter
- permutations
- powers
- prime numbers
- probability
- Pythagoras
- radius
- right angles
- Roman numerals
- score
- square root
- squares
- triangular numbers
- volume

Contexts

Crossnumbers can be used in the following ways:

- an item in an enrichment day, weekend or week
- as a differentiated homework
- as extension work for those ahead in normal work
- as a Mathematics Club activity
- as a competition for individuals or teams.

Extension

Pupils can be asked to design their own 'crossnumbers' piece of work, either with some necessary elements to be included or totally open-ended.

Solution

¹1	0	²0	1		³6	⁴3		⁵6	⁶2	⁷5
3		0		⁸5	0	4	0		⁹1	6	9	¹⁰
		¹¹4	¹²4	1				¹³5		¹⁴7	0
¹⁵1	¹⁶5		9			¹⁷9	9	9			
	¹⁸5	3	1		¹⁹4	9		²⁰1	²¹1	6	²²4
²³4	5		3		²⁴3	9		²⁵3	2		0
	²⁶5	²⁷4		²⁸4		²⁹9	3		³⁰1	³¹2	0
³²3		³³7	1	6		9		³⁴1		5	
³⁵6	7	5		3		9		³⁶8	2	6	4
0		³⁷2	4	2		³⁸1	2		3		

Single Surprise

One evening Gillian went round to see her friend, Katie. When she arrived, Katie was listening to the Top 30 Programme on the radio. Katie said how much she had liked the single that had just finished and she made it clear that she would buy it when her pocket money allowed. Gillian thought no more about it for the time being, especially as Katie switched the radio off.

When Gillian got back home she remembered that it was Katie's birthday the following week. She wanted to surprise her friend by buying the single she had liked. The problem was that Gillian did not know which single it was – it had finished just before she had arrived. She sat down to think if there was a way of working it out.

Your Task

Can you work out which single Gillian should buy for Katie, by using the information provided?

GILLIAN'S JOURNEY TO KATIE'S HOUSE

1. Gillian left home just as the 6 o'clock news started.
2. It was a ten-minute walk to the bus-stop at Green Corner.
3. She waited for the next 139 bus, which was on time.
4. The bus kept to its schedule.
5. Gillian got off the bus at Rowley Road.
6. It was then a three-minute walk to Katie's house.

BUS TIMETABLE – SERVICE 139 TO DEN PARK

TOWN CENTRE	GREEN CORNER	WREN AVE.	LONG LANE	ROWLEY RD.	DEN PARK
17.05	17.15	17.22	17.30	17.38	17.45
17.35	17.45	17.52	18.00	18.08	18.15
18.05	18.15	18.22	18.30	18.38	18.45
18.35	18.45	18.52	19.00	19.08	19.15
19.05	19.15	19.22	19.30	19.38	19.45
19.35	19.45	19.52	20.00	20.08	20.15
20.05	20.15	20.22	20.30	20.38	20.45
20.35	20.45	20.52	21.00	21.08	21.15
21.05	21.15	21.22	21.30	21.38	21.45
21.35	21.45	21.52	22.00	22.08	22.15

Single Surprise

TIMING

The programme that night started at 6.15 pm.

ORGANISATION OF THE PROGRAMME

The order of play is from position 30 to number 1.

Any single used is played in its entirety. The title and artist are given during playing time and therefore no extra time needs to be added.

Not all the singles in the Top 30 are played – only those that are new entries or have 'gone up' in the chart. The single in the number 1 position is always played. Any other single that has stayed in the same position as last week, or which has fallen in position, is not played on the programme.

Any single not played still takes about 15 seconds of programme time because the presenter makes a short comment about it.

Additional Task

Perhaps you would like to create your own 'Fun Chart' with suitably named singles. Here are some suggestions by one ten-year-old:

- ★ *You're Just Lying*, by The Pretenders
- ★ *Early Morning Noise*, by The Stray Cats
- ★ *Write Soon*, by The Post Office
- ★ *Handy Man*, by Doug Ivor Young
- ★ *My Life Is Over*, by The Dead
- ★ *I'm Going To Beat You*, by The Bullies
- ★ *Heart Of Time*, by The Love Clock
- ★ *The Alphabet Song*, by Adam Barry Crutch

Single Surprise

The Top 30 Programme

The Chart That Night

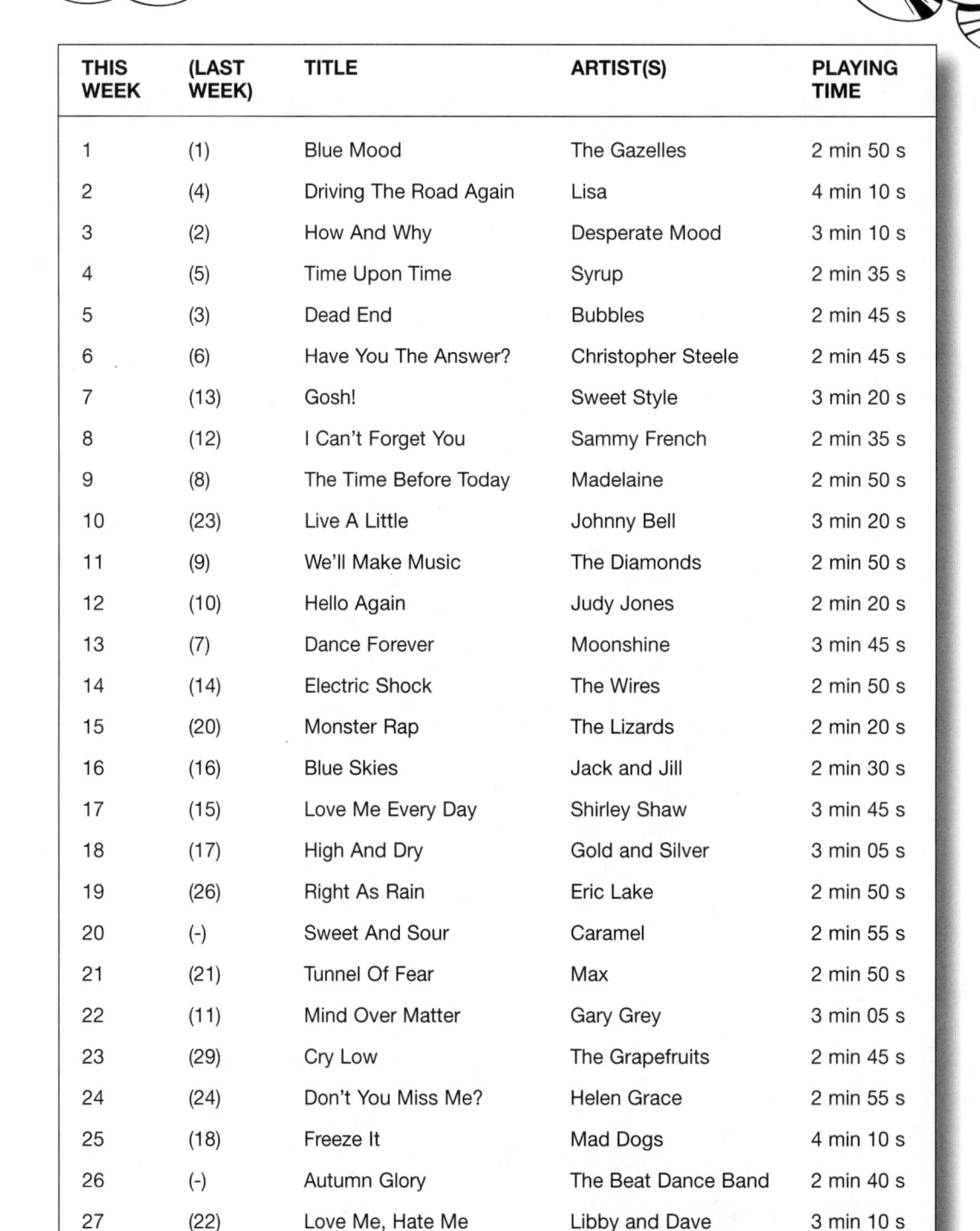

THIS WEEK	(LAST WEEK)	TITLE	ARTIST(S)	PLAYING TIME
1	(1)	Blue Mood	The Gazelles	2 min 50 s
2	(4)	Driving The Road Again	Lisa	4 min 10 s
3	(2)	How And Why	Desperate Mood	3 min 10 s
4	(5)	Time Upon Time	Syrup	2 min 35 s
5	(3)	Dead End	Bubbles	2 min 45 s
6	(6)	Have You The Answer?	Christopher Steele	2 min 45 s
7	(13)	Gosh!	Sweet Style	3 min 20 s
8	(12)	I Can't Forget You	Sammy French	2 min 35 s
9	(8)	The Time Before Today	Madelaine	2 min 50 s
10	(23)	Live A Little	Johnny Bell	3 min 20 s
11	(9)	We'll Make Music	The Diamonds	2 min 50 s
12	(10)	Hello Again	Judy Jones	2 min 20 s
13	(7)	Dance Forever	Moonshine	3 min 45 s
14	(14)	Electric Shock	The Wires	2 min 50 s
15	(20)	Monster Rap	The Lizards	2 min 20 s
16	(16)	Blue Skies	Jack and Jill	2 min 30 s
17	(15)	Love Me Every Day	Shirley Shaw	3 min 45 s
18	(17)	High And Dry	Gold and Silver	3 min 05 s
19	(26)	Right As Rain	Eric Lake	2 min 50 s
20	(-)	Sweet And Sour	Caramel	2 min 55 s
21	(21)	Tunnel Of Fear	Max	2 min 50 s
22	(11)	Mind Over Matter	Gary Grey	3 min 05 s
23	(29)	Cry Low	The Grapefruits	2 min 45 s
24	(24)	Don't You Miss Me?	Helen Grace	2 min 55 s
25	(18)	Freeze It	Mad Dogs	4 min 10 s
26	(-)	Autumn Glory	The Beat Dance Band	2 min 40 s
27	(22)	Love Me, Hate Me	Libby and Dave	3 min 10 s
28	(30)	Danger Man	David Troy	2 min 50 s
29	(-)	Wild, Wild, Wild	Eggbox	3 min 05 s
30	(25)	Too Sad	The Brown Twins	2 min 40 s

Single Surprise

Teaching Notes

This exercise contains some mathematics but it is very much concerned with following instructions and information processing. It places great emphasis upon accuracy and the correct use of details.

GILLIAN'S JOURNEY

The first task is to work out the time that Gillian arrived at Katie's house. She left home at 6.00 pm. The walk to the bus-stop takes the time to 6.10 pm. The next bus at Green Corner is 6.15 pm (18.15), arriving at Rowley Road at 6.38 pm (18.38). The three-minute walk means that Gillian got to Katie's house at 6.41 pm.

THE TOP 30 PROGRAMME

The programme started at 6.15 pm. By the time Gillian arrived at 6.41 there had been 26 minutes of the programme. We need to work from number 30 upwards by means of a cumulative total.

Number	Played	Time	Cumulative time
30	✗	0.15	0.15
29	✓	3.05	3.20
28	✓	2.50	6.10
27	✗	0.15	6.25
26	✓	2.40	9.05
25	✗	0.15	9.20
24	✗	0.15	9.35
23	✓	2.45	12.20
22	✗	0.15	12.35
21	✗	0.15	12.50
20	✓	2.55	15.45
19	✓	2.50	18.35
18	✗	0.15	18.50
17	✗	0.15	19.05
16	✗	0.15	19.20
15	✓	2.20	21.40
14	✗	0.15	21.55
13	✗	0.15	22.10
12	✗	0.15	22.25
11	✗	0.15	22.40
10	✓	3.20	26.00

By the time Gillian got into the house the single that had just finished was Number 10, *Live A Little* by Johnny Bell and therefore that was the one she should buy for Katie's birthday.

Additional Task

This is included as a fun item and acts as a contrast to the detailed and accurate work involved in the main task. Playing on words is an activity that a great number of able children enjoy.

Ancient Romans

A remarkable citizen of Ancient Rome lived until he was 107 years old. He had a five-letter palindromic name, which was made up of Roman numerals. The five separate numerals added together equalled the age at which he died. Perhaps this wasn't surprising as his father had lived to 112 years of age. His name was constructed in the same way and again the numerals added together gave a total to equal his age at death.

Your Task

What was the Roman citizen's name and what was the name of his father?

Ancient Romans
Teaching Notes

Ancient Romans is a short fun piece. It involves looking at a different number system – that of ancient Rome. The simple calculations are carried out in an unusual setting.

Contexts

Ancient Romans can be used for a variety of purposes:

- as an enrichment item for those well ahead on normal number work
- as differentiated homework
- as an activity within an enrichment session, summer school or cluster day
- as an activity for the Mathematics Club or Society.

Some Solutions

The man is	**LIVIL**	50 + 1 + 5 + 1 + 50	= 107
His father was	**VICIV**	5 + 1 + 100 + 1 + 5	= 112
or	**LIXIL**	50 + 1 + 10 + 1 + 50	= 112

Have you found any other solutions?

PROFESSOR REMAINS

Professor Remains keeps his own records on places of interest. He also uses his own symbols and among them there are:

Site of antiquity   **Battle site**   **Church**

The professor gives an historical interest rating to each town depending upon the places that can be visited there.

Your Task

If the town of Ruins is rated at 31, Maps at 23, and Plans at 32, what rating would be given to the town of Excavation?

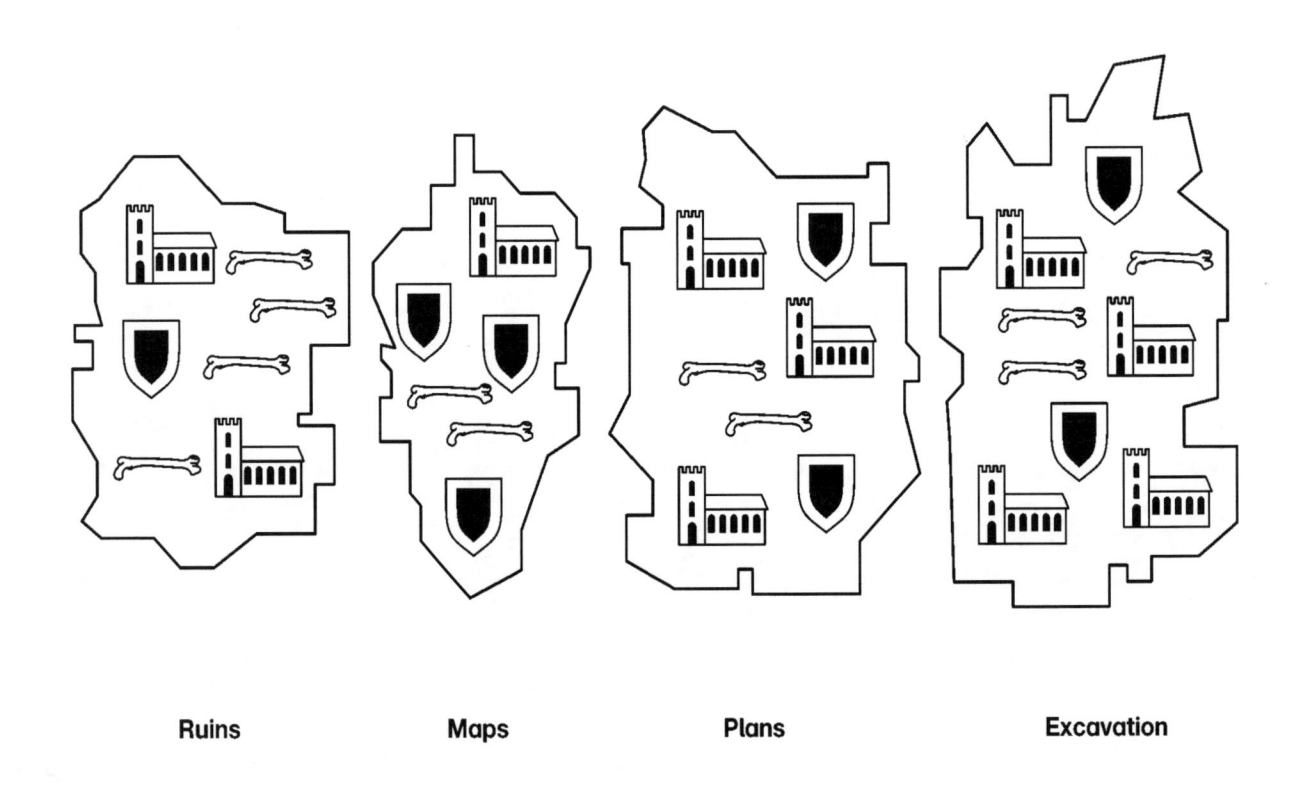

Ruins   **Maps**   **Plans**   **Excavation**

PROFESSOR REMAINS

Teaching Notes

Professor Remains fits an area of mathematics curriculum guidelines – symbols and equations, particularly simultaneous equations. It is an abstract piece, an important element for many able pupils. The setting is unusual and the first task is to explore the data and to decide upon which mathematical route to follow.

Contexts

Professor Remains can be used in the following ways:

- as extension material to work on algebra
- as an enrichment item for those ahead in normal classroom work
- as differentiated homework
- as an activity within an enrichment session, summer school or cluster day
- as an activity for the Mathematics Club or Society.

Solution

Below is one method of solving the problem. There may be others.

1. Let a stand for Sites of Antiquity, b for Battle Sites and c for Churches.

RUINS	$4a + b + 2c$	$= 31$	(1)
MAPS	$2a + 3b + c$	$= 23$	(2)
	$\therefore c = 23 - 2a - 3b$		(4)
PLANS	$2a + 2b + 3c$	$= 32$	(3)

2. Substitute (4) into (1)

	$4a + b + 46 - 4a - 6b$	$= 31$
	$-5b$	$= -15$
	$\therefore b$	$= 3$

3. Substitute (4) into (3), with $b = 3$,

	$2a + 6 + 69 - 6a - 27$	$= 32$
	$-4a$	$= -16$
	$\therefore a$	$= 4$

4. Put $a = 4$, $b = 3$ into (1),

	$16 + 3 + 2c$	$= 31$
	$2c$	$= 12$
	$\therefore c$	$= 6$

5. **EXCAVATION'S** rating $= 3a + 2b + 4c = 12 + 6 + 24$ $\qquad = 42$

WATCH CAREFULLY

Jimmy was delighted when he was given a new watch for his birthday in 1979. He was particularly pleased when he realised that it showed the date as well as the time.

After a number of weeks he was upset to find that the date he used on his work at school was underlined in red as being incorrect. In disgust he stopped using the watch to tell him the date. On October 9th, 1980, he took his watch back to the shop where it had been bought. 'It doesn't give the date properly,' he complained bitterly to the assistant. 'Look, it says October 4th.'

The assistant took the watch into the workroom at the back of the counter. Two minutes later he returned, smiling. 'There's nothing wrong with the watch,' he said. 'You haven't read the instructions properly.'

Your Tasks

1. What had Jimmy done wrong?

2. In which month was Jimmy's birthday?

3. What was the first day on which the date was incorrect?

WATCH CAREFULLY

Teaching Notes

Mathematical content needs to be delivered in a challenging and enjoyable way. ***Watch Carefully*** involves the months of the year, leap years and simple calculations but within a problem solving format.

Teaching Hints

Pupils may ask the teacher a number of questions to gain additional information on the watch. They need to know that the time was correct at all times – only the date was wrong. Both date and time were accurate on Jimmy's birthday. The date changes at midnight but there is no automatic setting to take account of the differing lengths of the months. It would be better to await pupil questions and then answer, when appropriate, rather than giving this additional information too early before children think for themselves.

The problem revises work on the calendar. Pupils need to know the lengths of the months. That allows mention of the 'rhyme' (*'30 days hath September…'*) or the 'knuckles' method of remembering the month lengths (a clenched fist on the left hand gives months with 31 days as the knuckles with the other months in between. After July go back to the knuckle on the left for August).

Contexts

Watch Carefully can be used in a variety of ways:

- as extension material to work on time
- as an enrichment activity for those ahead on normal work
- as differentiated homework
- as an activity within an enrichment session, summer school or cluster day
- as an activity for the Mathematics Club or Society.

Solution

Jimmy did not put his watch forward at the ends of months shorter than 31 days.

The watch is five days wrong. Working back from October there is one day at the end of September, one at the end of June, one at the end of April and two at the end of February (pupils need to calculate that 1980 was a leap year). There is the temptation to say the birthday was in February. However, January and December both have 31 days and therefore they also could be the birthday months. Of the three possibles the correct answer is December as that is the only month in 1979 (see the first sentence in the problem).

March 1st is the first day on which the date is incorrect. Jimmy's watch would have said '30' (February 30th).

Running Total

Bill Walker enjoyed running for the school cross-country team and he was quite successful. The team ran at a number of different venues and Bill's favourite was Grange Park. During the season there were five races at Grange Park. For individual medals and certificates, each competitor's best four positions of the season were used to give a 'Running Total'. The lower the total the better, because that means that the runner has finished in a good position in the races.

In the first four races Bill finished 6th, 2nd, 8th and 19th. He realised that on the last Saturday of the season he needed a good run to replace the rather disappointing 19th. In that final race Bill finished 10th and his best four positions therefore added up to 26. As there were medals for the first three and certificates for the first ten in the final placings, Bill felt that he should be well within the awards.

When the presentations were made Bill found that he was in 9th place. He was very pleased to have got a certificate but he felt that with counting scores of 2, 6, 8 and 10 he should have finished higher than 9th. He came to the conclusion that a mistake had been made.

Do you agree? Had a mistake been made?

Points To Consider

1. Work out whether or not it was mathematically possible for Bill to have finished 9th with his race positions of 2, 6, 8 and 10.

2. Bill later realised that although he did not know many of the other runners' scores, he did know that a boy called Mark Brown had won four of the five races. Mark had not run in the final race because he was competing in an area championship. His total of 4 was unbeatable anyway. Does this additional knowledge, that one runner had four of the five possible first places, make any difference to the calculations you have made above?

3. So far you have been working on possible solutions in a mathematical sense. Is there any change in your views about Bill's final position when you consider the realities involved? Remember that although many of the runners were the same in each race there were variations due to illness, other commitments, children moving to another area, and so on. Without being able to measure these factors accurately, what difference do you think that they would have made to Bill's 'Running Total'?

Running Total

Teaching Notes

Running Total is based upon a real-life situation although the figures have been 'manipulated' for the sake of the problem. It is an example of mathematics in the wider world.

Key Elements

- ❖ synthesis of data
- ❖ a real-life context
- ❖ estimation
- ❖ problem solving
- ❖ finding the 'correct mathematics' to tackle the problem
- ❖ investigative skills

Solution

1. Yes, it is mathematically possible for Bill to have finished 9th. In fact with positions of 2, 6, 8 and 10 he could have finished anywhere between 1st and 14th inclusive. He would be 14th if the 13 runners above him in the final table had between them all the other lowest scores possible.

    Here is the way in which 13 people could get less than the 26 points Bill scored:

1 + 6 + 6 + 12 = 25		1 + 6 + 6 + 11 = 24		1 + 5 + 7 + 11 = 24	
1 + 7 + 11 + 5 = 24		1 +11 + 5 + 7 = 24		2 + 5 + 7 + 11 = 25	
2 + 5 + 7 + 10 = 24		2 + 4 + 8 + 10 = 24		2 + 8 + 10 + 4 = 24	
3 + 4 + 8 + 10 = 25		3 + 4 + 8 + 9 = 24		3 + 4 + 9 + 9 = 25	
3 + 3 + 9 + 9 = 24					

    In that case Bill would have finished 14th. (The route to the key figure of 14 is to work out how many low places there were available outside Bill's scores: for example, 5 × 1, 4 × 2, 5 × 3, 5 × 4, 5 × 5, 4 × 6 ... 5 × 12. This gives 56 places that would between them add up to 364 place points. With 4 results to count, 56 places would mean 14 other competitors and they average 26 final points each – the same score as Bill).

2. The additional knowledge does change the calculations. Mark Brown scored 4 final points and if he is taken out the other combinations available now include one 1st only. The table given above is altered accordingly. The same type of calculation gives 48 places scoring 312 points; that is, 12 competitors averaging 26 plus the outright winner, Mark Brown. Amazingly even with this additional piece of information Bill could fill any place from equal 2nd to 13th.

3. Mathematically we have seen that certain combinations were available so that Bill could have finished 9th. Common sense, however, suggests that other factors would have played a part. Some of the low scores are likely to have gone to runners outside those finishing well up the final table; for example, some children had one good run that was far better than their normal performances. Some high places in individual races are likely to have been gained by children who did not attend 4 of the 5 races due to illness, leaving the school, moving home, injury, and so on. In other words Bill's final position was almost certain to be higher than the one that was mathematically possible.

And That Leaves One!

Thirty-two children entered the fancy dress competition in the seaside resort of Babbington on August Bank Holiday Monday. The winner was Alice. From the details given below, it is possible to identify the winner by asking exactly five questions, in a particular order, and receiving the answer 'yes' without naming individual children or items in the questions.

Your Task

List the five questions, in the particular order that produces a mathematical pattern, that would identify Alice as the winner from the details below.

Extension Tasks

1. Describe the mathematics involved in the process.
2. Explain how you would write a similar exercise with different data.

The Costumes

Name	Costume	Colours	Special features
Alan	policeman	dark blue jacket and trousers, white shirt, black tie	carrying a police whistle
David	Hercule Poirot	white hat, shirt and jacket, black trousers, 'dicky bow' tie and shoes	black moustache and carrying a walking stick
Ruth	fortune-teller	red and white headscarf, white blouse, red shawl, blue skirt, white socks, black shoes	carrying a crystal ball
Roger	pirate	black headscarf, jerkin and boots, red shirt, white trousers	black eye patch and carrying a cutlass
Alice	Little Bo Peep	white bonnet, socks and shoes, blue dress	carrying a crook in one hand and a cardboard sheep in the other
Harry	David Beckham	red shirt, white shorts, black socks and boots	none
Derek	Sherlock Holmes	brown and white shirt, checked deerstalker hat, cloak and trousers, brown shoes	carrying a curved pipe

And That Leaves One!

Name	Costume	Colours	Special features
Rosemary	nurse	blue nurse's uniform, white hat and shoes	none
Paul	Noddy	blue hat and trousers, red jumper with yellow necktie, yellow shoes	bell on hat
Richard	Darth Vader	black mask and costume	carrying a laser
Dorothy	Rupert Bear	white face mask and shoes, red jumper, red and yellow check trousers, yellow shoes	none
Asif	dragon	green head and costume	none
Lucy	Humpty Dumpty	yellow head, white shirt, blue trousers, brown shoes	none
Nigel	Little Boy Blue	blue hat, shirt and trousers, black shoes	carrying a horn
Daniel	Elton John	red, gold and white glittery hat, suit and shoes	carrying a miniature black piano
Henry	postman	blue cap, jacket and trousers, black shoes	carrying a brown sack of letters
Laura	the Queen	blue hat, coat and shoes	pulling a cardboard corgi on a lead
Simon	snowman	white head and body with eyes, nose, mouth and buttons marked in black and orange	none
Tina	Florence Nightingale	white hat and apron, old fashioned blue nurse's uniform, black shoes	carrying a lamp
Graham	scarecrow	brown hat, trousers and shoes, blue jersey	straw sticking out from arms and legs
Denise	Little Red Riding Hood	red cape, dress and shoes	carrying a basket of food
Amy	clown	red pointed hat and shoes, blue and white costume with white lace cuffs	red cheeks and nose
Sheila	juggler	blue and yellow shirt, blue trousers, red shoes	juggling three silver balls
Gordon	Mad Hatter	black top hat and shoes, white shirt, blue jacket, red trousers, yellow waistcoat	none
Terence	toy soldier	red jacket, blue hat and trousers, black shoes	carrying a toy rifle
Gina	Little Miss Muffet	red dress and shoes, white pinafore	carrying a bowl and spoon
Tommy	Peter Rabbit	brown head, trousers and shoes, blue jacket	carrying a carrot
Joan	The Queen of Hearts	red and white hat and dress, white shoes	carrying a large card of her namesake
Billy	busker	white shirt, black jacket, trousers and shoes	carrying a violin and a black hat with small coins in it
Greta	rock star	red and gold shirt, white trousers, silver shoes	carrying a guitar
Hazel	conductor	white shirt, black bow tie, jacket, trousers and shoes	carrying a baton and sheaf of music
Sally	'tree protestor'	brown shirt, trousers and shoes	green leaves sticking out from clothes and carrying a placard saying 'no you don't'

And That Leaves One!

Teaching Notes

Perhaps it would be best to start with the mathematics first. Pupils are considering the numbers 32, 5 and 1. They start with 32 possibilities and end up with 1 winner by asking 5 questions. The solution is not too difficult: 1 doubled 5 times is 32 (2, 4, 8, 16, 32) or alternatively 32 halved 5 times is 1 (16, 8, 4, 2, 1).

Solution

The five questions need to be able to reduce the field by one half on each occasion. Therefore pupils are looking for combinations that answer 16, 8, 4, 2 and finally 1. A certain amount of trial-and-error is needed.

Here is one pathway that works – there may be others, including some of no obvious pattern!

Question	'Yes' for ...
1 Does blue feature in the costume?	Alan, Ruth, Alice, Rosemary, Paul, Lucy, Nigel, Henry, Laura, Tina, Graham, Amy, Sheila, Gordon, Terence, Tommy (16)
2 Is the winner a girl?	Ruth, Alice, Rosemary, Lucy, Laura, Tina, Amy, Sheila (8)
3 Is the winner dressed as a named character rather than a general category?	Alice, Lucy, Laura, Tina (4)
4 Is the winner dressed as a nursery rhyme character?	Alice, Lucy
5 Does this character carry an object?	Alice – the winner.

Extension Tasks

Pupils creating their own exercise have to create a scenario involving the same mathematics. It is best to start with the one final answer and work outwards.

Key Elements

- logical thinking
- working with mathematics in a wider context
- looking for patterns
- synthesis of data
- an unusual item
- fun and enjoyment
- challenge

Contexts

And That Leaves One! can be used in a variety of ways:

- as a piece of enrichment work in the classroom
- as an unusual piece of homework
- as a differentiated homework
- as part of an enrichment session
- as a competition between teams
- as a Mathematics Club activity.

Par For The Course

For those who think that golf is all about driving, chipping and putting, think again! A great deal of mathematics is involved, most noticeably in the scoring of matches and competitions.

Scoring in golf has many features all of its own. Each hole has a 'par' – the expected number of strokes for the expert player. One less than par is a 'birdie', two less is an 'eagle'. In the same way, one more than par is a 'bogey' and two more is a 'double bogey'. The first nine holes are known as 'out' or the 'front nine'; holes ten to eighteen are known as 'in' or the 'back nine'. Each nine holes is totalled to give a par score and all eighteen added together produce the par for the course.

In some competitions (not the professional events) all players are given a chance by means of the 'handicap' system. Regular players have a handicap – the number of shots over par in which they are expected to complete the course. When playing against better golfers, with lower handicaps, the less proficient golfers receive shots on some of the holes.
'Scratch' is the term given to playing at par for the course.

Holes on a course are par 3, 4 or 5 depending upon the length and difficulty, with the majority being par 4.

Are you ready to tee off?
If you get 'bunkered' at any time, ask for further guidance on
the golf terms and their application.

---

1 Brian and Gordon were playing at Lexington Golf Club. The par for the course is 71. As the two men were of similar ability, no shots were to be given.

At the end of the eighteen holes Brian had scored 1 eagle, 2 birdies, 12 pars, 1 bogey and 2 double bogeys. Gordon did not get an eagle; he got one more birdie but also one more bogey. He scored 11 pars and 2 double bogeys.

What were the scores for Brian and Gordon, and who won the game?

2 In professional tournaments, four rounds are played, one each day for four days. After two days comes the 'cut' when the field is reduced for the final two rounds. Often the players to continue are decided by a system that says that all those no worse than 10 strokes off the leader, or 50% of the field, whichever is the larger, are included.

Par For The Course

Nancy Davies was competing in the Open Championship at Wobirch. The par for the course was 73. On the first day Nancy finished 3 over par and in the second round she scored a 77. The total number of players in the field was 144. After two days this was the position.

Score	Number of players
4 under par	2 players
3 under par	5 players
2 under par	8 players
1 under par	7 players
par	7 players
1 over par	9 players
2 over par	4 players
3 over par	6 players
4 over par	6 players
5 over par	4 players
6 over par	4 players
7 over par	8 players
8 over par	5 players
9 over par	20 players
10 over par	21 players
11 over par	14 players
12 over par	10 players
13 over par	2 players
14 over par	1 player

a Did Nancy make the cut to play on the final two days? Explain your answer.

b There is something odd about the totality of the field. What is it? Have you got a possible explanation?

3 The scorecard for the Dissington golf links includes the following information.

HOLE	YELLOW YARDS (MEN)	PAR	STROKE INDEX	RED YARDS (LADIES)	PAR	STROKE INDEX
1	291	4	10	256	4	15
2	175	3	11	160	3	12
3	426	4	1	436	5	2
4	383	4	4	373	4	1
5	289	4	18	245	4	18
6	197	3	3	154	3	11
7	328	4	13	306	4	7
8	520	5	8	457	5	3
9	325	4	14	292	4	17
OUT	2934	35		2679	36	
10	486	5	12	449	5	4
11	296	4	17	260	4	14
12	331	4	6	291	4	8
13	426	4	2	412	5	6
14	164	3	16	143	3	16
15	353	4	5	306	4	5
16	177	3	7	152	3	10
17	322	4	9	290	4	9
18	271	4	15	260	4	13
IN	2826	35		2563	36	
OUT	2934	35		2679	36	
TOTAL	5760	70		5242	72	

The stroke index column indicates the difficulty of the holes, with that marked 1 hardest to achieve par and 18 the easiest. The holes with the lowest stroke index are those where less able players receive strokes. Thus, if a player is to receive 12 strokes, it is one for each of the holes with stroke index 1–12 inclusive.

Par For The Course

Len and Roger were playing in a men's club tournament, with full handicap allowance to be deducted from the final scores rather than using the stroke index system. Len was playing off a handicap of 8 and his less expert partner off double that.

Their respective scores at each hole were as follows.

Len	4	4	5	4	4	3	4	5	5	5	4	4	5	2	5	3	5	4
Hole	1	2	3	4	5	6	7	8	9	10	11	12	13	14	15	16	17	18
Roger	5	4	6	5	4	3	5	6	5	5	4	5	4	6	4	4	4

a Who did better in the placings, Len or Roger?

b Was this a good performance for one or both of the two players?

c If Len and Roger continued to perform at this level for several events what was likely to happen?

d Julie and Janet played a singles match on the same Dissington course. Julie was a 10 handicap player whereas Janet was 22. As a singles match it was agreed that the normal convention of three-quarters of the difference in handicaps would apply to calculate the number of strokes to be received by Janet. These strokes would be allocated on the stroke index system. Match play was to be followed; that is, the result depended upon holes won by each player rather than adding up the scores to a grand total. The players actual scores, before the handicaps and stroke index are taken into account, were as follows.

Julie	4	4	7	5	4	4	4	6	4	5	4	5	6	2	5	3	6	5
Hole	1	2	3	4	5	6	7	8	9	10	11	12	13	14	15	16	17	18
Janet	5	4	7	6	7	3	5	7	4	7	4	5	6	4	6	3	5	5

After the adjustment for the handicap differences, who won most holes and therefore won the match?

e (i) In this particular match why did the players need to complete all eighteen holes?

(ii) Explain a singles match situation where play stopped after the 15th hole.

(iii) Explain a singles match situation where one player knew he could not lose after completing the 14th hole but he did not yet know that he would win.

f According to their official handicaps, who played better, and why?

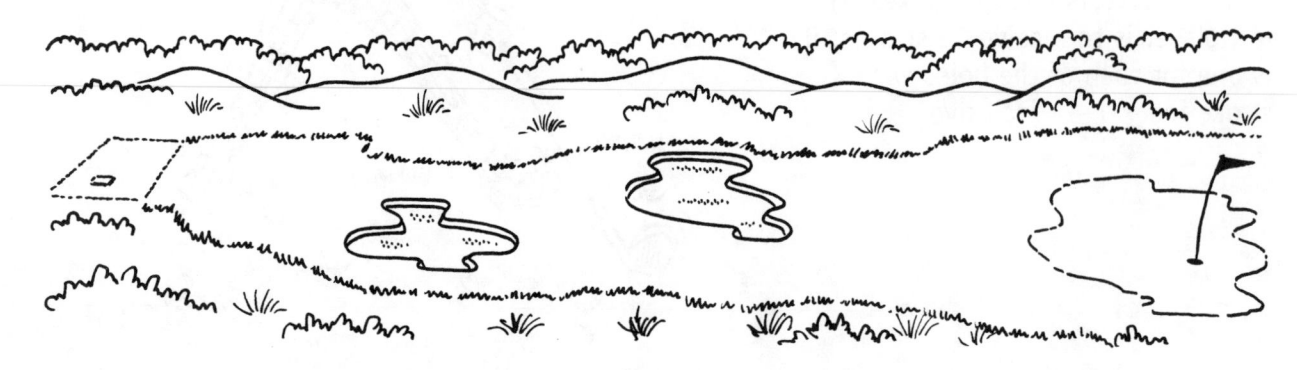

g At about the same time a men's Stableford competition was held at the Dissington course. It was played off the men's yellow tees as the white competition tees were under repair. In a Stableford, players are awarded points on the basis of:

- 2 points for par or nett par
- 1 point for a score or nett of one over par
- 3 points for a birdie or nett birdie
- 4 points for an eagle or nett eagle.

The 'nett' means 'after adjustment for handicap and stroke index', as used in previous situations. The convention here is that stroke allowance is calculated as seven-eighths of the handicap and then applied by the stroke index system.

Paul, with a handicap of 16, played in the Stableford at Dissington with the following actual scores; that is, before any allowances were made.

Hole	1	2	3	4	5	6	7	8	9	10	11	12	13	14	15	16	17	18
Score	6	4	6	4	4	3	5	6	5	7	4	4	7	3	6	4	7	5

Calculate his nett scores and then his Stableford points, and work out Paul's total.

h With the scoring systems in mind, explain why many inconsistent and average players prefer to play in a Stableford competition rather than a stroke play competition where all the eighteen hole scores are added together, even though they are still given a handicap allowance on the total.

Par For The Course

Teaching Notes

The mathematics involved in **Par For The Course** is not demanding in itself but it has to be carried out in a setting that will be unfamiliar to most pupils – the world of golf. One of the challenges is to work with information from different sources, and the synthesis that is required. The work fits one of the criteria laid down in the National Curriculum:

> *'... to use and apply mathematics ... in solving real-life problems.'*

Contexts

Par For The Course can be used in the following ways:

- as an enrichment item for those ahead in normal classroom work
- as extension work to exercises on fractions
- as differentiated homework
- as an activity within an enrichment session, summer school or cluster day
- as an activity for the Mathematics Club or Society.

Answers

1 Brian
   - 1 eagle = 2 less
   - 2 birdies = 2 less
   - 1 bogey = 1 more
   - 2 double bogeys = 4 more
   - ∴ 1 over par, a total of 72

   Gordon
   - 3 birdies = 3 less
   - 2 bogeys = 2 more
   - 2 double bogeys = 4 more
   - ∴ 3 over par, a total of 74

   Brian won by two shots.

2 a Nancy scored a 3 over par 76 on day one and a 77 or 4 over par on day two. She was therefore 7 over par by the end of the second day. The leaders, at 4 under par, were eleven shots better and therefore Nancy did not qualify under the 'Ten-Shot Rule'. 50% of the field (144) is 72. Adding up the number of players either above Nancy or on the same score comes to 70. Nancy did therefore qualify as part of the top 50%.

   b Only 143 players are accounted for in the figures, one less than the total field. The most likely explanation is that one player had retired injured.

Par For The Course

3 a Len's gross score was 75. His nett score when the handicap of 8 was taken off was 67. Roger's gross score was 83. His nett score when the handicap of 16 was taken off was also 67. Therefore Len and Roger finished in the same position in the tournament.

b They both did extremely well. Len's expected gross score would be 78 (par + his handicap of 8) and Roger's would be 86 (par + his handicap of 16). They both performed 3 shots better than their normal game.

c Their handicaps would be reduced – to 5 for Len and 13 for Roger.

d The difference in handicaps was 12. The 'three-quarters' convention for singles matches gives 9. Thus Janet would receive 9 strokes, one each at the end of the holes marked 1–9 inclusive in the ladies' stroke index; that is, holes 3, 4, 7, 8, 10, 12, 13, 15 and 17.

The play hole-by-hole was as follows.

Hole	Stroke allowed?	Result
1	no stroke allowed	win for Julie
2	no stroke allowed	halved (shared)
3	one stroke for Janet	win for Janet
4	one stroke for Janet	halved
5	no stroke allowed	Julie won the hole easily
6	no stroke allowed	Janet won the hole anyway
7	one stroke for Janet	halved
8	one stroke for Janet	halved
9	no stroke allowed	halved
10	one stroke allowed	Julie still won the hole
11	no stroke allowed	halved
12	one stroke for Janet	win for Janet
13	one stroke for Janet	win for Janet
14	no stroke allowed	Julie won the hole well
15	one stroke for Janet	halved
16	no stroke allowed	halved
17	one stroke allowed	win for Janet
18	no stroke allowed	halved

Therefore 9 holes were halved, Julie won 4 and Janet 5. Janet won the match.

Par For The Course

e (i) The match was still in the balance until the last hole. Neither player ever went up by more holes than were left to play. If Julie had won the 18th hole she would have halved the match.

(ii) After 15 holes 3 were left to play. If one player was 4 holes up then the match was decided. In golfing parlance this is called 4 and 3; that is, 4 up with 3 to play.

(iii) The player was 4 up with 4 holes left to play. Therefore he could not lose but the match could be halved if his opponent won all of the last 4 holes. In golfing parlance this is called 'dormie 4'.

f Julie scored 83 and with a handicap of 10 this would be reduced to 73. Janet scored 93 and with a handicap of 22 this would be reduced to 71. Janet therefore played better according to their official handicaps.

g Paul's handicap was 16. He gets seven-eighths of that – that is, 14 – for stroke allowances. This gives him a stroke on the holes with an index 1–14 inclusive; that is, all bar the 5th, 11th, 14th and 18th.

His scoring hole-by-hole was as follows:

Hole	Gross score	Nett score	Par	Stableford points
1	6	5	4	1
2	4	3	3	2
3	6	5	4	1
4	4	3	4	3
5	4	4	4	2
6	3	2	3	3
7	5	4	4	2
8	6	5	5	2
9	5	4	4	2
10	7	6	5	1
11	4	4	4	2
12	4	3	4	3
13	7	6	4	-
14	3	3	3	2
15	6	5	4	1
16	4	3	3	2
17	7	6	4	-
18	5	5	4	1
			TOTAL	**30**

Paul scored 30 points.

h At stroke play, some really bad holes – with scores of, say, 8 – can really ruin the card, but the worst that happens in a Stableford competition is that no points are scored. Other holes, though, can still score very well.

CANNY CRAG

Crag is a dice game that is scored in categories, such as Yahtzee, but here only three dice are used and the players are allowed just one throw and one re-throw each turn.
Here is the score sheet and the explanation for each of the 13 categories.

CATEGORY	EXPLANATION	SCORE
Crag	a total of 13, which includes a pair	50
Thirteen	any three dice totalling 13	26
High Straight	4, 5, 6	20
Low Straight	1, 2, 3	20
Even Straight	2, 4, 6	20
Odd Straight	1, 3, 5	20
Three Of A Kind	any three dice the same	25
Sixes	any sixes	number of dice × 6
Fives	any fives	number of dice × 5
Fours	any fours	number of dice × 4
Threes	any threes	number of dice × 3
Twos	any twos	number of dice × 2
Aces	any ones	number of dice × 1

NOTE

- If Crag is thrown and the category is already filled, the throw can be entered in Thirteen.
- Each turn leads to filling in a category, even with a score of 0.

QUESTIONS

1. Describe the different ways in which Crag could be achieved.
2. You have thrown 1, 3, 6 with the first throw. If you want to get a straight, any straight:
   a which one dice do you pick up?
   b What are the chances of getting a straight with the re-throw and what possible straights would that give?
3. What are the total number of spots on the dice being used in Crag?
4. You have thrown 3 and 5 the first go and you re-throw the third dice. This is your first turn in the game and therefore none of the categories have yet been scored.
   a How many different categories (ignoring a 0 for crossing out a category) could be produced by the re-throw of the third dice?
   b Which categories could not be produced?
   c How many different scores could result?
   d What would those scores be?
5. You have thrown 6 and 5 the first go and you re-throw the third dice. You want a Thirteen to complete your scoring sheet.
   a What is your chance of doing so?
   b After the re-throw the face pointing down towards the table is a 5. Has the top face given you Thirteen?
   c Explain why this is so.
6. What is the perfect or maximum score after the thirteen rounds?

CANNY CRAG

Teaching Notes

Many games, especially those that take place indoors, have strong mathematical content. The various dice games certainly fit that description. Curriculum guidelines ask that teachers use as many vehicles as possible, including games and competitions.

Key Elements

- deduction
- logical thought
- following instructions
- basic calculations
- analysis of data
- probability
- an unusual setting

Answers

1. a 6, 6, 1
   b 5, 5, 3
   c 4, 4, 5

2. a the 6
   b A 2 gives 1, 2, 3 (Low Straight) and a 5 gives 1, 3, 5 (Odd Straight); thus, the chances are 2 in 6 or 1 in 3.

3. Each dice = 21 ∴ 3 × 21 = 63 spots.

4. a A 1 gives an Odd Straight (score 20) or a score for Aces (1), Threes (3) or Fives (5).
   A 2 gives a score (2) for Twos (Threes and Fives as above).
   A 3 gives no new categories but a new score (6) for Threes.
   A 4 gives a score (4) for Fours (Threes and Fives as above).
   A 5 gives Crag (50) or Thirteen (26) or (10) for Fives (Threes as above).
   A 6 gives a score (6) for Sixes (Threes and Fives as above).
   b The categories that could not be produced are High Straight, Low Straight, Even Straight and Three of a Kind.
   c There are 11 different scores that could result.
   d The different scores are: Crag (50), Thirteen (26), Odd Straight (20), Sixes (6), Fives (10) or (5), Fours (4), Threes (6) or (3), Twos (2), Aces (1).

5. a 1 in 6
   b Yes
   c 2 on the top (faces opposite always add up to 7)

6. 181 for the first seven categories, plus 63 for the final six categories = 244.

Aerial Noughts And Crosses

Teaching Notes

There are no pupil sheets for **Aerial Noughts And Crosses**, which is a game demanding concentration, spatial awareness, visualisation and mental agility. Co-ordinates are a key element.

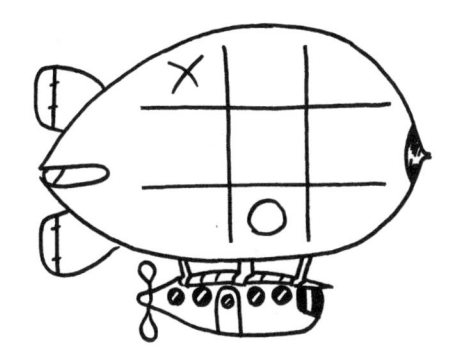

The Game

Most children know the normal game of noughts and crosses. Remind them of the rules. Now explain that you are going to describe moves played alternately by the two players by means of their co-ordinates on a 3 × 3 grid (or the normal written version). Show them this on a flipchart.

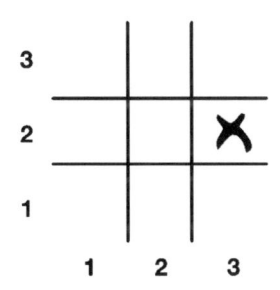

On this occasion the move would be described as 'a cross at 3, 2'.
Explain that you will read out moves for all nine spaces even when a line of noughts or crosses has been completed. This is to avoid identifying which player has won and at which point.

The Objective

The idea is to name the winning player – noughts or crosses – and to identify the winning line by naming the three spaces using their co-ordinates.

Rules Of The Game

1. The game can be played individually or in teams.
2. No child is allowed to write anything down until the teacher has described the nine complete entries.
3. Then *either* the individual or teams write down the answers, or they mark a pre-drawn grid with the three key entries.
4. One point is awarded for whether noughts or crosses are named correctly as the winners and one point for each of the three spaces described correctly by their co-ordinates – thus a total of four points is available for each grid. If teams are established, points can be awarded for the first group to give the correct answers.

Aerial Noughts And Crosses

EXAMPLE

```
3   O¹ | O⁷ | O⁹
    ---+----+---
2   X⁴ | X² | O⁵
    ---+----+---
1   O³ | X⁶ | X⁸
    1    2    3
```

The teacher called

1 a nought at (1, 3)
2 a cross at (2, 2)
3 a nought at (1, 1)
4 a cross at (1, 2)
5 a nought at (3, 2)
6 a cross at (2, 1)
7 a nought at (2, 3)
8 a cross at (3, 1)
9 a nought at (3, 3)

RESULT
Noughts won with a line passing through (1, 3), (2, 3) and (3, 3).

NOTE
❖ Clearly the teacher has to have completed grids with the order of play ready before the game is played with the pupils.

MAKE A DATE

Peter was sitting at the table doing his homework. Two subjects were completed and he had only a design assignment to do. He would be finished in good time to watch his favourite television programme. Five minutes later he threw down his pencil in disgust.

'This is stupid. There is no way to make it work,' he fumed.

Peter's mother came over to the table.

'What is the problem?' she asked.

Peter explained that his homework was to design a system to show the day and the date by the use of three wooden cubes and a small stand.

'One block is for the day of the week and the other two are supposed to show the date, but there aren't enough sides on a cube to include all the numbers.'
His mother brought him a drink of orange and a cake.

'Don't get in a panic,' she said. 'Your teacher would not have asked you to do something that is impossible. Think about the numbers you need while you have that cake.'

Ten minutes later Peter was watching television, his homework done.

The Tasks

1. What was the problem that was worrying Peter?
2. How did he solve it?
3. Make three paper cubes from the materials provided and test the system you have designed.
4. How would you extend the wooden equipment so as to indicate the month also?

MAKE A DATE

CUBE TEMPLATE

Fold along all lines. Starting at the bottom of the template, fold in all the triangular flaps, finishing at the top of the template, to form a cube. The cube can be glued together if required.

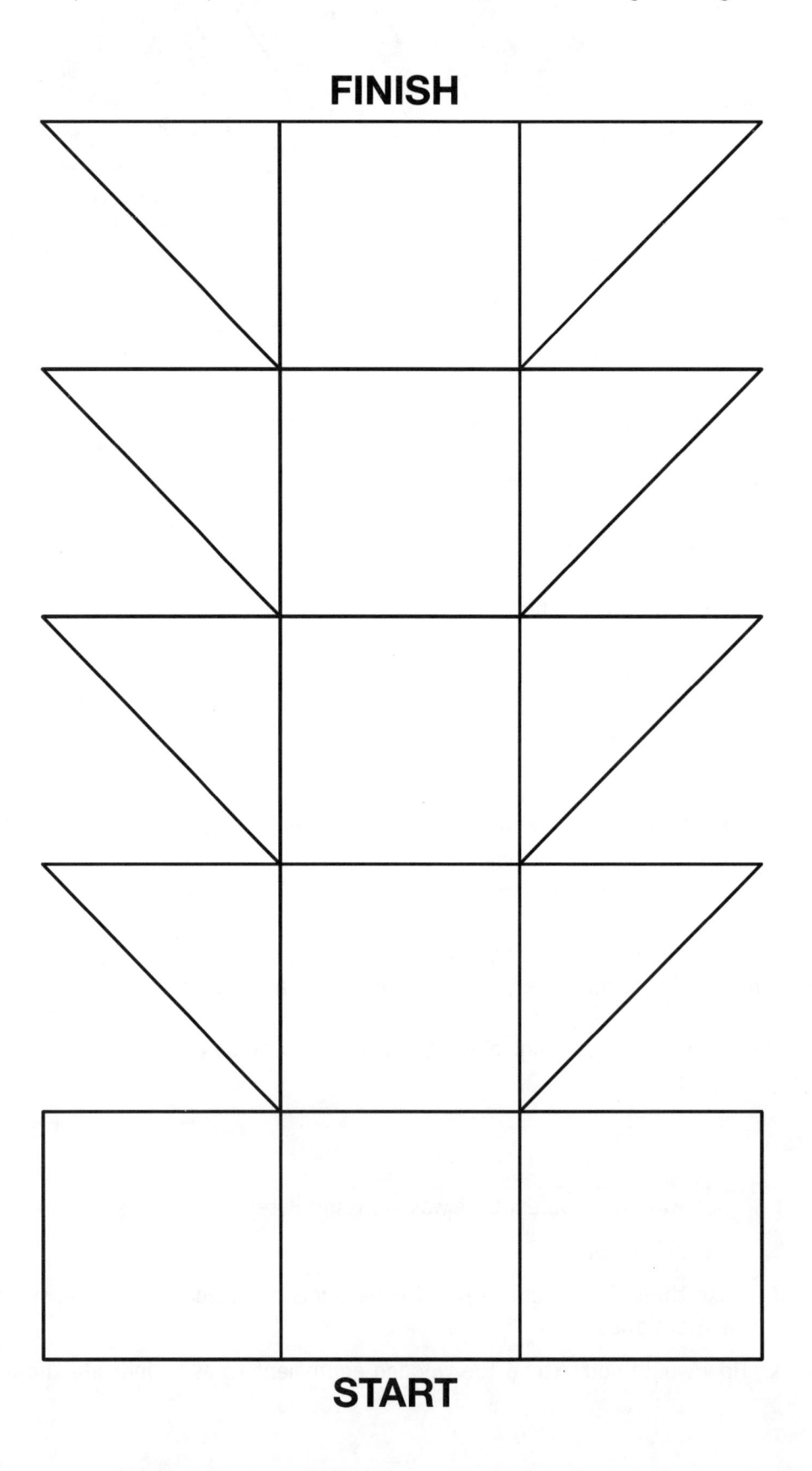

FINISH

START

MAKE A DATE

Teaching Notes

Make A Date has both number and space involved in it. It allows some practical work as the cube template (on a separate sheet, page 78) can be photocopied and each pupil given three copies so that the equivalent of the three wooden blocks can be constructed. This allows the system designed by each pupil to be tested out to see that it really does work. **Make A Date** fits the 'non-routine problem' description advocated in *Improving Mathematics Education 5–14* (Scottish Education and Industry Department, 1997).

Answers

1. Peter believed that he had to place 10 numbers (0–9 inclusive) on each cube, which is impossible.

2. 0 must be on both cubes to get all the numbers from 01 to 09. 1 must be on both to allow the 11th and 2 must be on both to allow the 22nd. That has already taken up six of the twelve sides and there are 7 more numbers to place. The solution is to use a 6 upside down as a 9. The two numbers are never used at the same time. The remaining five numbers can go anywhere on the sides remaining.

   There can be different solutions to the days of the week. Whatever is used, one side at least must be doubled up with the two names printed the opposite way up to each other. A small ledge on the stand covers the day not in use.

3. Pupils tend to guess solutions without thinking the problem through. Making the cubes allows an accurate test.

4. A fourth cube would be needed and therefore a longer stand. The months could all be included by putting two on each face, printed different ways up. The wooden ledge then conceals the month not in use.

Theme Three: Science

There is extensive content to be covered in science but that does not mean that challenging and thought-provoking methods need to be ruled out – in fact the reverse is true. It is important that content does not restrict the use of thinking skills. CASE (Cognitive Acceleration in Science Education) has taken that point on with good results, not only in science but in other subjects like English as well.

Curriculum guidelines offer many encouraging themes, including the following:

> '… creative thought in the development of scientific ideas.'
>
> '… consider anomalies in observations or measurements and try to explain them.'
>
> '… make predictions, where appropriate'
>
> '… ask questions [for example, 'How?', 'Why?', 'What will happen if…?'] and decide how they might find answers to them.'

The National Curriculum (DfEE/QCA, 1999)

> '… a more developed ability to make hypotheses and test these or take up a particular viewpoint and justify it.'
>
> '… greater empathy with and imaginative response to a variety of social and cultural situations or technological issues.'

Scottish 5–14 Guidelines on Environmental Studies

A major element in the curriculum guidelines for both England and Scotland is the place of science within society and the debate that ensues on advantages and disadvantages of scientific and technological advance. **Thanks To Science** (page 83) concentrates upon this area, which is also given an important place in *Improving Science Education 5–14* (Scottish Executive Education Department, 1999):

> '… need to have the skills and critical awareness to interpret and make sense of what they see and read about science in the media, where messages are often conflicting and where topics increasingly cut across a range of social, ethical and moral issues.'
>
> 'As responsible citizens they will need to be able to evaluate the benefits and risks associated with developments in science and their applications.'

The National Curriculum (DfEE/QCA, 1999) contains a similar message, at all Key Stages, including this quote from single science Key Stage 4:

> *'... to consider the power and limitations of science in addressing industrial, social and environmental questions, including the kinds of questions science can and cannot answer, uncertainties in scientific knowledge, and the ethical issues involved.'*

Thanks To Science explores these issues, allows prediction and hypothesising and involves a sustained piece of scientific writing.

Subject-specific language is pressed hard in curriculum guidelines for all subjects, and science is no exception. The Scottish 5–14 Guidelines acknowledge that one of the characteristics of more able pupils is:

> *'... a wider understanding and use of specialist language and terminology.'*

Talking Science (page 85) gives cryptic paragraphs containing key concepts and facts to identify a range of substances, objects, processes, scientific terms and pieces of equipment. Encouraging pupils to write their own paragraphs along similar lines is an important extension. One of the component aspects of Talking Science is that children are taken across many areas of the syllabus in the same piece.

Alternative answers are important for able pupils to explore. *The Spider That Loves Mozart* (page 89) asks pupils to speculate upon the reasons behind particular aspects of animal behaviour. They use their imagination but within scientific parameters. If children do not research too much to start with they are placed at the 'frontier of knowledge' and have to think for themselves. The title indicates that this is also a fun piece, and how we need increased enjoyment in the classroom!

Presenting content in an unusual and demanding way to engage able pupils is one of the greatest challenges to all teachers. *Carol Catalyst The Cryptic Chemist* (page 92) uses the vehicle of a code to deliver material on chemical elements, atomic numbers and the periodic table.

The same theme is at the heart of *Running Rings Round Saturn* (page 94). Major content is involved – the whole area of 'the Earth and beyond' – as well as a good number of technical terms from physical processes, thus playing to greater use of scientific language. The method this time is through a lengthy logical thought exercise pulling material together from different sources and therefore using the higher order thinking skill of synthesis. The fact that *Running Rings Round Saturn* is detailed and lengthy is also important. In our 'soundbite society', it is vitally important for children to have opportunities to develop a span of concentration.

ATTENTION

See also the resources suggested below.

Book	Theme or Section	Activity
Elsewhere in this book	Theme Four: Humanities, Citizenship …	Groundwork
	Theme Six: Young Children	One Thing Leads To Another
	Theme Seven: Logical Thought	Birds Of A Feather
	Theme Nine: Lateral Thinking	Eureka
		Classified Information
Effective Provision For Able And Talented Children, Network Educational Press, 1997	Section Six	What if?
Effective Resources For Able And Talented Children, Network Educational Press, 1999	Theme Two: Language Across The Curriculum	Quintessential Qualities
	Theme Six: Science	Property To Let
		Professor Malaprop
		Ruby Red
		In The Swim
	Theme Eleven: Alternative Answers, Imagination …	The Question Is … Science

Thanks To Science

'Thanks to science' is a phrase often heard in the media in connection with an advance or development. Sometimes it is linked to a particular adjective, such as 'thanks to medical science' when discussing a new treatment or cure. Our lives have been enhanced by scientific and technological advancements in many ways.

However, the work of scientists is carried out in a spirit of gaining more knowledge. The consequences are not always good in all people's eyes. This piece of work explores the area of differing opinions about scientific and technological developments.

Your Task

Either: Consider the list below and then choose the one scientific or technological development that you believe it would be better not to have occurred. Explain, in detail, why you have made this choice.

Or: Put the list into order of desirability of having taken place, with the most favoured at the top. Explain, in detail, why you have placed them in this order.

THE LIST OF DEVELOPMENTS

- Ω Splitting the atom
- Ω Being able to tell a baby's gender during pregnancy
- Ω Genetically modified crops
- Ω Fishing vessels that 'hoover up' everything in their path
- Ω Cloning sheep
- Ω World travel that is relatively cheap and quick
- Ω Transplant surgery
- Ω The development and use of wind power
- Ω The capacity to drill for oil in remote places
- Ω Putting human beings into space and onto the Moon

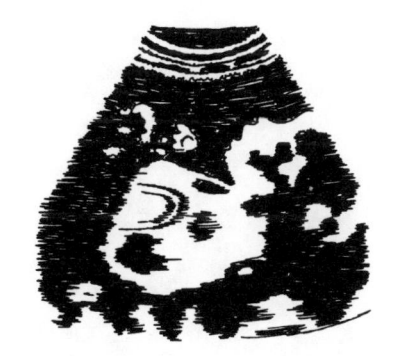

Extension Tasks

1. Name a development not in this list that you are very happy has occurred. Name one that you are unhappy about. Give your reasons.

2. Identify a possible future advance
   a that you *do* want to happen
   b that you *don't* want to happen.
   Again, explain your choices.

Thanks To Science
Teaching Notes

Thanks To Science explores an area that figures prominently in curriculum guidelines in both England and Scotland:

> '... a better understanding of the interaction between social, economic and political institutions and the environment.'
>
> '... greater empathy with, and imaginative responses to, a variety of social and cultural situations or technological issues'

Scottish 5-14 Guidelines on Environmental Studies

> '... considering and evaluating the benefits and drawbacks of scientific and technological developments, including those related to the environment, personal health and quality of life, and those raising ethical issues.'

National Curriculum (DfEE/QCA, 1999)

Key Elements

- research
- analysis of the issues
- evaluation of evidence
- synthesis of data
- taking a wider perspective of subject information
- hypothesising and predicting
- putting together a reasoned and sustained written statement

Contexts

Thanks To Science can be used in a number of ways:

- as extension work to areas of content already covered
- as enrichment work in the classroom
- as differentiated homework
- for debate within a single school or as a cluster activity
- as part of an enrichment session
- as a science competition
- as an activity for the Science Club.

TALKING SCIENCE

In dealing with some questions about chemical equations, the information is presented in the form of a sentence that tells the 'story' very briefly. Let us now extend that process to explain several areas of science by telling a story in the first person. When we give human attributes to objects, ideas, animals, plants and so on, we are using the literary device of 'personification'.

Your Task

Read the following 'extracts'. Each describes a substance, an object, a process, a scientific term or a piece of scientific equipment. Identify the subject of each, explaining the clues in the science personification stories that led you to your conclusion.

NOTE
- Most clues are given in a cryptic form.

EXTRACT ONE
I have the equivalent of the Arctic and Antarctica but not the equivalent of the sun rising and setting. Arctic and Antarctica get on well but two Arctics push away from each other. Around me there is an area that a farmer would use for grazing or cultivation.

EXTRACT TWO
I can be dangerous and destructive if I am not handled carefully. Water and I don't get on well and our meetings generate a lot of heat. If you like mysteries then I answer the gap below:

$$Mg + ? \rightarrow MgSO_4 + H_2$$

EXTRACT THREE
To inhabitants of Earth, I only appear from time to time. I share a physical feature with the cat but the proportions and appearance are very different. I, and my kind, get our names from the Earth-dweller who discovered us – really it makes us sound as though we are popular musicians! A very famous cousin of mine is due to reappear in 2062, as far as you are concerned – he will be there all the time as far as he is concerned.

EXTRACT FOUR
I am impatient and like to get a move on. Although my presence is important for quick change to take place, I myself remain unaltered.

EXTRACT FIVE
When put on trial many of us do not receive a verdict due to hostility along the way. We are very controversial and cause arguments. Some people believe that we are the future but others believe that we are a threat.

TALKING SCIENCE

EXTRACT SIX

I could write my own story. When I bond both strongly and uniformly I feel that I could last for ever. You can date with me but not at the cinema!

EXTRACT SEVEN

I believe in a measured approach to a solution. The end point of my work is clearly indicated by a change of colour. Definite concentration is a part of my process and I have to know exactly what is needed to bring about a result.

EXTRACT EIGHT

I am interested in current issues. When I protect property and people it is unfair because I am replaced – what a blow!

EXTRACT NINE

My key fellow-workers are K and P. You can't say that I am totally responsible for producing an atmosphere. Although odourless and colourless I am very important. My life goes in cycles.

EXTRACT TEN

Red or blue,

It depends on you,

You'll see me in the paper.

EXTRACT ELEVEN

I work in stations but I'm not Thomas The Tank Engine. Some people use my name for the changing of situations. Two of my components are spirally constructed and take their names from the two main phases of education. The control of power is my contribution to the supply of domestic bliss.

EXTRACT TWELVE

Although essential to good health I have a bad name. The story in circulation is that my harmful effects are hereditary only in the sense that I'm in the blood. But that is going to excess and taking a narrow and hard view of my effects.

Extension Task

Construct your own science personification stories on other items, substances, processes and so on. Remember to write the clues in such a way that key vocabulary about the subject is used.

TALKING SCIENCE
Teaching Notes

Talking Science is a piece where the extension work may well turn out to be rather more important and useful than the main item. In constructing their own examples, children really do have to play to the essential ingredients and to work with scientific vocabulary.

Key Elements

- analysis of data
- synthesis of data
- scientific terminology
- word play
- a mixture of lateral and logical thinking
- running across a range of topics at the same time
- essential ingredients

Contexts

Talking Science can be used in a variety of ways:

- as an enrichment item in the classroom
- as part of an enrichment session
- as differentiated homework
- for discussion work in groups
- as an open-access competition
- as an activity for the Science Club or Society.

PRACTICAL POINT
It is important that it is stressed to pupils that we are not just looking for an answer but for an analysis of the clues that support the answer. Otherwise, much of the worth is lost.

Solution

NOTE
Planned answers are given but are there others that satisfy the descriptions?

EXTRACT ONE: MAGNET
Arctic and Antarctica stand for north and south poles but we do not talk of east and west poles. Arctic and Antarctica attract (unlike poles) whereas two Arctics, as like poles, repel. The farmer would use a field – in this case the magnetic field.

EXTRACT TWO: SULPHURIC ACID
'Dangerous and destructive' could refer to a number of substances, some of which would not be safe with water, but it is clearly H_2SO_4 that is the missing component in the equation.

TALKING SCIENCE

EXTRACT THREE: COMET
A comet is there all the time, in an elliptical orbit around the Sun, but is only visible from the Earth at set times. The tail is the feature shared with the cat. Each comet is named after the discoverer; for example, Halley's comet 'appears' every 76 years and is next due in 2062.

EXTRACT FOUR: CATALYST
A catalyst speeds up a reaction without being changed itself. Some might argue that slowing down can occur and, in that case, the name given is 'inhibitor'.

EXTRACT FIVE: GENETICALLY MODIFIED CROPS
Many trial fields have been destroyed by protestors. There is a very lively debate between those who see GM crops as being important in meeting food demands and those who regard them as a serious threat to biodiversity and possibly human health.

EXTRACT SIX: CARBON
In the form graphite, carbon will write. Diamond is a form with strong and uniform bonding. Carbon dating is used extensively in archaeology.

EXTRACT SEVEN: TITRATION
One solution has to be released in exact known quantities into the other that is of known concentration. The 'end point' is the technical term for the moment when the colour change occurs.

EXTRACT EIGHT: FUSE
'Current' refers to electricity. When the current is too great the fuse 'blows'; that is, the wire overheats and melts, thus requiring a replacement.

EXTRACT NINE: NITROGEN
K and P are potassium and phosphorus, which – together with nitrogen – are the three most important elements required by plants. Nitrogen forms not all the atmosphere, but 80%. Biologists refer to the 'nitrogen cycle' – the regular circulation of nitrogen due to the activity of organisms.

EXTRACT TEN: LITMUS PAPER
It turns red to indicate the presence of acid, and blue in alkali.

EXTRACT ELEVEN: TRANSFORMER
'Stations' refers to power stations, where the two spirally constructed coils of a transformer are known as primary and secondary. A transformer changes the voltage of an alternating current; for example, reducing the voltage at substations for domestic supply.

EXTRACT TWELVE: CHOLESTEROL (OR SALT?)
Cholesterol is needed for surrounding a layer of cells and other essential functions, but in excess it inhibits the flow of blood by hardening and narrowing the arteries.

THE SPIDER THAT LOVES MOZART

Animal behaviour is fascinating. Some of it is odd but normally with good purpose. What is the reason behind a distinctive habit or action? Do we know all the answers?

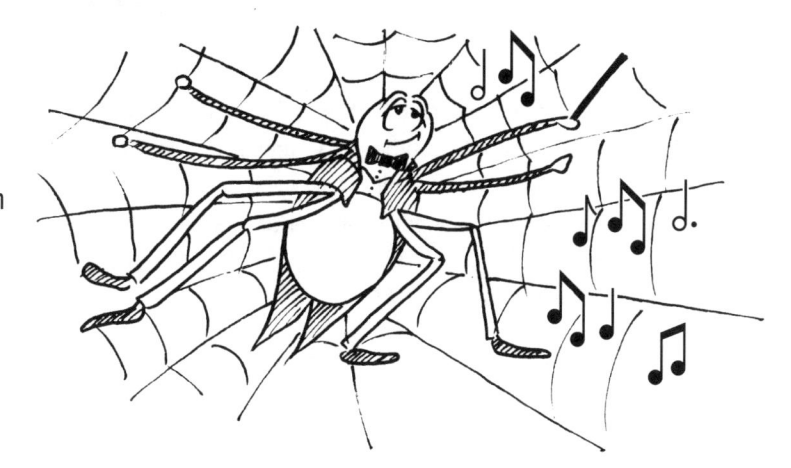

Your Tasks

Listed below are questions about animal behaviour.

* For each one, write down as many explanations as you can through a 'brainstorming' process.
* Now become more critical – indicate which explanation you believe to be the most likely reason for the behaviour, stating why.
* Research the twelve situations and see what the experts say. You will find that in some cases there is genuine doubt.

THE QUESTIONS

1. Why do water voles construct entrances to their burrows that are narrow and restricted?
2. Why are spiders fond of music?
3. Why do hares 'box'?
4. Why is the badger a social animal, which is not typical of flesh-eating carnivores?
5. Why do otters slap the water with their tails?
6. Why do bees dance?
7. Why do lizards 'sunbathe'?
8. Why do moles dig numerous burrows in their fortress (home)?
9. Why do bats hang upside-down when at rest?
10. Why do deer rub their antlers up and down trees?
11. Why do foxes make spine-chilling calls, especially on winter days and nights?
12. Why do hedgehogs 'self-anoint'; that is, produce large quantities of frothy saliva, which they spread over their spines?

Extension Task

Research other fascinating examples of animal behaviour and set them as questions for other members of your class. Perhaps you might find the monkey that loves Picasso!

THE SPIDER THAT LOVES MOZART

Teaching Notes

It is important that the tasks are carried out in their suggested order. Then children think for themselves to produce a number of possible explanations, rather than just regurgitating an already-known fact. They are then working at the 'frontiers of their knowledge'. Some of these situations do not have one fully-accepted explanation in any case.

Key Elements

- brainstorming
- evaluation
- analysis of situations
- synthesis of data
- hypothesising
- research
- consideration of alternatives
- intuitive thinking – using knowledge of a more general nature

Contexts

The Spider That Loves Mozart can be used in a variety of ways:

- as an enrichment activity in the classroom
- for classroom discussion
- as an extension item to other work on animal behaviour
- as a differentiated homework
- as a fun open-access competition
- as an activity for a Science Club or Society
- as part of an enrichment session.

Some 'Answers'

1. As the water voles struggle through the narrow space, they squeeze water from their fur so they are warmer and drier in the burrow.

2. Spiders aren't really fond of music. However, the vibrations produced by a musical instrument excite the spider because the web is made to tremble and the spider believes that prey is struggling to get away. Anything that makes the web tremble achieves the same result.

3. This is something of a mystery. It may well be that 'boxing' is part of the courtship ritual of hares.

4. There are various factors. Badgers are flesh-eating carnivores (they eat hedgehogs, for instance) but they also eat vegetable matter. Living in groups allows sensible exploitation of rich sources of food, rather than use by one pair. It is also helpful to have numbers to defend the territory.

5. In some circumstances slapping the water with the tail assists the otter to drive fish into shallow pools, where they can be caught more easily. (A number of explanations made by children, showing their 'free' thinking, are listed below this section, overleaf).

6   Bees dance to show where there is food. A circle dance indicates that the source is close, whereas a figure-of-eight dance means that the source is further away. Direction is also indicated.

7   Lizards are dependent upon external factors for body heat. They bask in the sun to warm their bodies to a temperature at which they can become active.

8   There is a difference of opinion as to whether moles dig several burrows to give a choice of escape routes or to provide a good system of ventilation.

9   Bats' muscles cannot support their weight in other positions due to the design of the limbs for flying.

10 The antlers of deer are covered with a furry skin called 'velvet'. When the antlers are fully grown this velvet dies and the deer rub it off on the trees.

11 The foxes' calls are part of courtship, which occurs in winter. From the dog fox's point of view it also serves to warn off rivals from the territory.

12 Nobody really knows why hedgehogs behave in this way. It does not seem to be related to keeping clean. One suggestion is that a substance in the saliva is intended to give protection against predators but the argument is far from convincing.

'WHY DO OTTERS SLAP THE WATER WITH THEIR TAILS?'

Some answers from children:

- To attract a mate.
- As a warning to other otters of danger.
- To let others know where they are.
- To tell other otters that they are about to jump in.
- To attract fish.
- To disturb the fish so that they can catch them.
- Make a splash so that curious fish come.
- Because they are angry.
- To let other creatures in the water know that they are coming.
- Cool themselves down on a hot day.
- Because they are frightened.
- To enable them to swim more quickly.
- To clean their tails.
- To refresh themselves with spray.
- To swim quickly away from danger.
- When they are washing.
- To wash each other.
- They go further forward when they splash their tails.
- To scare off predators.
- So that they can spray water over their bodies.
- To slap water at their enemies.
- To test the temperature of the water.
- Because they are learning to swim.
- It exercises their tails.
- They want to wash their tails but cannot reach.
- It attracts their prey with the vibrations.
- It can whack fish in the water.
- This rotates water straight to a friend's home.

Carol Catalyst The Cryptic Chemist

Carol Catalyst's favourite subject is chemistry but she also loves puzzles, brainteasers, codes, anagrams and cryptic clues. She produced the entry below and sent it to a puzzle magazine for possible publication. The editor returned it saying that although the puzzle was very good it would be better in a science magazine, given the specialist knowledge required.

Your Task

Being clued-in chemists like Carol, you have the knowledge required. Are you also a creative chemist so that you can crack the message below using Carol's Cryptic Hints, explaining in detail what the hints indicate?

Carol's Cryptic Hints

▲ Dmitri would, from time to time (cryptic), bleat (anagram) in Russia.

▲ Important is the number of times of being in favour of heavy weights (cryptic).

▲ Capital letters may create a funny appearance in the words due to the representation of the component elements.

▲ Cadmium is worth two of chromium.

The Message

```
4 – 18 – 16      20 – 43 – 1      9 – 53 – 16 – 1
74 – 53 – 90     56 – 75          91 – 74 – 16
```

Extension Task

Create other messages using the same system.

What problems do you encounter?

Carol Catalyst The Cryptic Chemist

Teaching Notes

Here is a fun piece that visits an area of the curriculum in a most unusual way.

Key Elements

- practice with the Periodic Table, atomic numbers and chemical symbols
- abstract feature through codes
- synthesis
- word play
- enjoyment

Contexts

Carol Catalyst The Cryptic Chemist can be used in a variety of ways:

- as extension work
- as an enrichment activity for those ahead with basic work
- as differentiated homework
- as part of an enrichment session
- as an activity for the Science Club or Society
- as an open-access competition with the extension work allowing judging

Solution

CAROL'S CRYPTIC HINTS

- 'Dmitri' refers to Mendelyev or Mendeleev, the Russian chemist who devised the Periodic (from time to time) Table (anagram) in a form close to the one we use today.
- 'In favour of heavy weights' gives 'protons', the number of which in an atom determines the atomic number.
- Some chemical elements (pun) are represented by two letters, some one, giving a mixture of capital and lower case letters within a word when used for decoding purposes.
- The atomic number of cadmium is 48 and chromium is 24.

THE MESSAGE

Clearly, then, the numbers in the message refer to atomic numbers as given below (but not set out as in the Periodic Table), with the chemical symbols.

1	hydrogen	H
4	beryllium	Be
9	fluorine	F
16	sulphur	S
18	argon	Ar
20	calcium	Ca
43	technetium	Tc
53	iodine	I
56	barium	Ba
74	tungsten	W
75	rhenium	Re
90	thorium	Th
91	protactinium	Pa

Be Ar S   Ca Tc H   F I S H   W I Th   Ba Re   Pa W S
4 – 18 – 16   20 – 43 – 1   9 – 53 – 16 – 1   74 – 53 – 90   56 – 75   91 – 74 – 16

Bears catch fish with bare paws.

RUNNING RINGS ROUND SATURN

'Universal Knowledge' is a society for people who love science, especially physics and – most of all – space, the planets, stars and associated matters. The latest project is to establish a website with basic data to help children at school with assignments and examination preparation.

Your Task

By using the information sheets on 'The Earth And Beyond' and on the details of the society members' contributions, together with the clues below, work out which member was responsible for compiling each section of 'The Earth And Beyond' material for the website.

Notes

- Each of the 14 members compiled one section of 'The Earth And Beyond'.
- You are advised to equip yourself with a science dictionary.

THE MEMBERS OF THE UNIVERSAL KNOWLEDGE SOCIETY

Name	Normal occupation	Other contributions to website
Pauline Pressure	dentist	analogue recording; digital recording
Sally Spectrum	engineer	electromagnetism
Alan Ampere	fashion designer	speed, velocity and acceleration
Elizabeth Eclipse	journalist	elasticity
Julian Joule	engineer	the reflection of light; the refraction of light
Fiona Fission	doctor	the behaviour of gases
Michael Mass	computer programmer	force and momentum
Christopher Charge	teacher	electricity in the home; electric current
Laura Lens	shopkeeper	radioactivity
Roger Resistance	bricklayer	kinetic theory of matter
Donna Dynamo	bus driver	heat transfer
Violet Velocity	detective inspector	magnetism
William Wave	meteorologist	specific heat capacity
Irene Inertia	journalist	sound

THE CLUES

1. The member whose name refers to the splitting of a heavy nucleus such as uranium into two parts, did not write a section on an individual star, planet or satellite (moon).

2. One of the other contributions of a member includes information on the periscope – a good example of the application of the principle he is writing about. The second of his other contributions has material that involves the use of a piece of equipment that is the name of another member. These two members wrote the sections on two planets (but not necessarily in this order) one of which is similar in size to the Earth and the other was discovered by William Herschel.

3. Two members sharing an occupation wrote sections on the planet normally eighth from the Sun but sometimes ninth and on the specific example, linked with Neil Armstrong, of a general feature associated with many planets.

4. The woman whose name refers to the characteristic of an object that causes it to resist any change in its state of movement unless it is being acted upon by some outside force, did not write a section on a planet.

5. One of the other contributions to the website concerned material that involved discussion of alpha rays, beta rays, gamma rays and half-life. The member who wrote this also wrote the section on an inhospitable planet with an atmosphere of carbon dioxide gas and clouds of strong sulphuric acid. This may be inhospitable but it is the brightest planet.

6. The planet with the eccentric orbit was written about by the member who also wrote about the theory explaining the behaviour of solids, liquids and gases in terms of the movement of the particles (atoms and molecules) from which they are made.

7. The two remaining of the four 'gas giants' were written about by two women whose other contributions were similar in subject matter apart from the fact that the detective inspector did not necessarily need the use of an electric current.

8. The member whose name describes the quantity of matter a body contains wrote a dramatic section in which something that is very large and coloured could finish up much smaller, a different colour, from where you would never escape.

9. If you could find a stretch of water large enough, this planet would float. It was written about by the member whose average would be found by dividing the distance moved in a particular direction by the time taken.

10. Two planets with the same initial letter were written about by a dentist and a meteorologist. One of these two members joked that as his/her other contribution concerned raising the temperature and heat, it was likely that he/she would see red.

11. It takes planet A 24 hours to complete one rotation on its axis, thus producing night and day due to the relation to source B. The member linked to source B wrote another section on the website where he advises to be live about brown and neutral about blue and that the colour of the earth is actually green and yellow. Planet A is linked to the member whose name measures the quantity of electric current.

12. Conduction, radiation and convection are covered in her other contribution to the website by the member who wrote the section for 'The Earth And Beyond' that explained the early misconceptions about what goes around what.

RUNNING RINGS ROUND SATURN

THE EARTH AND BEYOND

NOTE
- Some measurements vary in different texts. For the purposes of this work use the data provided.

SECTION ONE: THE SUN

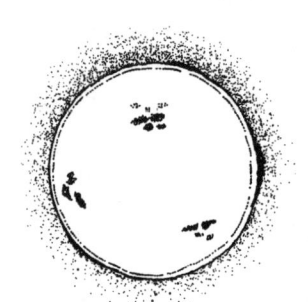

The Sun is a star. Its diameter is approximately 1.4 million kilometres; that is, 109 times the diameter of the Earth. It would take a million Earths to produce a body the same size as the Sun, which gives some idea of comparative size.

The temperature of the surface of the Sun is 6000 °C – absolutely nothing relative to that near the centre, where nuclear reactions occur around the core, producing a temperature estimated to be some 15,000,000 °C. Sunspots are areas of cooler gas and they appear dark in contrast to their brighter surroundings. Sunspots are connected with magnetism.

Intense explosions known as flares send out radiation that is absorbed by the Earth's atmosphere but, even so, affects radio waves. Prominences are huge up-rushes of hot gas, some shaped like giant arches. Sunspots, flares and prominences follow a pattern of activity known as the solar cycle.

SECTION TWO: THE SOLAR SYSTEM

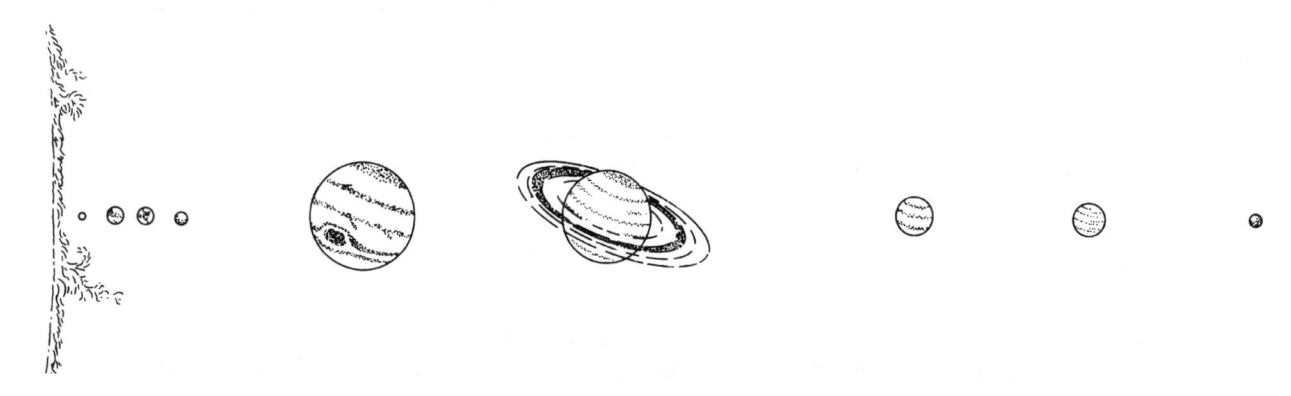

Astronomers agree that the Sun and planets were formed about 4600 million years ago. In ancient times it was believed that the Earth lay at the centre of the universe. This view began to change in the sixteenth century when Copernicus and Galileo disputed the old ideas and began to develop the notion of a Sun-centred planetary system. Later astronomers added to what was known, to finally end the controversy.

There are nine planets in our Solar System, which are – in order of nearness to the Sun – Mercury, Venus, Earth, Mars, Jupiter, Saturn, Uranus, Neptune and Pluto. Some people use a mnemonic, or memory aid, to remember the order. One such could be Most Very Enjoyable Mathematics Join Several Unusual Number Puzzles. As well as the planets, the Solar System includes some 66 moons and millions of asteroids and comets.

SECTION THREE: THE EARTH

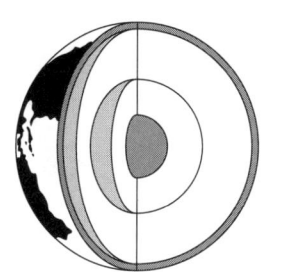

At the centre of the Earth is an inner core of molten iron at 4000 °C. Around that is the mantle – solid and molten rock between 1500 and 4000 °C. Next comes the crust or rocky surface layer. Of huge importance is the atmosphere some 200 km high and made up of various layers, most dense at the bottom and gradually thinning out into space.

Day and night result from the fact that, as the Earth rotates on its axis, different parts of the surface face towards the Sun, which is the source of light. As it takes the Earth 24 hours to rotate once on its axis, this gives the length of day and night.

As it spins on its axis, the Earth also revolves around the Sun. The Earth's axis is tilted at $23\frac{1}{2}°$ to the vertical, which dictates how much sunlight falls on different parts of the Earth at different times. When the Northern Hemisphere is tilted toward the Sun it is summer there and winter in the Southern Hemisphere. When the Northern Hemisphere is tilted away from the Sun the opposites are true. Here we have the explanation for the seasons of the year.

SECTION FOUR: THE MOON

The Moon is the satellite of the Earth. It orbits the Earth every $29\frac{1}{2}$ days. The Moon spins on its axis only once during each orbit and therefore the same side always faces the Earth. Only from spacecraft has it been possible to see the far side of the Moon.

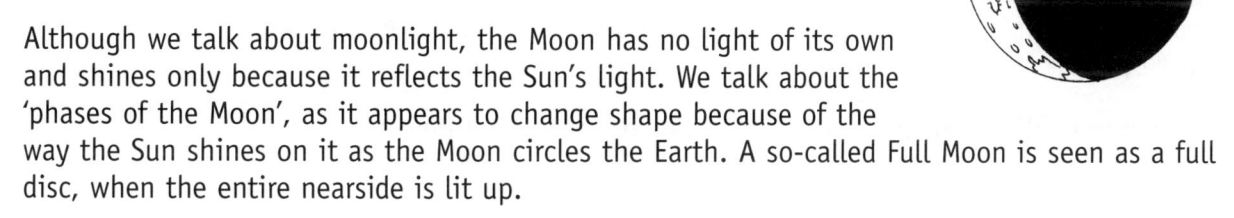

Although we talk about moonlight, the Moon has no light of its own and shines only because it reflects the Sun's light. We talk about the 'phases of the Moon', as it appears to change shape because of the way the Sun shines on it as the Moon circles the Earth. A so-called Full Moon is seen as a full disc, when the entire nearside is lit up.

The Moon is lifeless, with no oceans, no atmosphere and no vegetation. The lunar landscape is made up of craters, flat plains and mountain ranges. The craters are very different in size. Most planets have moons much smaller than themselves but the Earth's Moon is relatively large, being one-quarter the diameter of the Earth.

SECTION FIVE: MERCURY

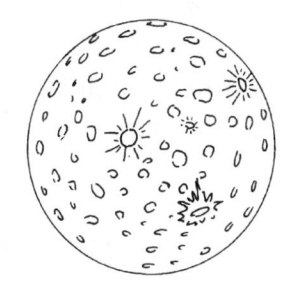

Mercury is the closest planet to the Sun and has no moons. It orbits the Sun in 88 days. Mercury is a small planet with a diameter of 4878 km. Astronomers' belief that Mercury was like the Moon was proved correct by the 1974 Mariner 10 space probe, which showed the surface to be covered by lunar-like craters. The planet is airless and waterless and a further reason for the lack of life is the intensity of radiation from the Sun.

Running Rings Round Saturn

SECTION SIX: VENUS

With a diameter of 12,103 km, Venus is close in size to the Earth. It is the brightest planet and is known as the Morning or Evening Star. Venus is very hot with a surface temperature in the region of 470 °C. The atmosphere is almost entirely made up of unbreatheable carbon dioxide gas. The clouds are not made of water vapour, as on Earth, but of strong sulphuric acid. The surface has craters, mountains and valleys.

This, the second planet from the Sun, has no moons and is unusual in being the only planet to spin on its axis in the opposite way to the path of its orbit.

SECTION SEVEN: MARS

Fourth from the Sun, Mars is the planet closest to the Earth. The diameter is 6786 km, with Mars being approximately half the size of the Earth. Mars is known as the Red Planet as it has a dusty, reddish surface strewn with rocks. This red colour results from the high content of iron oxide – otherwise known as rust! The planet is dotted with many craters but there are also some very large volcanoes, the biggest of which is called Olympus Mons and is three times the height of Mount Everest.

Much has been made of the possibility of life on Mars, and 'Martians' have figured prominently in science fiction. So-called canals on the planet surface turned out to be optical illusions. Mars is very cold with minimum surface temperatures reaching –100 °C. Water may have been present in the past but now Mars is gripped by ice.

There are two small, irregular-shaped moons called Phobos and Deimos.

SECTION EIGHT: JUPITER

Jupiter, with a diameter of 142,984 km, is the giant among the planets. It weighs two-and-a-half times as much as all the other planets put together. Jupiter is made mainly of a liquid mixture of hydrogen and helium. There is no solid surface. Its atmosphere is made up of hydrogen, helium and traces of water, ammonia and methane. The cloud pattern is ever-changing with violent storms including the Great Red Spot that is three times the size of the Earth. Jupiter spins very rapidly and this causes a bulge at its equator. The outermost layers are very cold, approximately –150 °C, but this is not as cold as might be expected considering the planet's distance from the Sun. This is due to the fact that the interior is very hot.

Jupiter has a total of sixteen known moons although others may yet be discovered. Some are as large as the Earth's Moon. Two of the moons, Ganymede and Callisto, have craters pitting their surface.

SECTION NINE: SATURN

Saturn, the sixth planet from the Sun, is a gas giant similar to Jupiter, although not as large. Its diameter is 120,536 km, between nine and ten times greater than that of the Earth. Saturn rotates very quickly and this causes it to flatten at its poles and bulge at the equator.

Saturn is made mainly of hydrogen and helium. It has the lowest density of all the planets, less in fact than the density of water. Saturn is a cold planet and has a surface temperature in the region of −170 °C. The planet is very well known for its rings, which are not solid but are composed of billions of ice-covered particles.

Some 23 or 24 moons have been discovered but there may well be others. Titan is the largest and has an atmosphere of dense orange clouds.

SECTION TEN: URANUS

Uranus is another of the gas giants. It is the seventh planet from the Sun. The diameter is 51,118 km. The planet was discovered by William Herschel and it was the first to be observed through a telescope. The greenish colour he saw is caused by considerable amounts of methane. It is composed mainly of gases with a thick atmosphere of methane, helium and hydrogen. Like Saturn, Uranus has rings but they are narrower and have wider gaps. Unlike any other planet, Uranus is tilted on its side.

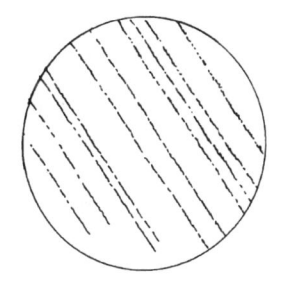

There are fifteen moons orbiting above the equator. The largest is Titania. Ariel has deep valleys, and Miranda – the smallest moon – has a mass of canyons, rocks and a towering cliff higher than Mount Everest.

SECTION ELEVEN: NEPTUNE

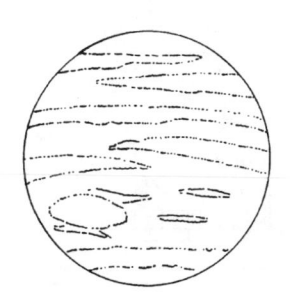

Astronomers were interested to see that Uranus did not keep to its predicted path. The most likely explanation was that it was being pulled out of position by another planet. Mathematicians worked on this theory and pinpointed the position of Neptune. With a diameter of 49,528 km, Neptune is a similar size to Uranus.

Neptune is regarded as the eighth planet from the Sun but the orbit of Pluto is so eccentric that for a few years in every 248 years, its distance from the Sun is less than Neptune.

Neptune is extremely cold with a surface temperature of approximately −200 °C. The atmosphere consists mainly of methane, hydrogen and helium. Neptune has dramatic, changing weather patterns. The great Dark Spot is a gigantic storm.

One of Neptune's moons, Triton, has a frozen surface with icy volcanic mountains. It has been described as the coldest place in the Solar System.

Running Rings Round Saturn

SECTION TWELVE: PLUTO

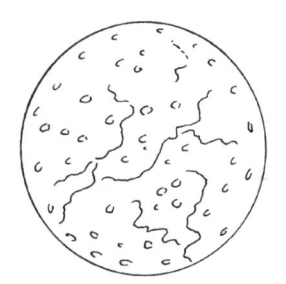

The farthest planet from the Sun, Pluto, has a tilted oval orbit that differs from those of all the other planets of the Solar System. This is the ninth and smallest planet. It was discovered in 1930 by Clyde Tombaugh years after its existence was predicted by Percival Lowell. Little is known about it but it probably has an iron core and a rocky surface with a covering of methane gas. More recently a moon, Charon, was discovered to be circling the planet. One theory is that Pluto is a satellite of Neptune that has escaped.

SECTION THIRTEEN: STARS

Stars have interesting life histories. A cloud of dust and gas called a nebula accumulates, consisting mainly of hydrogen and heavy hydrogen. The gas is pulled together by its own gravity and the particles collide as they are drawn ever closer. Thermonuclear reactions occur and a star is born. Young stars can be seen still surrounded by gas.

For a long time the star shines steadily. It is powered by nuclear reactions at the centre, which turn hydrogen into helium, releasing energy in the process. Eventually the supply of hydrogen runs out. The core collapses and heats up, while the star's atmosphere expands and cools. Considerable expansion occurs and the star becomes a red giant. The unstable atmosphere drifts away leaving the small collapsed core as a blue or white dwarf. Eventually the light fades completely leaving a cold black globe.

Massive stars die in a different way. They explode spectacularly forming a supernova. Then one of two things happens. If the core survives the blast and is between one-and-a-half and three times heavier than the Sun it becomes a ball of neutrons, known as a neutron star or pulsar. If the core is more than three times heavier than the Sun it just keeps on collapsing. Gravitational pull prevents light escaping. A black hole is formed where anything falling into it is trapped forever.

SECTION FOURTEEN: SPACE EXPLORATION

The first artificial Earth satellite, Sputnik 1, was launched by the USSR in 1957. The speed of launch of any rocket must be great enough to take the rocket out of the Earth's gravitational pull. Rockets can carry artificial satellites that are then set in orbits around the Earth or other planets. Some are used for communications, others have been deliberately targeted on gaining information about space, including the planets. Planetary probes have included unmanned missions to the Moon, orbiting Mars, photographic missions to Saturn and Jupiter and landings on Venus.

Manned flights started with Yuri Gargarin on Vostok 1 in 1961. In July 1969, Neil Armstrong became the first man to set foot on the Moon. Colonisation of the Moon faces many problems, since there is no air, no water and no food supplies. In July 1975, a joint American–Soviet space mission culminated in a successful link-up between Apollo and Soyuz spacecraft. Space stations have been launched successfully where astronauts have carried out experiments for a period of months. The American Space Shuttle has been an important development, as it comes back to Earth like an aeroplane and can be used again, thus reducing the considerable costs involved in space exploration.

Running Rings Round Saturn

Teaching Notes

This detailed piece of work is linked not only to a major content area, 'The Earth And Beyond', but also many other sections of content.

Key Elements

- scientific vocabulary
- use of a scientific dictionary
- delivery of content in an unusual way
- span of concentration
- analysis of data
- synthesis
- word play
- good recording habits
- cover of many sections of content simultaneously

Contexts

Running Rings Round Saturn can be used in a variety of ways:

- as extension work to content on planets, space and so on
- as an enrichment item for the classroom
- as differentiated homework
- for revision purposes for many areas of a syllabus
- as part of an enrichment session
- as an activity for the Science Club.

Solution

Clue 1 The person is Fiona Fission who wrote one of the sections on The Solar System, Stars or Space Exploration.

Clue 2 A periscope is a practical application of the reflection of light. The member is Julian Joule who also contributed material on the refraction of light. This second topic involves lenses for refraction at a spherical surface. The two members are therefore Julian Joule and Laura Lens. The two planets are Venus and Uranus but we do not know yet which way round.

Clue 3 The sections are Neptune and the Moon. Occupations are shared by two pairs of members – engineers and journalists. It cannot be 'engineer' as Julian Joule, one of them, is linked to other planets. The two journalists are Elizabeth Eclipse and Irene Inertia.

Running Rings Round Saturn

Clue 4 The description refers to inertia and therefore from Clue 3 it is Irene Inertia who wrote about the Moon and Elizabeth Eclipse who contributed a section on Neptune.

Clue 5 The planet is Venus. The website section also described is that on radioactivity, contributed by Laura Lens. It is she, therefore, who wrote the section on Venus and from Clue 2 Julian Joule is linked with Uranus.

Clue 6 The planet with the eccentric orbit is Pluto, which was written about by Roger Resistance who also contributed the section on the kinetic theory of matter.

Clue 7 Uranus and Neptune have already been sorted. The other two 'gas giants' are Jupiter and Saturn and the members are Sally Spectrum (electromagnetism) and Violet Velocity (magnetism) but we do not know yet which way round.

Clue 8 The description refers to mass and it was Michael Mass who wrote the section on Stars where a red giant could become a black hole. This also eliminates one of the possibilities for Fiona Fission (Clue 1).

Clue 9 Saturn has a lower density than water. The member is Violet Velocity. From Clue 7, therefore, it was Sally Spectrum who contributed the section on Jupiter.

Clue 10 Mercury and Mars share an initial letter. The dentist and the meteorologist are Pauline Pressure and William Wave. William Wave's other contribution was specific heat capacity and seeing red would lead to the 'red planet', Mars. Mercury and Pauline Pressure therefore go together.

Clue 11 Planet A is of course the Earth, written about by Alan Ampere. Source B is the Sun, contributed by Christopher Charge whose advice on the correct wiring of plugs comes into his other contribution, 'Electricity in the Home'.

Clue 12 These units are part of heat transfer, contributed by Donna Dynamo who was also responsible for the section on the Solar System. From Clue 1 we are now left with the pairing of Fiona Fission and Space Exploration.

The Final Outcome

Contributor	Contribution
Pauline Pressure	Mercury
Sally Spectrum	Jupiter
Alan Ampere	Earth
Elizabeth Eclipse	Neptune
Julian Joule	Uranus
Fiona Fission	space exploration
Michael Mass	stars
Christopher Charge	Sun
Laura Lens	Venus
Roger Resistance	Pluto
Donna Dynamo	Solar System
Violet Velocity	Saturn
William Wave	Mars
Irene Inertia	Moon

Theme Four: Humanities, Citizenship, Problem Solving, Decision Making, Information Processing

The Geography Guidelines of the National Curriculum (DfEE/QCA,1999) point out that children should learn, among other skills, to:

> '... ask geographical questions.'
>
> '... use an extended geographical vocabulary.'

Both that document and the Scottish 5–14 Guidelines on Environmental Studies place emphasis upon map work.

Shipping Forecast (page 106) uses geographical concepts and language in real-life situations before getting pupils to apply the skills to an imaginary area. *Anachorisms* (page 112) is an unusual and enjoyable way of looking at classification and the geographical correctness of place.

The History Guidelines of the National Curriculum (DfEE/QCA, 1999) have as a comment in the foreword:

> 'History is an unusual discipline. Its core is hard fact that you cannot get away from and have to learn to master. At the same time you have to be deductive, perceptive and imaginative in the use of that fact.'

Dr Christine Carpenter, University of Cambridge

Finders Keepers ... Sometimes (page 114) gets pupils to use documentary evidence on treasure and metal detecting, and to apply rules to certain situations. Careful analysis of the data is necessary. *Groundwork* (page 119) is also about archaeology and the many methods now used to locate and date finds. This is certainly based upon hard fact but pupils are required to be creative and imaginative in the use of the material. Selection is an important element.

Problem solving, decision making and information processing are linked skills that are fundamental not only to many aspects of education but to life itself. Whether at work, or in our private lives, most people need to process information, solve problems and make decisions. The quality involved in the first activity has a great influence upon the success of the others. Indeed with an explosion of information around us, through the Internet especially, there has never been a greater need to be able to extract what is essential and relevant from the huge mass of what is available. Able children, in particular, need to resist being seduced by quantity and instead concentrate upon quality data.

Problem solving comes in several formats. There are models, such as the Bulmershe project of some years ago, that concentrate on real-life situations, which are seen as the only valid problems to solve. Many other programmes involve simulation or fictional scenarios. In between, comes a category combining the two, in which activities are based on actual situations but some of the elements are changed to assist the setting of the problem – a form of poetic licence. The author's view is that it is profitable to draw examples from each of the three categories of problem solving activities.

Problem solving and decision making feature heavily in the National Curriculum. They are fundamental elements within the new document on Citizenship. Some quotes from Scottish 5–14 Guidelines also stress their importance:

> '... apply a problem-tackling process in relevant situations.'

Personal And Social Development

> '... as a source of challenge, satisfaction and pleasure, where creativity and inventiveness are seen to link with everyday problem solving.'

Mathematics

> '... selected national and international disputes and ways of resolving them.'

Social Subjects

> '... ways in which individuals can influence health and the quality of the environment.'

Health Education

Peace Treaty (page 124) is a demanding piece involving complex issues and decisions. It has a specific setting but the principles can be applied far more generally. *Peace Treaty* fits closely one strand of the National Curriculum Citizenship programme of study:

> '... the wider issues and challenges of global interdependence and responsibility.'

Silence In Court (page 133) enacts a murder trial, involving the consideration of conflicting evidence and a difficult decision for the jury. The skills involved are vital to many areas of the curriculum, especially humanities subjects. This piece also ties in closely with a theme of the National Curriculum Citizenship programme of study:

> '... the legal and human rights and responsibilities underpinning society and how they relate to citizens, including the role and operation of the criminal and civil justice systems.'

Tournament (page 150) takes the intermediate of the three problem solving formats described above. The basic scenario comes from real life and the main tasks were those required at the time. However, details have been changed for technical reasons. A strong feature of this activity is organisation – again a major skill for us all to master, both at work and at home. Able pupils need the challenge of the density and complexity of information in pieces like *Tournament*, *Peace Treaty* and *Silence In Court*.

ATTENTION

See also the resources suggested below.

Book	Theme or Section	Activity
Elsewhere in this book	Theme Two: Mathematics, Numeracy	Running Total
		Single Surprise
		Make A Date
		Watch Carefully
	Theme Three: Science	Thanks To Science
	Theme Eight: Detective Work, Codes	Cliffhanger
		Critical Clues
	Theme Nine: Lateral Thinking	One Question, Many Answers
		Classified Information
	Theme Ten: Competitions	The People Of Britain
Effective Provision For Able And Talented Children, Network Educational Press, 1997	Section Six	What If?
Effective Resources For Able And Talented Children, Network Educational Press, 1999	Theme Two: Language Across The Curriculum	Depict
		Quintessential Qualities
	Theme Five: Numeracy, Mathematics	Acute
		A Calculated Risk
		In The Balance
		Lucky Programme
	Theme Six: Science	Ruby Red
		In The Swim
	Theme Nine: Humanities	Decision Makers
		Eyam
		On The Map
	Theme Ten: Detective Work	According To The Evidence
		An Arresting Problem
		Seeing Is Believing
		Vital Evidence
	Theme Eleven: Alternative Answers, Imagination …	The Question Is
		Who Am I?
		Just Imagine

Shipping Forecast

Many of you who listen to the radio will have heard shipping forecasts like this one:

> '... Cromarty, Forth, south westerly 5 occasionally 6, showers, moderate ...'

Cromarty and Forth are sea areas. Some forecasts include coastal stations, such as Tiree, rather than sea areas. Varied data is given, including air pressure, wind direction, windspeed, weather and visibility. There are also warnings of bad weather, such as:

> 'Attention all shipping in sea areas Faeroes, Bailey, Hebrides and Fair Isle. Gale force 9 imminent.'

Task One

Explain why such messages are broadcast on the radio. Who listens to them? What is their value?

Task Two

The waters around the British Isles are divided into named sea areas, as shown on the map below. Some of the names sound familiar, others less so. Explain why these divisions have been made and why they have been named.

Shipping Forecast

Task Three

Look at detailed maps covering the British Isles and surrounding areas, in an atlas. Explain how the sea areas got their particular names.

Task Four

Now look at the separate sheet that shows a map of Tranland and the surrounding waters. Using the blank outline map provided, divide the waters up into suitable sea areas and name them using the same principles as those that applied in the case of the British Isles.

> **You may find this short glossary of terms helpful.**
>
> **Bank**   Part of the sea bed raised above its surroundings. There is, however, still enough water to allow navigation.
>
> **Point**   A headland; a pointed piece of land jutting out into the sea.
>
> **Strait**   A narrow stretch of sea connecting two much larger areas of sea.
>
> **Bight**   An indentation in the sea coast, which is larger than a bay or which has a gentler curvature.
>
> **Headland** A steep cliff jutting out into the sea.
>
> **Sound**   A narrow passage of water that is usually a little wider than a strait.
>
> **Gulf**   A large, deep bay.

Follow-Up

1. Listen to the shipping forecast on the radio.
2. Have a look at Peter Collyer's wonderful book *Rain Later, Good*, (Thomas Reed Publications, 1998).

Shipping Forecast

Map Of Tranland And Surrounding Waters

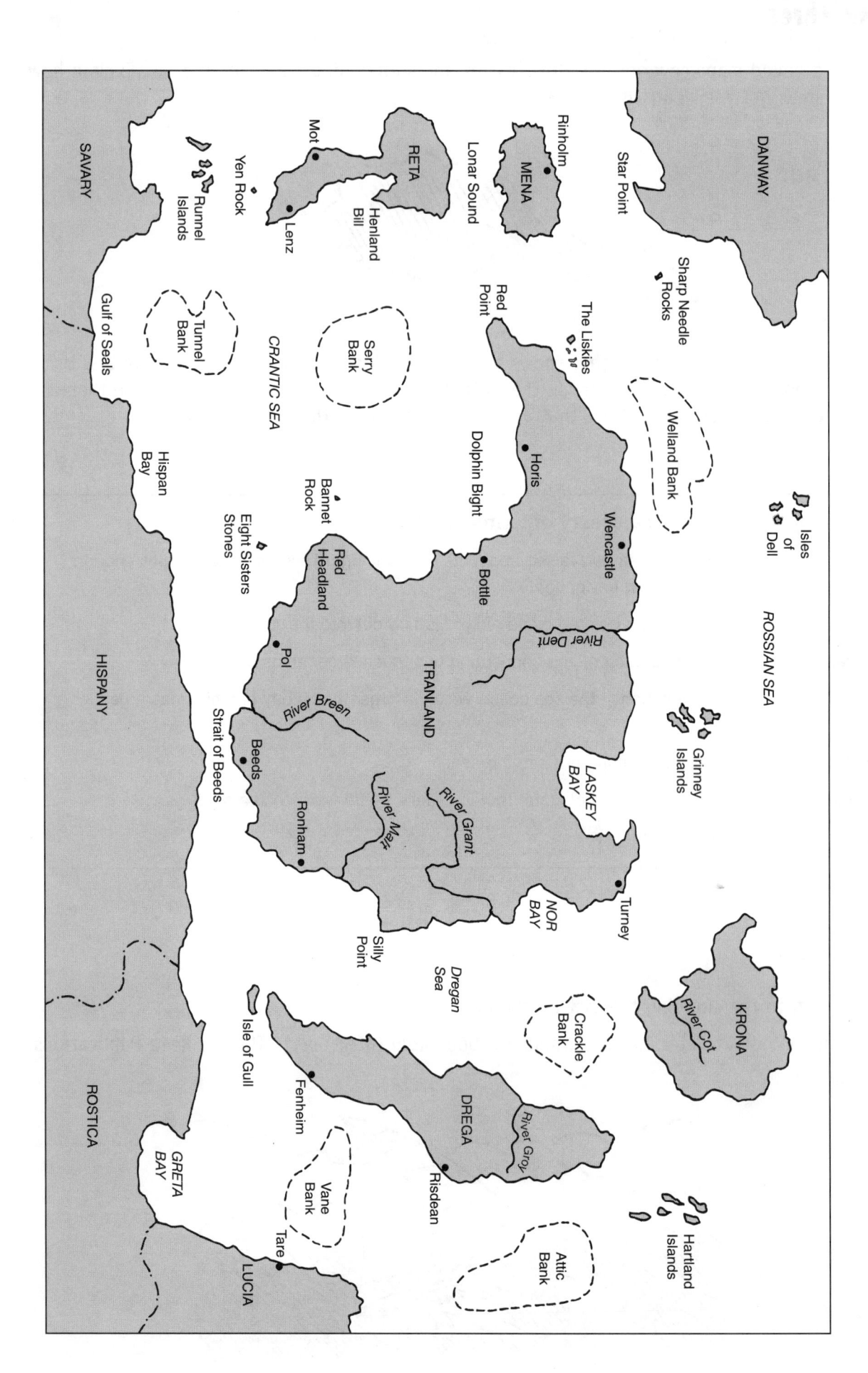

Landmasses/Regions: SAVARY, DANWAY, RETA, MENA, HISPANY, HISPAN BAY, TRANLAND, ROSSIAN SEA, CRANTIC SEA, ROSTICA, DREGA, KRONA, LUCIA

Places on RETA: Rinholm, Mot, Lenz, Henland Bill, Lonar Sound

Islands/Rocks (north): Runnel Islands, Yen Rock, Sharp Needle Rocks, Star Point, The Liskies, Isles of Dell

Banks: Tunnel Bank, Serry Bank, Welland Bank, Crackle Bank, Vane Bank, Attic Bank

Tranland features: Red Point, Dolphin Bight, Horis, Wencastle, Bottle, Bannet Rock, Eight Sisters Stones, Red Headland, Pol, River Breen, River Dent, River Melt, River Grant, Ronham, Beeds, Strait of Beeds, Silly Point, LASKEY BAY, NOR BAY, Turney, Dregan Sea

Southern features: Gulf of Seals, Isle of Gull, Fenheim, GRETA BAY, Tare, Risdean, River Groy, River Cot, Grinney Islands, Hartland Islands

108 More Effective Resources for Able and Talented Children © Barry Teare (Network Educational Press, 2001)

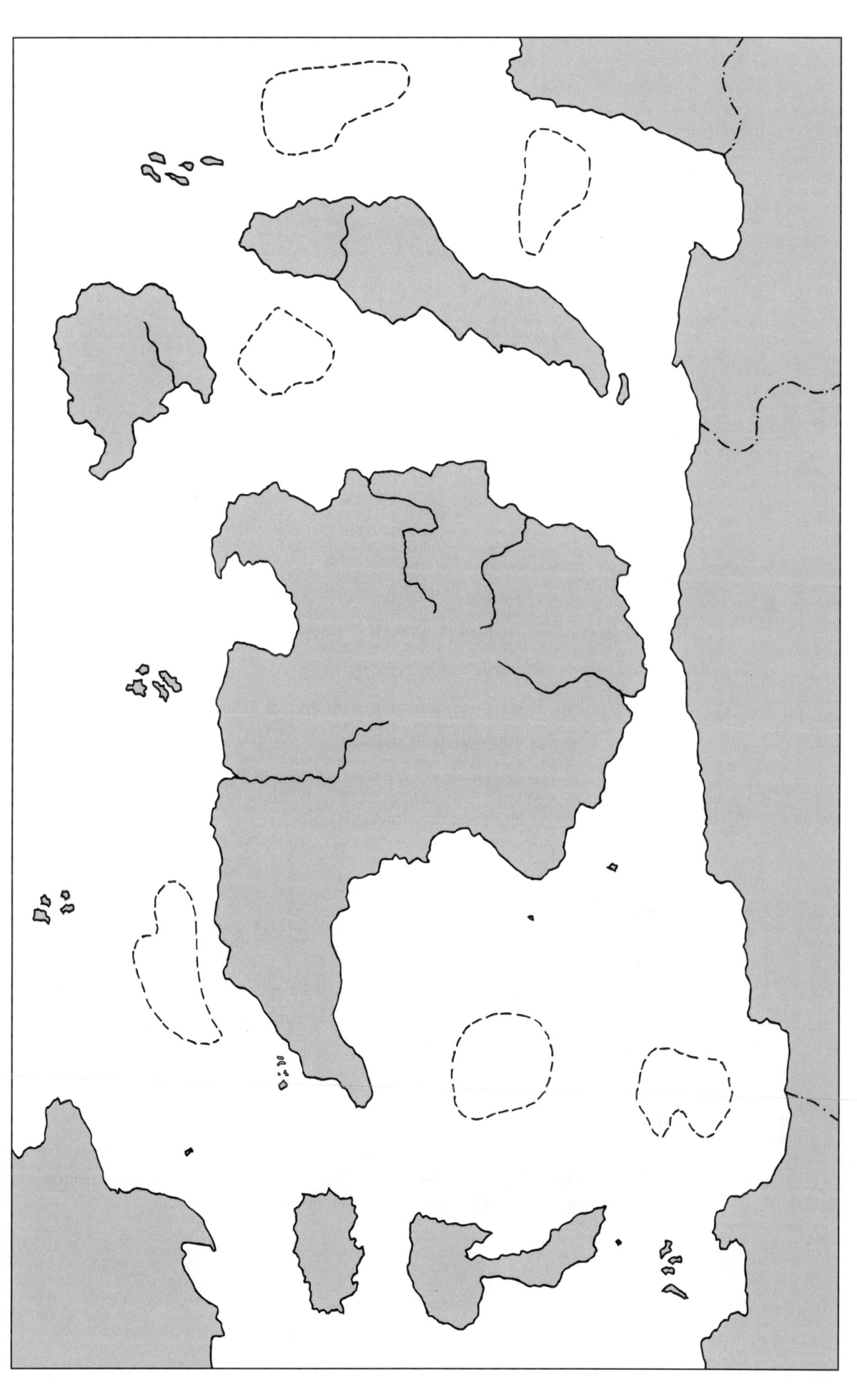

Shipping Forecast

Sea Areas Around Tranland

Shipping Forecast

Teaching Notes

Shipping Forecast starts with work on existing areas around the British Isles and then moves onto an activity involving an imaginary area.

Key Elements

- map work
- geographical terms
- analysis
- evaluation
- word play
- application

Contexts

Shipping Forecast can be used in a variety of ways:

- as enrichment material for those ahead in standard tasks
- as extension material to map work or geographical vocabulary
- as differentiated homework
- as an activity in an enrichment session, summer school or cluster day
- as an open-access competition.

Answers

TASK ONE
Shipping forecasts are intended for sailors, fishermen and any other users of the sea. The information is very important in terms of sea conditions, weather and any accompanying hazards or dangers such as fog.

TASK TWO
Sailors and others need to know exact details and locations. Divisions allow areas of a reasonable size to be dealt with individually. The names are linked to the areas and allow easy identification so that messages can be delivered quickly and efficiently.

Shipping Forecast

TASK THREE

South East Iceland:	obviously, the area is to the south east of Iceland
Faeroes:	named after the islands
Fair Isle:	named after one of the group of islands
Bailey:	named after Bill Bailey's Bank (sand bank)
Rockall:	named after a tiny island of the same name close to Rockall Bank
Shannon:	named after the River Shannon
Hebrides:	named after the group of islands
Malin:	named after Malin Head, Northern Ireland
Irish Sea:	named after the waters of the same name
Fastnet:	named after Fastnet Rock
Sole:	named after a sand bank
Lundy:	named after Lundy Island
Finisterre:	named after Cape Finisterre on the coast of Spain
Biscay:	named after the Bay of Biscay
Plymouth:	named after the city of the same name in south west England
Portland:	named after Portland Bill and the Isle of Portland
Wight:	named after the Isle of Wight
Dover:	named after the port in south east England
Thames:	named after the River Thames
Humber:	named after the River Humber
Tyne:	named after the River Tyne
Dogger:	named after Dogger Bank
German Bight:	off the coast of Germany, a wide indentation of the shoreline
Forth:	named after the Firth of Forth
Forties:	named after the greater part of the waters, that are forty fathoms or more deep
Fisher:	named after two sand banks – Great Fisher Bank and Little Fisher Bank
Cromarty:	named after Cromarty Firth, and the town of Cromarty
Viking:	close to Norway and a reference to the Vikings
North Utsire:	named after the small isolated island of Utsira
South Utsire:	named after the small isolated island of Utsira

NOTE

- ❖ **Trafalgar** is off the map to the south, off the coast of Portugal. It is not included in all shipping forecasts.

TASK FOUR

There are of course many possible answers but due note should be taken of the division of the seas into reasonably-sized areas, and the allocation to each of an appropriate, distinctive name based on a relevant local feature.

ANACHORISMS

Many people know the term 'anachronism'. It refers to objects, events or people out of their correct time, historically. Also coming from a Greek origin is the term 'anachorism' – a geographical misplacement, or something located in a wrong position (khoros = place, khronos = time).

For each of the groups below, identify the anachorism or misplacement and give the reason for your choice in each case.

1   adder, cobra, smooth snake, grass snake
2   gerbil, jerboa, caracal, hedgehog
3   kangaroo, lion, cheetah, elephant
4   North Sea, Ocean of Storms, Sea of Tranquillity, Sea of Crises
5   oak, beech, ash, mangrove
6   meadow brown, monarch, orange tip, peacock
7   cormorant, jay, gannet, guillemot
8   parrot fish, damsel fish, butterfly fish, dragon fish
9   dragonfly, cricket, locust, grasshopper
10 cod, whiting, roach, mackerel

ANACHORISMS

Teaching Notes

Anachorisms is a light geographical exercise but it does have some important key elements.

Key Elements

- classification
- concepts
- word play
- content, which could be extended into any topic

Extension Task

Pupils can be asked to construct examples of their own, either with a free choice of subject matter or with a list of designated themes that explore sections of the syllabus.

Contexts

Anachorisms can be used in the following ways:

- as enrichment for those ahead with normal work
- as differentiated homework
- as an activity for an enrichment session, summer school or cluster day
- as an open-access competition where the extension task would act as the 'discriminator'.

Answers

Number	Anachorism	Reason
1	cobra	the others are to be found in the British Isles
2	hedgehog	the rest are from the Sahara
3	kangaroo	this is the only one not native to Africa
4	North Sea	the others are on the Moon
5	mangrove	the mangrove is a tropical tree, unlike the others, which are woodland trees in Britain
6	monarch	the others are common British butterflies; the monarch lives in the USA or is a rare migrant to Britain
7	jay	the jay is a woodland bird, while the others are found on cliffs and the sea
8	dragon fish	this lives in seas off Antarctica, while the others are coral reef inhabitants
9	locust	the locust is present in Africa and Asia, while the others are found in the British Isles
10	roach	this is the only freshwater fish; the others are marine species

Finders Keepers... Sometimes

In recent years there has been an upsurge of interest in archaeology, fuelled by television programmes like those involving 'The Time Team'. Metal detectorists, either singly or as members of clubs, have made many finds. However, the rules about what to do with such finds are not as simple as the famous saying 'Finders Keepers'.

Your Task

Read the extract from The Treasure Act, together with key points summarised from the rest of the Act and the Code of Practice, on the separate sheets.

Look at the list of finds below. Decide whether they are 'treasure', and what the finder should do, in each case. Explain, in detail, how your answer fits the terms of the Act.

The Finds

1. A Victorian brooch, gold-plated.
2. A wooden box containing eighteen sovereigns from the nineteenth century.
3. A single 100% gold coin from the reign of Elizabeth I.
4. Stones with fossils of plants.
5. Seven bronze Roman coins.
6. A purse of eleven copper halfpennies and farthings from the reign of Charles II.
7. A group of gold coins from the reign of Philip II of Spain, found on the foreshore on a beach in the south west of England following winter storms.
8. Twelve bronze Celtic coins found in a hole in the rock beside an ancient spring believed to have healing powers.
9. Six silver coins from a range of dates recovered separately over a large site where medieval trade was conducted.
10. Items of Tudor jewellery found during the laying of pipes from a site where previously four gold coins from the reign of Henry VIII had been discovered near the surface.

Extension Tasks

- Explain why you believe that the following sentence was inserted at the end of the new definition of treasure:

  'If you are in any doubt, it will probably be safest to report your find.'

- In the past, many archaeologists were hostile to metal detecting. Recently this attitude has changed to a more positive approach. Why do you think archaeologists held their original view? Why do you think it has changed?

- There are codes of practice advised in many situations. When you go for a walk in rural areas you are asked to obey 'The Country Code', for the benefit of all those who work in and enjoy the countryside. The Council for British Archaeology has issued advice to the users of metal detectors. Think about the issues involved and then write your own 'Metal Detecting Code'.

Information Sheet 1 on The Treasure Act

WHAT IS THE NEW DEFINITION OF TREASURE?
(taken from the leaflet prepared by the Department for Culture, Media and Sport)

> The following finds are treasure under the Act (more detailed guidance is given in the Code of Practice):
>
> 1. *Objects other than coins:* any object other than a coin, provided that it contains at least 10 per cent of gold or silver and is at least 300 years old when found. (Objects with gold or silver plating normally have less than 10 per cent of precious metal.)
>
> 2. *Coins:* all coins from the same find, provided they are at least 300 years old when found (but if the coins contain less than 10 per cent of gold or silver there must be at least 10 of them; there is a list of these coins in the Code of Practice).
>
>   An object or coin is part of the same find as another object or coin if it is found in the same place as, or had previously been left together with, the other object. Finds may have become scattered since they were originally deposited in the ground.
>
>   Only the following groups of coins will normally be regarded as coming from the 'same find': (a) hoards that have been deliberately hidden; (b) smaller groups of coins, such as the contents of purses, that may have been dropped or lost and (c) votive or ritual deposits.
>
>   Single coins found on their own are not treasure and groups of coins lost one by one over a period of time (for example, those found on settlement sites or on fair sites) will not normally be treasure.
>
> 3. *Associated objects:* any object, whatever it is made of, that is found in the same place as, or that had previously been together with, another object that is treasure.
>
> 4. *Objects that would have been treasure trove:* any object that would previously have been treasure trove, but does not fall within the specific categories given above. These objects have to be made substantially of gold or silver; they have to have been buried with the intention of recovery and their owner or his heirs cannot be traced.
>
>   The following types of find are not treasure:
>
>   – objects whose owners can be traced;
>
>   – unworked natural objects, including human and animal remains, even if they are found in association with treasure;
>
>   – objects from the foreshore, which are wreck.
>
> If you are in any doubt, it will probably be safest to report your find.

Finders Keepers ... Sometimes

Information Sheet 2 on The Treasure Act

OTHER KEY POINTS SUMMARISED FROM THE ACCOMPANYING CODE OF PRACTICE

1. All finds of treasure must be reported to the coroner for the district in which they are found.
2. Failure to do so could involve imprisonment for up to three months or a fine of up to £5,000 (current figure) or both.
3. Finders are normally asked to take the items to a local museum or archaeological body.
4. If the find is not treasure it is returned to the finder.
5. If the find is treasure but no museum wants it, it is returned to the finder.
6. If a museum wants the treasure the coroner holds an inquest after which the find will be valued by independent experts and a reward is paid.
7. The reward is paid to the finder if he or she had permission to be on the land unless there was a previous agreement between the finder and the landowner.
8. Even where finds are not treasure, finders are encouraged to report them to build up evidence of the past.
9. The foreshore is the area between mean high water and mean low water. The Treasure Act applies if the finds lay originally on land but if finds come from a wreck they are subject to regulations governing wrecks.
10. The government recognises that metal detectorists have been responsible for discovering many objects of great importance. The Act is not intended to restrict their hobby but metal detectorists are encouraged to join a club, to know the terms of The Treasure Act and to behave responsibly.
11. Permission is required to go on to any private land.
12. It is illegal to use a metal detector on a scheduled ancient monument unless permission has been obtained (very unlikely).
13. On cultivated land metal detectorists should only recover items from the plough-soil.
14. There is a real danger that finds could be damaged by inappropriate cleaning or that surrounding evidence could be destroyed.

Finders Keepers ... Sometimes

Teaching Notes

Archaeology is a fascinating area that can employ many important thinking skills.

Key Elements

- working with an official document
- analysis of evidence
- synthesis
- deduction and inference

Contexts

Finders Keepers ... Sometimes can be used in a variety of ways:

- as an extension to appropriate sections of work
- as an enrichment activity in the classroom
- as a differentiated or normal homework task
- as 'differentiation by content' – an item only covered by certain pupils
- as an activity within an enrichment session or summer school
- as an activity for the History Club
- as preparatory work for a Metal Detectors' Club.

THE FINDS

1. Not treasure, as less than 300 years old and not 10% gold or silver. Can be kept.

2. Such a collection looks as though it was deliberately hidden with the intention of recovery and the objects are gold. The coins are 'from the same find'. They are not 300 years old but come under the old treasure trove rules and are treasure. Report to the coroner. (Note: this is difficult because of the ambiguous wording of the document.)

3. Although over 300 years old and made of gold, this is not treasure as there is a single coin only.

4. Not treasure and no action needed as this goes under the heading 'unworked natural objects'. However a local museum might like the information.

5. Over 300 years old but less than 10% silver or gold. As there are less than ten of them, they are not treasure. Can be kept, depending upon any private agreement with landowner. Pass on information.

6. More than 300 years old and, although less than 10% gold or silver, there are at least ten of them. They are also 'of the same find'. This is treasure and must be reported to the coroner.

Finders Keepers ... Sometimes

7 Gold, over 300 years old, and found on the foreshore – therefore constitutes treasure *as long as the find originated on land and did not come from a wreck*. However, the circumstances suggest that the coins do come from a wreck (perhaps the Spanish Armada) and therefore the find is likely to come under special provisions associated with wrecks.

8 Over 300 years old, so they are treasure even though there is no gold or silver content, because there are at least ten and they would constitute 'the same find' as they look as though they are 'a ritual deposit'. Report to the coroner.

9 These appear to have been lost one by one over a period of time due to the nature of the area. They are not treasure and can be kept, depending upon any previous agreement with the landowner. Information to museum is recommended.

10 We do not know the content of the jewellery but these look like 'associated objects' with previous treasure and therefore become treasure themselves no matter what the composition. Report to the coroner.

Extension Tasks

- It is safest to report any find, because some objects may be difficult to identify without testing or more expert advice. In addition, damage could be done if the find is investigated without professional guidance.

- Many archaeologists were hostile to 'amateurs' because there was a danger that damage to a valuable site could be done. Also, valuable artefacts may have been removed, despite the previously-existing treasure trove regulations. However, metal detectorists have made many valuable finds that are now housed in museums. Co-operation with regulation may be much better than antagonism. The extra people out looking for finds are helpful, as archaeology is restricted financially.

- Pupils can deduce many obvious points of guidance to include in a 'Metal Detecting Code' from reading the information sheets (pages 115 to 116). For example, they may suggest that metal detectorists should not detect on an ancient site, should always get permission from the landowner, and so on.

Groundwork

Uncovering the truth about the past is fascinating. Archaeological techniques are being refined all the time. Dating procedures, in particular, are very sophisticated. Here is your chance to take advantage of this improved knowledge to design a 'dig' of your own that combines historical accuracy with your own creativity.

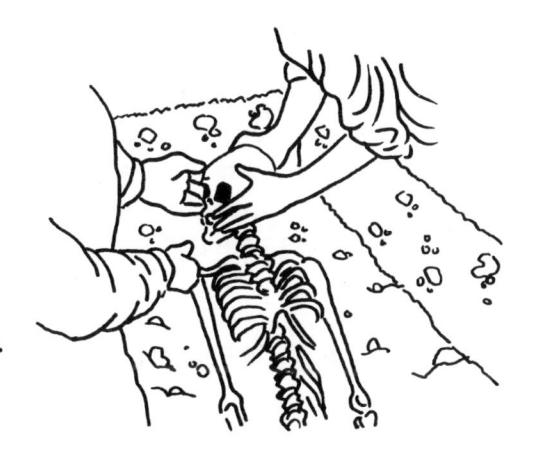

Your Task

Study carefully the accompanying sheets on archaeological methods.

Now choose a period or type of archaeology for the 'dig' you are going to create; for example, Roman, Medieval, Tudor, Victorian, Celtic, Ancient Egypt, Industrial, and so on.

Using at least six of the main methods described on the separate sheets, create the description and record of an archaeological excavation that is historically accurate but is the product of both research and your imagination. You can also use other methods not included in the information sheets.

Practical Points

1. You need to research carefully the period or type of archaeology chosen.
2. Diagrams are an important part of the archaeologists' work and they should be used appropriately.
3. The methods taken from the accompanying sheets should be appropriate for the period and the nature of the individual excavation.
4. The finished product should be realistic, albeit fictional.

Groundwork

A Summary Of The Archaeological Methods Available

DENDROCHRONOLOGY

By the eighteenth century, it was understood that trees produce annual growth rings allowing their ages to be calculated by counting those rings. The rings vary in thickness from year to year according to growing conditions. The work was advanced in the early twentieth century by A. E. Douglass who built up a series to which other examples could be compared. The overlapping or contemporary portions of the sample and the established series can be matched by observing similarities in the pattern of their rings. Computers can help the matching process. There are, however, some problems. There are regional and environmental variations in the growth of trees, and the storing and re-using of timbers cause difficulties.

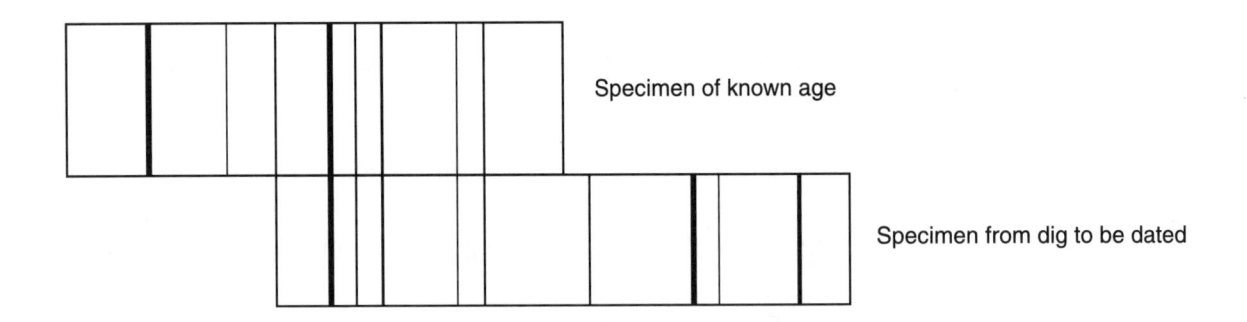

Specimen of known age

Specimen from dig to be dated

STRATIGRAPHY

This is based upon the principle that, in a series of layers below ground, those at the top contain the most recent archaeological deposits and older items will be in lower layers. Early excavations did not take sufficient notice of this principle but now the layers are removed very carefully so as to preserve the evidence. Layers could, however, have been disturbed. If, for instance, a post had been placed into a hole dug in the ground, soil from lower down could have been replaced closer to the surface.

POLLEN ANALYSIS

Palynology, or the study of pollen, provides useful information. Each grain of pollen has a tough outer shell that helps survival. Pollen is dispersed by birds, insects and the wind. Most can be identified to a genus although grasses cannot be separated. The grains in a soil sample are counted under a microscope to show the proportions of pollen of different plants. Pollen from cores extracted from peat bogs, for instance, help dating through layers. A picture is built up of the major changes in vegetation over time. Early farming activities can be identified. A change in the ratio of tree pollen to non-tree pollen points to the destruction of woodland.

Groundwork

RADIOCARBON DATING

Living things take up radiocarbon, or C-14, during life. This process stops at death. The C-14 then present decays at a known rate, with a half-life of 5730 years. A calculation can then be made of the time that has elapsed since the death of the organism. The process works best with charcoal and then wood.

The technique of radiocarbon dating changed views about many archaeological theories dramatically; for example, on how early agriculture developed. For some time, 40,000–50,000 years was as far back as the method of radiocarbon dating could be used, due to the weakness of C-14 still present. However, in the 1980s, an advanced form of radiocarbon dating called 'accelerator mass spectrometry' was developed to permit dating way beyond 50,000 years ago.

TYPOLOGY

Artefacts such as axes, pottery and beads can often be fitted into a pattern of classification, as the objects changed style or developed new characteristics over time. The classification of pottery can include a number of factors – handmade or wheel-made, size, shape, spouts, handles, colour and decoration. Similarly, early bronze axes were flat but the basic design went through a process of development to make the use more efficient. New finds can be placed against what has been excavated and dated previously.

AERIAL PHOTOGRAPHY

Aerial photography can give additional information on known visible sites, providing a better overall picture, as well as helping to identify previously unknown sites.

Ancient features such as walls and ditches produce shallower and deeper conditions of soil, which in turn affect the growth of plants. Crop-marks occur when buried features encourage or reduce the growth of plants. Cereal grains are particularly sensitive. In dry weather they need moisture and therefore grow better over buried pits and ditches where there is deeper soil that retains moisture. The opposite is true over buried walls and stone structures.

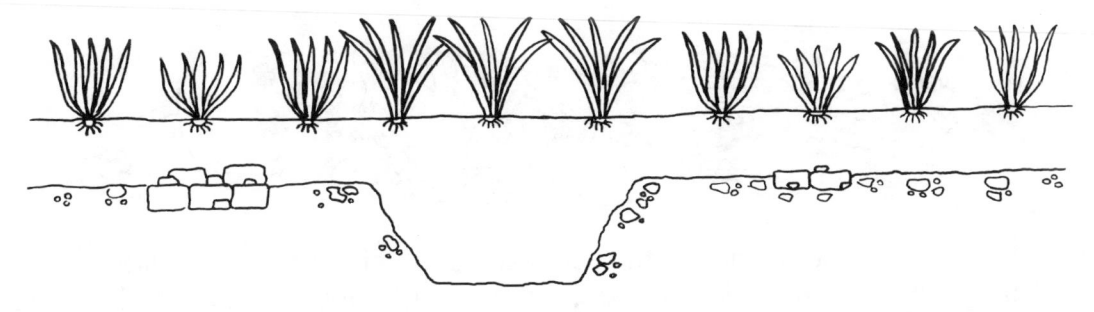

When the sun is low and long shadows are cast, aerial observation can pick up the remains of banks and ditches. Frost and light snow also produce favourable conditions.

Groundwork

GEOPHYSICAL SURVEYS
The methods involved in geophysical surveys are employed to give further details on a known site rather than to discover a new site. Resistivity meters are used to measure the resistance to the flow of an electric current passed through the ground between electrodes. Damp soil, perhaps indicating a pit, has low resistance whereas dry soil, perhaps pointing to a buried wall or road, shows a positive reading for high resistance.

Magnetometers give opposite readings – positive for pits and ditches and negative for roads and walls. They also detect metal objects such as iron axes.

Electromagnetic devices do not penetrate as deeply but can be helpful in detecting buried features. Metal detectors have allowed the 'lay person' to be involved in archaeological investigations but under strict rules and guidance, and not on scheduled monument sites. Sonar scanning is used for seabed surveys and was of major importance in the discovery of the Tudor warship 'Mary Rose'.

SOIL ANALYSIS
Different colours, textures and other features in soils are produced by natural and human activities. Knowledge can be gained about past climates. Colour is determined by reference to a Munsell Chart. Examination under the microscope may show very tiny pieces of charcoal, indicating that a fire has occurred there at some time. Chemical tests can identify elements; for example, phosphates point to human settlement, possibly with animals for food and milk, while sulphates often result from wood ash.

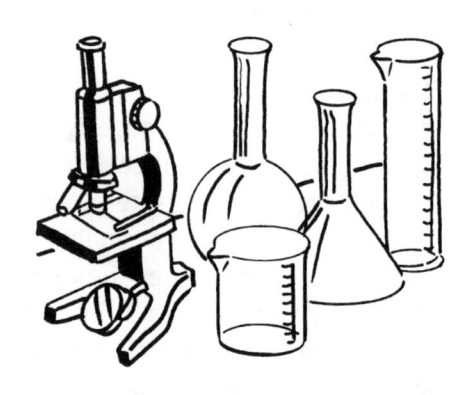

VARVES
During the summer, the melting of glaciers results in sediments being deposited on the beds of lakes. The thickness of the layers, which are called varves, depends upon the degree of melting. A Swedish geologist, Baron de Geer, used these varves to build up a sequence that helped to date the end of the last ice age. Pollen in the varves gives additional information.

THERMOLUMINESCENCE DATING
This method depends upon the presence of tiny amounts of radioactive matter in clay, and has been a great help in dating pottery. The sample is heated to over 300 °C, which causes the emission of light. This is measured and plotted on a graph where it is compared to other 'glow-curves'.

DNA

Tiny amounts of DNA can be taken from the bones and teeth of animals and humans. Analysis can reveal details about diseases and illnesses. Information is also gained about domestication of animals. Such analysis can also help decide whether bodies found in a cemetery come from family groups. Genetic information assists in understanding the movements and locations of ancient peoples. The archaeologists have to take great care not to contaminate the samples.

Groundwork

Teaching Notes

Many pieces of work in this book only need light teacher guidance but for *Groundwork* a stronger lead is required – not, that is, to give too many instructions including too much detail, thus reducing the pupils' thinking, but rather to make sure that various considerations are kept in mind so that the quality of the finished product is high. This piece of work could be completed without sufficient research and links being made, in which case the account would not fit together credibly. The teacher's role is to keep a watchful eye on proceedings and to drop appropriate hints when needed; it is not to guide the account strongly so that the pupil does not make the major input.

Key Elements

- research
- taking the general and applying to the specific
- using creativity but within a credible framework
- application
- synthesis of data
- good choice of material
- a sense of time
- logical thinking
- understanding the concepts behind archaeological techniques

Success Criteria

Groundwork accounts should be assessed with relation to:

- sensible choice and combination of methods
- skill in writing particular examples from general points
- the appropriateness of the methods to the period or type of archaeology selected
- the imagination and creativity displayed in the report without damage to historical accuracy and sense
- the use made, and application, of additional reading and research
- the authenticity of the report – does it look like the work of an archaeologist?

Contexts

Groundwork can be used in a number of ways:

- as extension to work on a particular period (in this case, the pupil may not be given the choice of period or type of archaeology)
- as enrichment work for pupils ahead in normal classroom tasks
- as differentiated homework
- as an activity within an enrichment session, a special weekend, summer school or cluster session
- as a project for members of the History Club
- as an open-access competition
- as a joint project with a local archaeological group
- as a piece of follow-up work to a trip to a museum or site.

Peace Treaty

A major war has just ended in the continent of Lamanda. The winning side consists of Fenland, Rubity and Grandi. Targary joined them after starting the war on the opposite side. Late in the war these allies received assistance from the large and wealthy country of Darca, which dominates the continent of Kransky. Lamanda and Kransky are separated by a thousand miles of sea known as the Rintic Ocean.

The defeated countries are Banland and Hanti. Banland is by far the more powerful and influential and in fact she defeated Rubity in a war only fifteen years ago. By the Treaty of Lummity, which ended that earlier conflict, Banland took a border area from Rubity called Milden.

Your Task

You are the representative of Fenland at the talks (to be held at Hargon, the capital of Rubity) that will draw up a peace settlement, dealing with Banland in particular. Let us assume that you have the final say in the peace terms.

Consider all the information presented on this and the accompanying sheets. Write out the clauses of your peace treaty. Explain why you have come to these decisions and include the arguments that you have used to persuade other countries.

The exercise is a complicated one. You need to read everything before you make any decisions. Extraction of key points in note form would be very advisable.

You have many **factors to bear in mind**. Among the most important may be:

1 **Public opinion** in your own country. An election is due shortly and, as a politician, you need as much public support as possible.

2 **Justice**. There is the question of punishing the 'guilty', if such a situation is relevant. 'Guilt' might be connected either with causing the war or with atrocities during the war.

3 The need to satisfy your **allies**. This will be particularly difficult as each country has differing views as to what should happen.

4 The **practicability** of the proposed terms. It is important that any decisions made should be capable of being put into operation.

5 The **security of Rubity**, especially in view of the two attacks made by Banland in recent years.

6 The need to maintain **peace** in Lamanda for as long as possible. If any country, including the defeated nations, feels very angry or upset at the terms, it will try to overthrow the settlement as soon as possible.

NOTE
- You may think of other factors that are equally important. If so, include them in your thinking.

Peace Treaty

Types of terms you may wish to include:

- **War-guilt clause.** This blames one or more countries for causing the war. Its inclusion allows other terms to punish a 'guilty country'.
- **Reparations.** Charges of money and/or goods such as timber, coal and iron are made to help pay for damage done during the war.
- **Territorial adjustments.** This involves the transfer of land to another country. Colonies may be dealt with in the same way.
- **Free Cities or Zones.** Areas of land are governed by international arrangement.
- **An Assembly of Nations.** An attempt to keep the peace by bringing the countries together in an organisation with set rules and arrangements.
- **Demilitarised Zone.** A country is forbidden to keep troops in a particular area.
- **Disarmament.** There is a complete ban or partial limitation on the quantity and quality of armaments and troops.
- **Army of Occupation.** For a set or unlimited time the victorious countries place an army in a defeated country to keep a close watch and/or to enforce the peace terms.
- **Form of government** in a defeated country. This may involve the banning of the past system of government and/or the imposition of a new system.

NOTE
Again, you may wish to consider other possibilities.

Individual decisions that you need to make may include the following:

- The **venue** (location) of the talks. (Remember that at the moment it is planned to use Hargon in Rubity.)
- The **representatives** who should play a major part in the discussions.
- The future of Emperor Carl of Banland and the form of **government** in that country.
- The level of **armaments** in Banland and other countries.
- The bill for the **damage** caused by the war.
- The border area of **Milden**.
- The importance to be given to **President Gilbert's Peace Programme**.
- The demands for **independence** of the Mandenians, Wullians and Dessians.
- The area of **Dangia**.
- The port of **Suga**.
- The future of the **Banlan colonies** of Raza, West Gola and South Liffen.
- The possible establishment of an **Assembly of Nations**. Consideration would need to be given to the membership and to the set of rules that would operate.
- A solution to the internal difficulties of **Hanti**.

Peace Treaty Information

THE CAUSES OF THE WAR

It is very difficult to see the causes of any conflict clearly. The following points are considered important by a number of historians, representing a variety of views.

1. The growth of an **alliance system**. Two major groups of countries were involved – Fenland, Rubity and Grandi formed the Triple Complex; Banland, Hanti and Targary joined to make the Triple Union. Any argument between two countries was likely to involve the whole continent because of the alliances and the promises of assistance contained within them.

2. The countries of Lamanda were involved in a struggle for **colonies** in the two distant continents of Manicia and Nenia. Banland was late to enter the search but eventually gained Raza, West Gola and South Liffen in Manicia. Fenland resented the rather aggressive way that Banland gained markets and colonies. The Banlans claimed that they had as much right as anybody else to extend their empire.

    There were also colonial arguments between Banland and Rubity, Targary and Rubity, Fenland and Rubity, and Fenland and Grandi.

3. Targary claimed that the area of **Dangia** in south east Rubity was really hers, as 60% of the people were of Targar origin. At the time of the unification of Targary an effort had been made, unsuccessfully, to include Dangia.

4. Grandi was in competition with Banland for use of the port of **Suga**. Many of Grandi's ports were on the eastern coast, which was badly affected by ice during the winter months. Grandi also wanted a corridor of land to the port to allow easy transport.

5. Three groups of people were struggling to gain **independence** as small nations. These were the areas of Mandenia and Wullia in Hanti and Dessia in Grandi. Other countries became involved. Banland gave help and encouragement to the Dessians while Grandi supported the peoples of Mandenia and Wullia.

6. Rubity wanted to regain the border area of **Milden**, which had been taken by Banland in an earlier war. Both countries claimed that the area should rightfully be theirs. The population was split almost exactly 50 : 50 in origin.

7. A **naval race** developed between Fenland and Banland. As an island, Fenland claimed that she needed a strong navy, for protection and for trade. She objected when Banland tried to build a large fleet of battleships, saying that as Banland had the strongest army, the increase in the Banlan navy could only be for aggressive purposes. In reply Banland said that her navy was needed to protect her overseas empire.

Peace Treaty 4/8

8 **Emperor Carl of Banland** made many aggressive speeches. He caused upset and annoyance on a number of occasions, especially in Fenland. He tended to speak first and think later. The Triple Complex countries accused him of being warlike. In reply he claimed only to be protecting his own country, which he felt was threatened by Rubity to the west and Grandi in the east.

9 The **immediate cause** of the war involved the assassination of Prince George of Hanti, the heir to the throne. On a visit to the city of Hevo in Wullia he was killed by men belonging to a secret society called 'The Wullian Liberation Army'. The assassins were Wullians who had previously fled to Grandi to avoid arrest. They planned the assassination in Grandi.

Hanti was outraged by the crime. They blamed the government of Grandi who denied that they had any previous knowledge of the plot. Hanti decided to take advantage of the situation to deal with their rival Grandi. They made impossible demands of the Grandians and when these demands were not met fully, Hanti declared war. The Hantian government was able to take confident action in the knowledge that they had a promise of help from Banland in the event of a war. Without such a promise they may well not have taken such a strong line.

10 **Banland** was worried that she would have to fight a two-front war against Rubity in the west and Grandi in the east. Feeling that war was inevitable, Banland launched an attack against Rubity through the small neutral country of Galtia. This was to avoid the main defences of Rubity. Banland hoped to knock Rubity out of the war quickly so that the war effort could then be concentrated against Grandi in the east. Within days all six countries involved in the two alliance systems were at war.

Peace Treaty

THE MAIN EVENTS OF THE WAR

1. At first there was great movement as Banland tried to capture Hargon, the capital of Rubity. The Galtians delayed the Banlan advance sufficiently to allow a Fenland army and redirected Rubitian troops to block the route.

2. A stalemate then developed in the west. Both sides lost great numbers of men in an effort to achieve a decisive breakthrough.

3. Banland was successful in the east where she gained a number of victories over the Grandians. Grandi may very well have been defeated if Banland's ally, Hanti had been stronger. Hanti struggled on but she was restricted by uprisings in Mandenia and Wullia which took away troops needed elsewhere.

4. Targary only entered the war on a promise from Banland and Hanti that Dangia would be taken from Rubity if the Triple Union was successful. She was not strong and failed to make any real impact.

   A year later Targary changed sides, joining the Triple Complex. She was promised the area of Dangia by both Fenland and Rubity. Although Targar troops did not make much ground, they did help to pin down Banlan forces.

5. At sea, the Fenland fleet was dominant although Banlan submarines did much damage to merchant shipping.

6. In the air, there were rapid developments as aircraft became more recognised as weapons of war. The pilots from both sides treated each other with great respect.

7. After three years there was a revolution in Grandi, which removed that country from the war. Banland forced a harsh peace treaty on Grandi, taking Dessia and other border territory further south. The Banlans were then able to concentrate their forces in the west.

8. In the same year Darca entered the war on the side of the Triple Complex. The Darcan government was angry at attacks made by Banlan submarines, which had cost Darcan lives. The involvement of this rich and powerful country broke the deadlock in the west.

9. Banland made one last big effort before the arrival of the Darcan troops in any great number. They made ground before being halted again. The forces of Fenland, Rubity and Darca then started to push the Banlan army back.

10. Banland signed an armistice as her position seemed hopeless. Targary had deserted the Triple Union and Hanti was beaten. Darcan troops had made a great difference on the western front. At home, the Banlan people were badly affected by a blockade operated by the Fenland fleet. There were great shortages of food and supplies. Emperor Carl abdicated and a new temporary government started to negotiate peace terms. This surrender was on the basis of President Gilbert's Peace Programme (see elsewhere).

11. During the war there were the normal atrocity stories on both sides but nothing was really proved. Banland used poisonous gas first but both Rubity and Fenland soon followed suit. There was an outcry about the sinking of a passenger liner from Fenland called the 'Middity', which involved the deaths of many women and children. Banland defended the sinking with a claim that the 'Middity' was not such an innocent victim as it was carrying munitions.

The war ended on a bitter note. As Banlan troops withdrew from Rubity they were responsible for deliberate damage.

Peace Treaty 6/8

Public Opinion And Official Views

DARCA

Darca had hoped to stay neutral but eventually the government felt obliged to intervene. In the final stages of the war President Gilbert published a Peace Programme, which he hoped would provide the basis for a treaty. The main points in the Peace Programme were as follows.

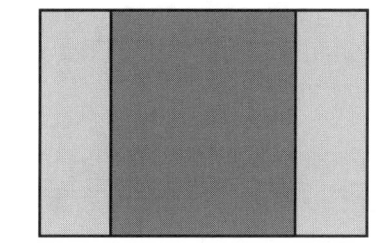

- Self-determination; that is, that all peoples should govern themselves rather than be ruled by another country.

- All nations should have equal rights at sea.

- Each country should reduce its armaments to a level consistent with national security.

- An Assembly of Nations should be established in an effort to maintain peace in the future.

- Grandi should have access to better port facilities.

- No country should indulge in secret diplomacy that was likely to provoke trouble.

President Gilbert will represent his country at the talks, but he has a difficult public opinion situation at home. Many Darcans feel that their country should play no part in the affairs of Lamanda. Another complicating factor is that Darca is fundamentally opposed to the new Ranbist government in Grandi.

President Gilbert would like to see peace negotiated on the basis of 'fairness and justice' so that no country will wish to overthrow the terms. He can, of course, take a sympathetic view of Banland as Darca is a thousand miles from Lamanda.

RUBITY

Rubity is very angry at Banland. The damage done by retreating troops in the final days of the war has not helped the situation. Public opinion is strongly in favour of a harsh peace treaty that will protect Rubity from further attack (Banland has invaded twice in the last 20 years).

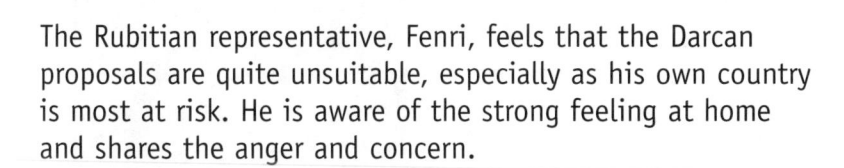

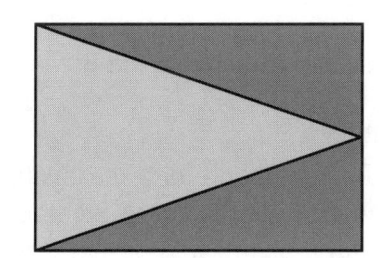

The Rubitian representative, Fenri, feels that the Darcan proposals are quite unsuitable, especially as his own country is most at risk. He is aware of the strong feeling at home and shares the anger and concern.

Some Rubitians want to see Banland divided up. They argue that the Banlans are very powerful and that only a division of territory will prevent further attacks. Others do not go that far but they would still press for reparations, for protection along Rubity's eastern frontier, for a drastic reduction in Banland's armaments and for some weakening of Banland's industrial strength, which is concentrated around Dendall.

All Rubitians are determined to recover the border area of Milden, which was taken by Banland in the previous conflict. They blame the outbreak of the war on Banland.

Peace Treaty

FENLAND
Your own country stands somewhere between Darca and Rubity. There is some support for President Gilbert's Peace Programme but Fenland feels that she needs special rights at sea. It is also acknowledged that Rubity needs protection against a possible Banland attack.

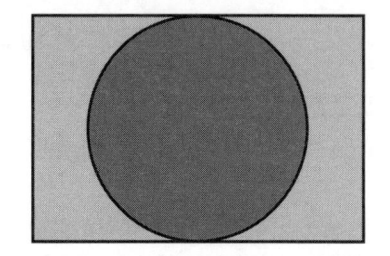

One possible way forward could be some form of guarantee from both Fenland and Darca. Most Fenlanders would support such a guarantee, provided that it was a joint venture with Darca. They would not want to give such an undertaking independently.

One complication for your government is that it is difficult to carry through a middle-of-the-road policy because of the ill-feeling towards Banland. During the war it was felt advisable to use propaganda against the Banlans. Now the war is over you cannot tell the people that they should ignore what has been said previously.

GRANDI
Grandi will not be represented at the talks. The new Ranbist government does not want to negotiate with countries who hold very different views on history and economics. The government is looking to the country's previous allies to make sure that Grandi gets a fair deal, and that the peace treaty negotiated with Banland at the time of the revolution is quashed.

TARGARY
The Targar representative, Bondrassy, wants, above all, to secure the area of Dangia. This territory was promised to Targary as reward for joining the Triple Complex but now that the war is over Rubity is not so keen to give up any land. Bondrassy knows that his voice will not be as strong as some other representatives as Targary started the war on the side of Banland. Public opinion in Targary is more interested in gains for themselves rather than any measures against the Banlans.

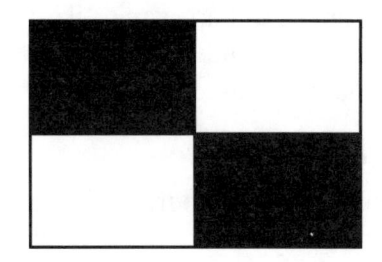

BANLAND
The Banlans hope for a reasonable settlement based upon President Gilbert's Peace Programme, which would stop any plans of Rubity for division or major territorial changes. They do not believe that any punitive measures are appropriate.
Banland has appointed a representative, Ligmund, but the government is very concerned at persistent rumours that he will not be entitled to take an active part in the talks.

HANTI
The Hanti Empire has broken up. During the war the areas of Mandenia and Wullia have been beyond the government's control. Emperor Bernard has fled the country. There is chaos inside Hanti and nobody knows what is going to happen. At the moment no representative will attend the peace talks.

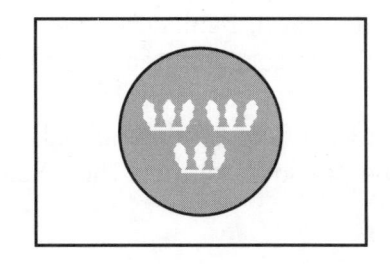

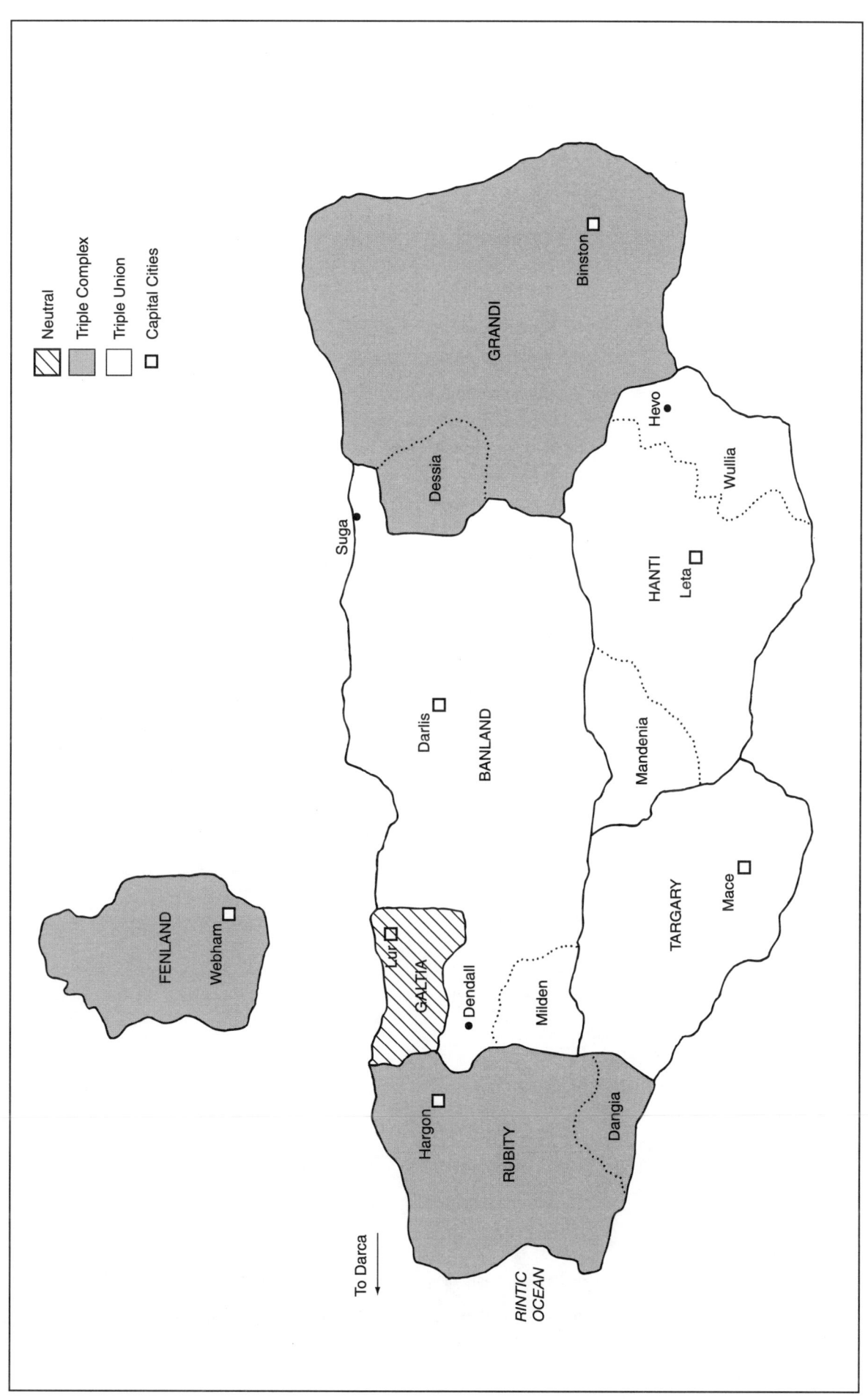

Peace Treaty

Lamanda

Legend:
- Neutral
- Triple Complex
- Triple Union
- □ Capital Cities

Countries and places:

- GRANDI (capital: Binston)
  - Dessia
- FENLAND (capital: Webham)
- BANLAND (capital: Darlis)
  - Suga
- HANTI (capital: Leta)
  - Hevo
  - Wullia
  - Mandenia
- GALTIA (capital: Lurz)
  - Dendall
  - Milden
- TARGARY (capital: Mace)
- RUBITY (capital: Hargon)
  - Dangia

RINTIC OCEAN

To Darca →

Peace Treaty

Teaching Notes

Many teachers will recognise that this piece of work is based loosely upon the Treaty of Versailles, the peace settlement at the end of the First World War. A fictional approach has been used for two main reasons:

- This makes it easier to make the unit self-contained, in terms of back-up information. This would be a far more difficult job if the First World War itself was used.
- There is the hope that pupils can be more objective in their views when they have no preconceived ideas about the countries involved.

Classes dealing with Modern World History may very well wish to compare these fictional events with the First World War. There are many parallels but there is certainly no exact duplication. This unit could be used as a revision exercise, looking to see what is the same, what is different and what is ignored.

The piece, however, stands in its own right and could be used to explore the difficulties of peace settlements in general. It would provide useful material for citizenship courses or general studies elements post-16.

Many of the ideas and concepts are difficult. This is inevitable because the nature of peacemaking is complex. Much discussion work will be needed so that ideas presented can be thoroughly tested. **Peace Treaty** would lend itself very easily to drama, with different pupils arguing out the views of the countries involved.

Key Elements

- analysis of data
- synthesis of data
- evaluation and judgement
- role play
- negotiation
- an alternative vehicle, if used in conjunction with the First World War

Contexts

Peace Treaty can be used in a variety of ways:

- as extension material to work on the First World War
- as an enrichment item in history
- as course material in citizenship
- as a differentiated homework
- as the basis of a group or class discussion
- as an activity for an enrichment session, summer school or cluster day.

SILENCE IN COURT

SILENCE IN COURT

CLERK	(*standing*) Put up the defendant.

A POLICE OFFICER ACCOMPANIES THE DEFENDANT TO HIS PLACE.

CLERK	All stand in court.

EVERYBODY STANDS. THE JUDGE ENTERS AND SITS DOWN, FOLLOWED BY OTHERS IN THE COURT.

CLERK	(*to the defendant*) Please stand. (*pause*)
	Josh Zenith Smith, you are charged that on Friday November 3rd you murdered John James Jones. How do you plead, guilty or not guilty?
DEFENDANT	Not guilty.
CLERK	You may sit down.

SWEARING IN OF THE JURY NOW TAKES PLACE.

CLERK	(*to 1st juror*) Take the book in your right hand and read the words on the card.
1st JUROR	(*stands up, sits after oath*) I swear that I will well and truly try and true deliverance make and give a true verdict according to the evidence.
CLERK	(*to 2nd juror*) Take the book in your right hand and read the words on the card.
2nd JUROR	(*stands up, sits after oath*) I swear that I will well and truly try and true deliverance make and give a true verdict according to the evidence.

3RD JUROR STANDS UP.

DEFENCE COUNSEL	(*standing up*) Objection. Your honour, this person lives on the same housing estate as the defendant and may well have heard prejudicial comments about my client. There has to be a real danger that the juror may be biased.
JUDGE	Very well. Replace the juror.

JUROR LEAVES AND SWEARING IN CONTINUES, UNTIL -

CLERK	(*to 5th juror*) Take the book in your right hand and read the words on the card.
5th JUROR	(*stands up*) There is something that I feel I ought to say. While other jurors have been sworn in, I have been looking around the court. The counsel for the prosecution is known to me. We went to school together, and although we have not met for some years I still feel that we are friends. Does that make a difference to my position?
JUDGE	Indeed it does. No member of the jury should know an advocate previously. Thank you for your honesty and alertness. If you had remained and your friendship had been discovered at a later stage, this trial could have been threatened. You are dismissed and you should return to the main jurors' assembly room.

THE 5TH JUROR LEAVES. THE REMAINING JURORS ARE SWORN IN.

CLERK	Members of the Jury, the prisoner stands indicted for that he on the 3rd day of November murdered John James Jones. To this indictment he has pleaded not guilty, and it is your charge to say, having heard the evidence, whether he be guilty or not guilty.

SILENCE IN COURT

CLERK SITS DOWN.

JUDGE Yes, Mr(s) Larch.

PROSECUTION COUNSEL (*standing up*) May it please Your Honour. Members of the Jury, in this case I appear to prosecute and my learned friend, Mr(s) Digby, appears for the defence.

The facts of this case are quite clear. The defendant is charged with murder – that is, causing the death of another human being with intent to cause his or her death or intent to cause grievous bodily harm. The defendant is known to have had a strong hatred for the murdered man. There is a long history of bad relations between them. Indeed, only days before the murder, the dead man received a threatening letter made up of words cut from newspapers. We shall show that there is no doubt that this was sent by the defendant. Other forensic evidence will place the defendant at the scene of the crime as, also, will the account of an eye witness. The defendant has lied to the police about essential points of the case. He claims to have an alibi for the key period of time, but this is another lie, supported by a person of dubious character. Members of the Jury, this is a dreadful crime committed by a spiteful man who was jealous of the success of a rival in business.

PROSECUTION COUNSEL SITS DOWN.

JUDGE Mr(s) Digby.

DEFENCE COUNSEL (*standing up*) Your Honour. Members of the Jury, this is indeed a dreadful crime as indicated by my learned friend. However, the facts of the case are far from clear. Indeed the defendant has lied, but there is a good explanation for that. We shall challenge the strength of the evidence against him. There is real doubt about key points in this case and as such we shall invite you to find the defendant not guilty.

DEFENCE COUNSEL SITS DOWN.

JUDGE Mr(s) Larch.

PROSECUTION COUNSEL (*standing up*) Thank you, Your Honour. Members of the Jury, we shall now lay the case for the prosecution before you. I now call Inspector Branch.

INSPECTOR BRANCH ENTERS THE WITNESS BOX.

CLERK (*stands, sits after oath*) Take the book in your right hand and repeat the words on the card.

INSPECTOR I swear that the evidence I shall give shall be the truth, the whole truth and nothing but the truth.

PROSECUTION COUNSEL You are Inspector Branch, Criminal Investigation Department, Hurlington?

INSPECTOR Yes, I am.

PROSECUTION COUNSEL Inspector Branch, on the evening of November 3rd, were you called to 24 Lacey Gardens, Hurlington?

INSPECTOR Yes sir/madam.

PROSECUTION COUNSEL Please tell the court what you found there.

THE INSPECTOR TAKES OUT HIS NOTEBOOK AND OPENS IT.

DEFENCE COUNSEL (*standing up*) Your Honour, there is here a point of law.

JUDGE Very well Mr(s) Digby. Clerk, please take the jurors out of court.

THE CLERK REMOVES THE JURY FROM THE COURT. PROSECUTION COUNSEL SITS DOWN.

SILENCE IN COURT

DEFENCE COUNSEL	Your Honour, it is normal to allow a police officer, or detective, to refer to a notebook while giving evidence. However, there is some doubt as to how soon these notes were made and therefore as to their reliability. Inspector, when did you write the notes down?
INSPECTOR	The following afternoon, November 4th.
DEFENCE COUNSEL	Why was there the delay?
INSPECTOR	After visiting 24 Lacey Gardens, I was called out to another incident, which lasted through the night. I then returned home to get some sleep. My notes were written up for both incidents during the afternoon of the 4th.
DEFENCE COUNSEL	Your Honour, I am concerned about the accuracy of these notes, given the time delay, and also the fact that the Inspector had been dealing with two major incidents, one after the other.
JUDGE	Inspector, do you feel that this delay impaired your memory and that, as a result, your notes may be inaccurate?
INSPECTOR	Your Honour, I am confident that there is no such inaccuracy. The delay was unfortunate but inevitable. The following afternoon I did confer with a colleague who had been present at the scene of the crime.
JUDGE	Mr(s) Digby, I appreciate your concern and wonder if perhaps there was an opportunity to record information earlier. However, I am satisfied that the Inspector should be allowed to consult his notebook.
DEFENCE COUNSEL	As it pleases Your Honour (*sits down*)
JUDGE	Bring the jurors back.

THE CLERK GOES, AND RETURNS WITH THE JURORS WHO TAKE UP THEIR PLACES AGAIN.

JUDGE	Members of the Jury, there has been a discussion on the correctness of the Inspector using his notebook as the notes were made after a delay. I am satisfied that their accuracy has not been impaired especially as a conference took place with a second officer. You may continue Mr(s) Larch.
PROSECUTION COUNSEL	(*standing up*) I am obliged, Your Honour. Now Inspector Branch, tell us what occurred at 24 Lacey Gardens on the evening of November 3rd.
INSPECTOR	I was in the police station when we received a call from PC Hawkes who explained that there had been a break-in at 24 Lacey Gardens. A man's body was found on the floor of the study area. He had been stabbed repeatedly. The man turned out to be John Jones, a local businessman. An upstairs room had been ransacked and a jewellery case had been broken open. The case was empty. After the doctor and scene-of-the-crime officers had finished their work, we carried out a search of the house and garden. Near the wall at the end of the garden we found items of jewellery hidden behind a shrub.

THE CLERK TAKES THE BAGS LABELLED EXHIBITS 1, 2, 3, 4 TO THE WITNESS BOX.

PROSECUTION COUNSEL	Would you please look at Exhibits 1, 2, 3 and 4. Are these the items of jewellery found near the garden wall?
INSPECTOR	Yes, they are.
PROSECUTION COUNSEL	Inspector Branch, please continue with your evidence.

SILENCE IN COURT

INSPECTOR	A downstairs window to the small store room off the kitchen had been broken. We also found in a drawer of the dead man's desk a sheet of paper with the message, 'You look out. You have ruined me,' spelt out by means of newspaper cuttings.
PROSECUTION COUNSEL	Inspector, please look at Exhibit 5.

CLERK TAKES EXHIBIT 5 TO THE WITNESS BOX.

	Is this the paper message to which you are referring?
INSPECTOR	Yes it is.
PROSECUTION COUNSEL	No further questions. (*sits down*)
DEFENCE COUNSEL	(*stands up*) Inspector Branch, in your search did you find any evidence directly linking the defendant to the scene of the crime – fingerprints, for instance?
INSPECTOR	No such fingerprints were found. Areas like the windowsill of the store room showed evidence that the intruder had worn gloves. However, we did link broken glass with the defendant's shoes.
DEFENCE COUNSEL	This is a charge of murder, Inspector. However, in your professional judgement, are the circumstances consistent with a break-in that went wrong? In other words, a burglar was disturbed and killed in panic.
INSPECTOR	Yes that is possible, but there are other explanations.
DEFENCE COUNSEL	No further questions.

DEFENCE COUNSEL SITS DOWN.

PROSECUTION COUNSEL	(*stands up*) Inspector, please tell the court how the circumstances would fit another explanation; that is, a case of murder.
INSPECTOR	The jewels that had been stolen were abandoned in the garden. They may well have been taken as a blind to the real crime – the murder of John Jones. The break-in was very amateurish – a broken window. This may have been deliberate to draw attention to a minor crime as a cover-up for murder.
PROSECUTION COUNSEL	Thank you, Inspector. I have no further questions. You may step down. I now call Dr Ross.

THE INSPECTOR LEAVES THE WITNESS BOX AND IS REPLACED BY DR ROSS.

CLERK	(*stands, sits after oath*) Take the book in your right hand and repeat the words on the card.
DOCTOR	I swear that the evidence that I shall give shall be the truth, the whole truth and nothing but the truth.
PROSECUTION COUNSEL	You are Dr James/Janice Ross?
DOCTOR	Yes, that is so.
PROSECUTION COUNSEL	Please tell the court your current occupation.
DOCTOR	I am employed at the forensic science laboratory in Newton.
PROSECUTION COUNSEL	Doctor, your laboratory examined a piece of paper with a message on it made up from newspaper cuttings. Will you please look at Exhibit 5 and confirm that this is the said piece of paper.

CLERK TAKES EXHIBIT 5 TO THE WITNESS BOX.

DOCTOR	Yes, that is the paper that was examined.

SILENCE IN COURT

PROSECUTION COUNSEL	Members of the Jury, this is a vital piece of evidence in this case. Doctor, please describe to the court the tests carried out on this paper and how they were linked to other tests on items handed to you by the C.I.D.
DOCTOR	We carried out tests on the glue that had been used and on the paper itself. The glue was identical to a tube removed from the defendant's home. Other sheets of paper from the defendant's home matched exactly the sheet used for the message. Old sheets of newspaper found in the waste bin of the defendant had pieces missing which fitted exactly the slips used to make the message.
PROSECUTION COUNSEL	Thank you doctor. Now would you please inform the court about tests carried out on fragments of glass.
DOCTOR	We tested samples of glass from the broken window and fragments taken from between the ridges on the soles of the shoes found at the defendant's home. The samples from both the window and the shoes have the same refractive index. This index only applies to 20% of all such glass.
PROSECUTION COUNSEL	Can you please confirm that Exhibits 6 and 7 are the samples of glass from the window and the shoes respectively?

CLERK TAKES EXHIBITS 6 AND 7 TO THE WITNESS BOX.

DOCTOR	Yes I can confirm that.
PROSECUTION COUNSEL	Thank you Dr Ross. I have no further questions. (*sits down*)
DEFENCE COUNSEL	(*standing up*) Dr Ross, I do not wish to question you about the message on the paper. Members of the Jury, this evidence is not challenged, but I will provide you with an explanation later in the trial.
	Doctor, this glass that you examined – I am correct in saying that your tests only proved that the two samples of glass both come from the 20% of such glass in use, and not that the two samples are identical? In other words, the fragments from the shoes cannot be shown to have definitely come from the broken window?
DOCTOR	Yes, that is correct.
DEFENCE COUNSEL	Thank you, no further questions. (*sits down*)

PROSECUTION COUNSEL SIGNALS THAT NO RE-EXAMINATION IS NEEDED. THE DOCTOR LEAVES THE WITNESS BOX.

PROSECUTION COUNSEL	(*standing up*) I now wish to call Mrs Edith Seymour.

CLERK TAKES MRS SEYMOUR TO THE WITNESS BOX.

CLERK	(*stands, sits after oath*) Take the book in your right hand and repeat the words on the card.
MRS SEYMOUR	I swear that the evidence that I shall give shall be the truth, the whole truth and nothing but the truth.
PROSECUTION COUNSEL	You are Mrs Edith Seymour and you live at 22 Lacey Gardens, Hurlington?
MRS SEYMOUR	Yes, I am Mrs Seymour and I live at 22 Lacey Gardens.
PROSECUTION COUNSEL	Mrs Seymour, you live next door to the murdered man, John Jones. Tell the court what you saw on the evening of November 3rd last.
MRS SEYMOUR	At eight o'clock I was putting some rubbish into the dustbin at the side of my house. From there you can see between the houses to the road. As I was looking I saw a man stop and look around him, as though he was up to no good.

SILENCE IN COURT

DEFENCE COUNSEL	(*standing up*) Objection. Your honour, the witness is speculating about the behaviour of this man beyond what she can actually know.
JUDGE	Objection sustained. Members of the Jury, you will ignore that last comment. Mr(s) Larch, please endeavour to keep your witness to what she knows, not what she might suppose.

DEFENCE COUNCIL SITS.

PROSECUTION COUNSEL	As you please, Your Honour. Mrs Seymour, please continue but limit your comments to what you actually saw.
MRS SEYMOUR	Well, I saw this man – he stopped and hesitated and then went from my view.
PROSECUTION COUNSEL	Would you be able to identify this man?
MRS SEYMOUR	Yes I would. I got a good look at him.
PROSECUTION COUNSEL	Do you see that man in court?
MRS SEYMOUR	Yes – over there – the defendant.
PROSECUTION COUNSEL	Let the record state that the witness indicated the defendant, Josh Zenith Smith. Mrs Seymour would you now tell the court what happened during the next few minutes on that night.
MRS SEYMOUR	I went back inside to watch television. Five minutes later I heard a scream. Then there was the sound of breaking glass. I looked through the front window and I saw the shape of a man running off. I went out onto the street and as luck would have it I saw a police car parked up on the main road. I got there as quickly as I could and told the police officers inside the car. They entered 24 Lacey Gardens and found poor Mr Jones. I am sure that Mr Jones had had trouble with Josh Smith before – his name is familiar.
DEFENCE COUNSEL	(*standing up*) Objection. Your Honour, this is hearsay.
JUDGE	Objection sustained. Members of the Jury, Mrs Seymour has not witnessed this so-called trouble. Clearly we cannot question the dead man. This is therefore what we call hearsay. It cannot be tested in court. You must ignore Mrs Seymour's final comment.

DEFENCE COUNSEL SITS DOWN.

PROSECUTION COUNSEL	Thank you, Your Honour. Mrs Seymour, you are sure that the man you saw at the front of the house was the defendant?
MRS SEYMOUR	Yes, I am sure.
PROSECUTION COUNSEL	You are also saying that the man you saw running off was the defendant.
DEFENCE COUNSEL	(*standing up*) Objection. Your Honour, my learned friend is leading the witness.
JUDGE	Mr(s) Larch, you should know better than to use leading questions. Objection sustained. Members of the Jury, defence counsel has suggested, quite correctly, that prosecution counsel is putting words into the witness' mouth.

DEFENCE COUNSEL SITS DOWN.

PROSECUTION COUNSEL	I apologise, Your Honour. Mrs Seymour, did you get a reasonable view of the man running off?
MRS SEYMOUR	Yes I did

SILENCE IN COURT

PROSECUTION COUNSEL	Did you recognise him?
MRS SEYMOUR	Yes – it was the defendant. It was the same man that I had seen a few minutes before
PROSECUTION COUNSEL	Thank you Mrs Seymour. I have no further questions of this witness.

PROSECUTION COUNSEL SITS DOWN.

DEFENCE COUNSEL	(*standing up*) Mrs Seymour, you say that you got a good view of the man at the front of the house. How long did he hesitate there – one second, two seconds, ten seconds, a minute?
MRS SEYMOUR	Well – I suppose a couple of seconds, but I did see him clearly.
DEFENCE COUNSEL	Do you remember what the weather was like on that evening?
MRS SEYMOUR	Er ... I don't really know. My memory is not what it used to be.
DEFENCE COUNSEL	I have in court a written record of the weather from our local meteorological office. Your Honour, it is Exhibit 8.

THE CLERK TAKES EXHIBIT 8 FIRST TO THE JUDGE AND THEN TO THE JURY.

	This is what it says – 'The evening of November 3rd was wet and misty. A cold front was passing over the Hurlington area. Visibility was poor.' You still say you saw this man clearly at a distance of, what – some 25 or 30 yards?
MRS SEYMOUR	Yes I do say that. I can't remember such weather but if you say that's what it was like, I suppose it must have been. There is a little distance between my dustbin and the street front as the houses are set well back, but I saw what I saw. I've got good eyesight – that's what my optician said anyway on my last visit for new glasses.
DEFENCE COUNSEL	You returned from the dustbin to watch television?
MRS SEYMOUR	Yes, I love watching the TV. It's how I spend most evenings.
DEFENCE COUNSEL	Mrs Seymour would you tell us what you have in your left ear?
MRS SEYMOUR	You know what it is – it's a hearing aid.
DEFENCE COUNSEL	You have some trouble with your hearing. Do you therefore have the sound on your television set turned up?
MRS SEYMOUR	Perhaps – just a bit.
DEFENCE COUNSEL	Are you sure of the order of the noises on that night? A scream, then breaking glass?
MRS SEYMOUR	Yes, I am very sure.
DEFENCE COUNSEL	Thank you, no more questions.

DEFENCE COUNSEL SITS DOWN.

PROSECUTION COUNSEL	(*standing up*) I do not wish to re-examine. Your Honour, Members of the Jury, that concludes the case for the prosecution.

PROSECUTION COUNSEL SITS DOWN.

DEFENCE COUNSEL	(*standing up*) Members of the Jury, my learned friend has presented his case. Now it is the turn of the defence. Without any hesitation or delay I call the defendant, Josh Zenith Smith.

THE DEFENDANT COMES TO THE WITNESS BOX.

SILENCE IN COURT

CLERK	(*stands, sits after oath*) Take the book in your right hand and repeat the words on the card.
DEFENDANT	I swear that the evidence that I shall give shall be the truth, the whole truth and nothing but the truth.
DEFENCE COUNSEL	You are Josh Zenith Smith?
DEFENDANT	Yes I am.
DEFENCE COUNSEL	And you live at 14 Park Street, Hurlington?
DEFENDANT	Yes, that is correct.
DEFENCE COUNSEL	Mr Smith, you are aware that the defendant does not have to take the witness stand?
DEFENDANT	Yes I am, but I am keen to clear my name. I am not frightened to take the stand in my own defence.
DEFENCE COUNSEL	You have heard the prosecution discuss the paper found in the dead man's home that has on it a message made up of newspaper cuttings. Please look at Exhibit 5. Do you recognise this paper?
DEFENDANT	Yes I do. I was responsible for cutting words out of newspapers, making the message, and sending it to John Jones. It was a very stupid thing to do and I bitterly regret it.
DEFENCE COUNSEL	Members of the Jury, the defence does not contest this particular evidence. The defendant admits full responsibility for it. Mr Smith, why did you send this message to the dead man?
DEFENDANT	I won't say that I didn't hate John Jones. He was an awful man. He damaged my business badly by opening rival shops close to where I already had premises. His business and mine were concerned with cards and stationery items. He cut prices to force me out of business. Unfortunately, he had more capital behind him than me and could survive a price war more easily than I could. One or two of my shops had already closed down, and others were in trouble. I telephoned John Jones and tried to talk some sense into him but he wouldn't listen. He just laughed and said, 'May the best man win'. At the end of October I was feeling very low and very angry. In desperation I sent him the message. I know it was stupid but I wasn't thinking straight and I didn't mean anything by it.
DEFENCE COUNSEL	Mr Smith, did you murder your rival, John Jones?
DEFENDANT	No I didn't. I disliked him intensely but that's very different to taking action.
DEFENCE COUNSEL	The prosecution has made much of the glass fragments found between the ridges on the soles of your shoes. Have you any explanation as to the origin of these fragments?
DEFENDANT	Well they certainly did not come from the window of John Jones' house. I have been thinking hard about this and I believe I know the answer. On November 2nd I took a variety of rubbish to the council recycling centre on Leeming Road. While there I had a look round at the items for sale. There was quite a lot of broken glass scattered on the concrete. The man looking after the section said that a previous customer had dropped a pane of window glass and there had not been time to clear it up.
DEFENCE COUNSEL	Where were you on the fateful evening of November 3rd?

SILENCE IN COURT

DEFENDANT I went round to see a mate of mine – Luke Standish – who lives at 9 Knorr Road, close to my own house. I was there all evening.

DEFENCE COUNSEL Thank you Mr Smith for your frank and honest answers. I have no more questions to ask, but I expect my learned friend does.

DEFENCE COUNSEL SITS DOWN.

PROSECUTION COUNSEL (*standing up*) Indeed I do. Mr Smith, you admit sending the threatening letter to John Jones but claim that it does not mean that you would do anything to hurt him – a little difficult to believe, don't you think?

DEFENDANT Yes I do admit it, but no I had no intention of harming John Jones. We all dislike people without intending to kill them.

PROSECUTION COUNSEL That's as maybe, but we don't all see our livelihoods being threatened quite so clearly as in this case. Mr Smith, if you are so innocent, how is it that at first you denied anything to do with the threatening message when the police first interviewed you?

DEFENDANT Because I was frightened. People know that John Jones and I did not get on. When I heard of his murder I was worried that I would be accused. When the police asked me about the letter I panicked. I thought that they would see an admission as proof of my involvement in his death. I did later own up to sending the letter.

PROSECUTION COUNSEL Ah yes! Indeed you did, Mr Smith. Would it not be true to say that you agreed you had sent the letter when police tests proved its origin beyond any doubt?

DEFENDANT If you wanted to, you could say that.

PROSECUTION COUNSEL Yes you could, and indeed I do. Members of the Jury, I hope that you have noted the sequence of events relating to the threatening letter. Moving on, then. Mr Smith, this glass found on the soles of your shoes – it came from the window of John Jones' house, didn't it?

DEFENDANT No it didn't. I've told you where it came from.

PROSECUTION COUNSEL The convenient recycling centre and, of course, by the time you gave this story to the police, the evidence had been cleared up and no tests could be carried out upon this mythical glass.

DEFENCE COUNSEL (*standing up*) Objection. Your Honour, my learned friend is in no position to claim that there was no such glass.

JUDGE Perhaps, Mr(s) Larch, you could be a little more careful about your inferences. However, I am not going to strike the comment from the record. Pray proceed.

DEFENCE COUNSEL SITS DOWN.

PROSECUTION COUNSEL I am obliged, Your Honour. Members of the Jury, suffice it to say that no test of comparison was possible to try to match the fragments of glass on the shoes with any broken glass at the Leeming Road recycling centre. Let me move on. Mr Smith, you claim you had an alibi for the critical time. This was just a put-up job wasn't it?

DEFENDANT No it wasn't. Luke will back me up.

PROSECUTION COUNSEL I will have more to say on that particular subject, but I have no more questions for you, Mr Smith.

PROSECUTION COUNSEL SITS DOWN.

SILENCE IN COURT

DEFENCE COUNSEL	(*standing up*) Before you leave the stand, Mr Smith, let me ask you again – did you kill John Jones?
DEFENDANT	No I didn't, I really didn't. I'm not capable of such a thing.
DEFENCE COUNSEL	Mr Smith, are you telling this court that you did not visit 24 Lacey Gardens on November 3rd?
DEFENDANT	Yes I am, and anybody claiming different is mistaken or lying.
DEFENCE COUNSEL	Thank you, Mr Smith. You may leave the witness box. I now call Mr Luke Standish.

THE DEFENDANT LEAVES THE WITNESS BOX AND IS REPLACED BY LUKE STANDISH.

CLERK	(*stands, sits after oath*) Take the book in your right hand and repeat the words on the card.
MR STANDISH	I swear that the evidence that I shall give shall be the truth, the whole truth and nothing but the truth.
DEFENCE COUNSEL	You are Luke Standish of 9 Knorr Road, Hurlington?
MR STANDISH	Yes I am.
DEFENCE COUNSEL	How long have you known the defendant?
MR STANDISH	Many years – fifteen or sixteen. We are old friends.
DEFENCE COUNSEL	Tell the court where you were on the evening of November 3rd and what happened that evening.
MR STANDISH	I was at home. I had my tea about six o'clock and then settled down to read the evening newspaper. At about a quarter to seven there was a knock on the front door. I opened the door and there was Josh. He said that he was at a loose end and asked if he could come in. I was only too pleased to see him.
DEFENCE COUNSEL	What did you do during the evening?
MR STANDISH	We chatted for a while. Then we got out the cards and played a game. We had a beer or two during the game and before he went we had a bit of supper – ham sandwiches, crisps and pickled onions.
DEFENCE COUNSEL	What time did Josh Smith leave you?
MR STANDISH	At about half past ten.
DEFENCE COUNSEL	No further questions.

DEFENCE COUNSEL SITS DOWN.

PROSECUTION COUNSEL	(*standing up*) Mr Standish, you are an important witness in this trial. You have sworn to tell the truth and if you fail to do so you will be guilty of perjury and may face prosecution yourself. Do you understand that?
MR STANDISH	Yes. I am telling the truth.
PROSECUTION COUNSEL	Did anybody else see Josh Smith at your home on the evening of November 3rd?
MR STANDISH	No.
PROSECUTION COUNSEL	Did Josh Smith leave your presence during the evening?
MR STANDISH	No.

SILENCE IN COURT

PROSECUTION COUNSEL So what it amounts to is this, Mr Standish. Josh Smith's alibi for the fateful evening is entirely down to you and nobody else. Are you an honest man, Mr Standish?

DEFENCE COUNSEL (*standing up*) Objection. Your Honour, it is not Mr Standish on trial here.

PROSECUTION COUNSEL No, Your Honour, but the honesty, or otherwise, of this witness is vital to the case. With Your Honour's permission I wish to follow a line that will put Mr Standish's evidence in context.

JUDGE Objection overruled. Mr(s) Digby, you are right that Mr Standish is not on trial although he is sworn to tell the truth. The defendant's alibi depends upon the honesty of this witness. You may proceed Mr(s) Larch but go no further than you have to.

DEFENCE COUNSEL SITS DOWN.

PROSECUTION COUNSEL Thank you Your Honour, I am much obliged. Now Mr Standish, where were we? Ah yes! I was asking you if you were an honest man. Has there ever been a doubt about your honesty?

MR STANDISH I don't know what you mean.

PROSECUTION COUNSEL Oh, I think you do. Let me put it this way. Mr Standish, have you ever been found guilty of dishonesty in a court of law?

DEFENCE COUNSEL (*standing up*) Objection. Your Honour, my learned friend is trying unfairly to discredit a witness.

JUDGE Objection overruled. Mr(s) Digby you know only too well that if the defendant uses a witness in this way, that the prosecution is quite entitled to pursue this approach. Continue Mr(s) Larch.

DEFENCE COUNSEL SITS DOWN.

PROSECUTION COUNSEL Thank you Your Honour. Now Mr Standish, let me repeat my question. Have you ever been found guilty of dishonesty in a court of law?

MR STANDISH Yes.

PROSECUTION COUNSEL Am I correct in saying that you have been convicted twice for burglary and once for fraud?

MR STANDISH Yes.

PROSECUTION COUNSEL Thank you. No more questions.

PROSECUTION COUNSEL SITS DOWN.

DEFENCE COUNSEL (*standing up*) I have no more witnesses to call. That is the case for the defence.

DEFENCE COUNSEL SITS DOWN.

JUDGE Thank you Mr(s) Digby. Members of the Jury, you have heard the evidence in this case. There remains the closing speeches and my summing-up. However, given the time, we will take a short break.

THE COURT RISES AND THE JUDGE LEAVES. THERE IS A SHORT BREAK.

CLERK (*standing*) All stand in court.

THE JUDGE ENTERS AND TAKES HIS SEAT. EVERYONE SITS DOWN.

JUDGE Mr(s) Larch, we are ready for you now.

PROSECUTION COUNSEL (*standing up*) Thank you Your Honour. Members of the Jury, you have heard the evidence in this case. I am now about to make the closing

SILENCE IN COURT

speech for the prosecution, and a simple and straightforward affair it will be, given the clarity of the guilt of the defendant, Josh Zenith Smith.

This is a case of envy, anger and brutal murder. Not just brutal murder but the premeditated death of an innocent human being.

Members of the Jury, the defendant saw John Jones not only as an arch rival in business but as the cause of his own personal misfortunes. You have heard how the defendant's business was going downhill rapidly. We may never know how his mind was affected by the downturn in his fortunes, but he came to a fevered plan for ridding himself of his rival, namely the murder of John Jones.

The defendant admits putting together a threatening letter saying 'You look out. You have ruined me'. This is not in conflict. What is in conflict, according to the defendant, is that he took no action to follow up his threat.

Members of the Jury, can you really believe this? Look at the evidence. Glass fragments from the soles of Josh Smith's shoes match the broken window glass to the extent that only 20% of such glass shows the same characteristics. In other words there is a 4 in 5 chance of positive identification. The defendant comes up with an explanation of the glass which, conveniently, cannot be tested.

We have a reliable witness, Mrs Edith Seymour, who has identified clearly the defendant as being the man seen at the front of her property on the evening in question, and again running away a few minutes later. She heard a scream followed by breaking glass – a very strange sequence of events. There is however an explanation for this sequence. The defendant got into the property quietly, killed the unfortunate John Jones and, after getting back outside, he broke the window. Why? To give the appearance of a break-in. He strengthened that appearance by taking items of jewellery. Whether this jewellery was accidentally dropped or whether it was left deliberately, I cannot say.

Strong evidence indeed, Members of the Jury. What does the defendant offer as an alibi? The sole support of a dubious witness, a man whose honesty is very much in doubt – a man who has been found guilty in court of dishonesty on three separate occasions. What credence can you place upon the words of such a witness?

Members of the Jury, you have heard and seen clear evidence as to the defendant's guilt. This is beyond reasonable doubt.

PROSECUTION COUNSEL SITS DOWN.

DEFENCE COUNSEL (*standing up*) Members of the Jury, you have heard my learned friend give a superficially persuasive case for the prosecution, but in my closing speech I will expose its weaknesses.

The defendant has been very frank and honest with you. He took the stand when there is no legal compulsion to do so. Indeed, wild horses would not have kept him out of that witness box. He freely admitted to hatred of the victim and to sending him a threatening letter. That, however, Members of the Jury, is a long way from murder. How many of you have said at a moment of great anger, 'I could kill him'? Did you mean it? Of course you didn't!

SILENCE IN COURT

The evidence is pretty flimsy. The only forensic evidence linking the defendant to the scene of the crime is the glass. Yes, only 20% of glass has the same refractive index as the fragments on the soles of Josh Smith's shoes. That, Members of the Jury, is a long way from an exact match. No other forensic evidence has been offered – fingerprints, footprints, threads from clothing, not even the weapon. Indeed, during the case no mention has been made of the murder weapon. Why? Because it has not been traced, that's why.

It is alleged that Josh Smith deliberately set up a burglary to cover murder. In that case why leave the jewellery in the garden? If the crime was so well planned, why make such a mistake? Surely a more convincing burglary would be if the jewellery had disappeared entirely?

The prosecution has made much of the sequence of events – the scream and then the breaking glass. However this depends upon the sole evidence of one elderly woman. Members of the Jury, I have no doubt as to the honesty of that witness. She came to court to do her duty. That does not mean that she did not make mistakes. Mrs Seymour admitted that her memory is not what it was. She has to have the television on loudly due to hearing loss. What is more natural than that she should have made mistakes about the sequence of events that night.

Then there is the so-called sighting of the defendant. The night was dark, wet and misty (something that Mrs Seymour did not recall). She was some distance from the man on the street and he was soon gone. Her eyesight is not the best. After the murder the second sighting is even more in doubt – after all, the man was running away. By that time an elderly woman living on her own would have been confused and frightened. No wonder she made genuine mistakes.

Members of the Jury, the defendant has admitted to things that he knows are wrong – not, you might say, the actions of a dishonest man, let alone a murderer. The rest of the case is based upon superficial evidence that cannot be relied upon. The prosecution has dismissed the defendant's alibi on the grounds that Mr Standish has a record of dishonesty. Does that mean that he is incapable of telling the truth on this occasion?

Members of the Jury, your course of action is clear. You must acquit the defendant on the grounds of insufficient and conflicting evidence. There is no way that what you have heard in this courtroom constitutes guilt beyond reasonable doubt.

DEFENCE COUNSEL SITS DOWN.

JUDGE   Members of the Jury, it is now my duty to sum up the case before you retire to come to your verdict.

First I must make you aware of the law – that is my responsibility, and mine alone. This case has attracted considerable publicity. You, Members of the Jury, must pay no heed to things beyond this courtroom. Your decision must be based upon evidence, the evidence that you have heard in court, and nothing else.

In English law the guilt of a defendant must be proved 'beyond reasonable doubt'. The onus has been upon the prosecution. If you have reasonable

SILENCE IN COURT

doubt, it is your duty to acquit. However, you cannot look for absolute proof. There will always be alternative explanations for everything. 'Beyond reasonable doubt' is what you have to keep in mind, not fanciful nor fantastic doubts.

The defendant is charged with murder. This is defined as 'causing the death of another human being with intent to cause his or her death or intent to cause grievous bodily harm'. The intent must be there or murder has not been committed.

Secondly – the facts of the case. I, as judge, am the sole interpreter of the law but you, and you alone, have the duty of judging the facts. To help you, however, I will indicate key areas for your special attention.

There is no conflict about the authorship of the threatening letter but there is a major difference as to whether it led to action, in fact to murder. The glass fragments have been described by an expert forensic witness. You can take his/her evidence as factually correct but what element of doubt remains as to their significance? Are the statistics strong enough? Do you believe the defendant's explanation as to the undoubted presence of glass fragments on the soles of his shoes? There is no evidence to prove his assertion or otherwise.

There is a single eye witness. Her testimony is very important. You have seen and heard Mrs Edith Seymour in the witness box. Can you trust her sightings – one, or both – of the defendant? If so, this points towards his guilt. Or do you have sufficient doubts as to her evidence, not because she is trying to deceive but because she made genuine mistakes through impairment of her senses and the poor weather conditions prevailing on the night?

Finally, the defendant's alibi. Much depends upon Mr Standish. He is the only person who has placed the defendant away from the crime. His evidence is unsubstantiated but it is quite feasible that the two men shared an evening without the knowledge of other people. The honesty of the witness is crucial and that is why it was permissible for his criminal record to be brought into court. Do you believe Mr Standish or do his past misdemeanours make you doubt his word? Even people who are dishonest on occasions, do tell the truth. Was this one of those times? Only you can decide.

Members of the Jury, you have sworn to try the case fairly. Weigh up the evidence and reach your conclusion. You will need to appoint a foreperson to chair your deliberations. The discussions of the jury room are secret. You must not discuss the case with anybody else, now or in the future. To start with I ask you to reach a unanimous verdict, but if this proves impossible, I will give you further instructions. On behalf of our legal system I thank you for your efforts.

CLERK (*standing*) All stand in court.

THE JUDGE RISES, ALL STAND (S)HE LEAVES, THE JURY IS TAKEN BY THE CLERK TO THE JURY ROOM READY TO START THEIR DELIBERATIONS.

SILENCE IN COURT

Teaching Notes

Silence In Court enacts a murder trial. It holds considerable intrinsic interest for many pupils and provides an exciting challenge. The work fits the programme of study for the new citizenship course.

A great deal of research has gone into the preparation of ***Silence In Court*** so that an accurate picture has been given of the order of proceedings and the component parts of a trial. There are, however, some points to note:

- the piece is long in terms of the time framework of schools but even so it has been truncated to make it feasible to handle
- only limited evidence has been included – enough to give proper consideration but much, much less than for a real-life murder trial
- the names and events are fictional and any link to real people is accidental and coincidental
- some wording has been changed to avoid problems with pupils of particular beliefs or faiths. In particular the swearing-in of the jury and the taking of the oath by witnesses has been written so as to give a correct impression without any reference to religion.

The teacher should communicate these changes and limitations to the pupils so that they are aware of discrepancies with a proper court case.

Practical Points

The length of the piece means that it needs to be used in an extended time or over a number of lessons.

Teachers might find it helpful to carry out preliminary work on court procedures before starting the trial. Otherwise there could be a lack of understanding of the significance of some events and statements. Topics to be covered could include eligibility for jury service, the jury system, the order of a trial, objections, use of exhibits, hearsay, leading questions and reaching a verdict.

Silence In Court can be tackled as a written exercise but it loses much of its impact. It is designed to be acted out. In that case the teacher needs to prepare the exhibits, set out the room as a court, choose children to take various parts and, if possible, acquire some basic costumes – wigs, gowns and so on.

All of the class can be involved. Any pupils not involved in taking parts in the trial act as members of the jury. They make notes during the case and at the end of the trial appoint a chairperson, discuss the evidence and reach a verdict. Pupils who have had roles in court listen to the jury discussion. Their views can be sought after the verdict to see if they agree.

The case has been constructed in such a way that the verdict could go either way. There is some strong evidence but also room for doubt. It will be interesting to see the results over a number of hearings.

Getting members of the jury to discuss their experience and linking it to real life is a valuable activity. Pupils begin to understand the responsibility involved.

Key Elements

- detective work
- analysis of evidence
- synthesis of data
- evaluation and judgement
- role play
- decision making
- citizenship

Contexts

Silence In Court can be used in the following ways:

- as a written assignment for individuals or a group
- as an enrichment activity for a whole class
- as an assignment in drama
- as an activity in an enrichment session, summer school or cluster day.

NOTE

- Remember the time-scale involved.

Tournament

Miss Lesley is a very efficient organiser with a great interest in junior school games. It was no surprise, therefore, when the local sports federation asked her to organise a netball tournament for a Saturday morning at Castle View Sports Centre. Miss Lesley was told that six schools were definitely going to take part – Moat Junior School, Great Barn Junior School, Manor Junior School, Desmesne Junior School, High Hall Junior School and Gallery Junior School. Two other schools – Museum Road Junior School and Courtyard Junior School – were interested in the tournament but they would not be able to say definitely whether or not they were taking part until the night before the actual event.

Miss Lesley decided to follow the normal procedure of each team playing all the other teams once. Points would be awarded on the basis of two points for a win, one point for a draw and no points for a loss. The two teams with the most points would then play against each other in a final. In the event of two teams tying on points, the one with the best goal difference (that is, the number of goals scored minus the number of goals conceded) would go forward. Should this also be equal, the team who had scored the most goals would go forward. In the unlikely case that this still did not separate the two teams, a play-off would take place with the first team to score three goals going into the final.

Miss Lesley was concerned that she would not know whether six, seven or eight teams were going to compete until the night before the tournament. She decided to have plans ready for all three possibilities.

Tournament

Your Tasks

Put yourself in Miss Lesley's position. You have got to make decisions about the staging of the tournament and draw up detailed plans so that all the participating schools can have the information as soon as they arrive on the Saturday morning.

1. There are two courts available at Castle View Sports Centre so that two matches can take place at the same time. For each of the three possibilities – that is, that six, seven or eight teams may be involved – draw up a schedule of matches so that each team plays all the other teams once. Work out how many matches will be involved in the whole tournament, in each case. Draw up a timetable of matches using the two courts. To make it fair for each team you need to consider carefully the distribution of matches and the gaps in between matches for each of the competitors. Include in your working the method you have used to check that all the teams play each other once and once only. That same method will help you during the drawing-up of the timetable.

2. Which of the three tournament possibilities have you found

   a easiest to organise

   b most difficult to organise?

   Why?

3. The tournament is to start at 9.30 am. The building must be clear by 1.00 pm. For tournaments involving six, seven and eight teams decide how long each match should last. Explain your thinking. Bear in mind the time available, the number of matches to be played and the total amount of time each child would be expected to be on court. Two substitutes are to be allowed for each team but even so you, as organisers, must be careful about the physical demands on the players. They normally play a single match of 10 minutes each way, a total of 20 minutes. The matches need to be of a reasonable length to try to get a sensible result but you cannot ignore the other relevant factors.

4. A netball match is normally umpired by two people. In school matches this means that the two teachers in charge of the two teams do the umpiring. One school asked if Miss Lesley could organise umpires so that teachers were able to watch all the matches involving their own team with the umpiring being carried out by teachers from schools not involved in the particular match. Look at the six-, seven- and eight-school tournaments. Would it be possible to meet this request about umpires in any of the three possible tournaments? Would it be sensible to do so?

5. In the end both Museum Road and Courtyard Schools were able to compete and it became an eight-school tournament. The points gained by seven of the eight schools were – Great Barn 13 points, Manor 4 points, Demesne 7 points, High Hall 5 points, Gallery 5 points, Museum Road 3 points, and Courtyard 6 points. Which two teams met in the final? What results did these two teams achieve on their way to the final? Explain your reasoning.

6. The Football League now has a system of three points for a win and one point for a draw. If that same scoring system had been adopted for the Castle View Netball Tournament, why would it have been impossible to work out the two finalists from similar information (with the points correctly increased) as given in 5 above?

Tournament

Teaching Notes

Tournament primarily concerns problem solving and organisational skills in an exercise that was taken from an actual situation and then amended. There are a number of possible answers and it is the thinking behind the plans and the decisions that is of great importance.

Some 'Possible Solutions'

(There are many others that can be credited.)

QUESTION 1

A   Six teams
One possible timetable is as follows.

Court A	Court B
Moat v Great Barn	Manor v Desmesne
Moat v High Hall	Manor v Gallery
Great Barn v High Hall	Desmesne v Gallery
Moat v Desmesne	Great Barn v Manor
Gallery v Moat	Manor v High Hall
Gallery v Great Barn	High Hall v Desmesne
Moat v Manor	Great Barn v Desmesne
High Hall v Gallery	
PLUS The Final	

	Moat	Great Barn	Manor	Desmesne	High Hall	Gallery
Moat	✗	✔	✔	✔	✔	✔
Great Barn	✔	✗	✔	✔	✔	✔
Manor	✔	✔	✗	✔	✔	✔
Desmesne	✔	✔	✔	✗	✔	✔
High Hall	✔	✔	✔	✔	✗	✔
Gallery	✔	✔	✔	✔	✔	✗

Tournament

With six teams involved, the number of matches in the main part of the tournament is 15 (6 × 5 = 30, divided by 2 = 15 (because Moat v Manor is the same as Manor v Moat for the purposes of the competition)). With a final, the total number of matches is 16. A matrix is shown as one way of checking that all the matches are included and no match is repeated. Crosses are used to show where the column for a team coincides with the row for that same team (Moat cannot play Moat!). Where a match is arranged (for example, Gallery v Desmesne) two ticks are placed – one where Gallery and Desmesne meet and one where Desmesne and Gallery meet. The chart should be full when all 15 games are timetabled.

As the matrix is being constructed it makes it easy to see what matches are left to arrange. With six teams using two courts, you can use four teams on each line of the timetable, and then repeat two of the teams in the next line and add to them the two teams temporarily left out. In this way you can ensure that no team plays more than two matches without having a break.

NOTE
- Other methods are to be credited, provided that they show a sensible and accurate way of working.

B Seven teams

Please note that Museum Road is used as the seventh team in these fixtures. If the other acceptor was Courtyard then that name could simply be put into the places occupied by Museum Road.

One possible timetable is as follows.

Court A	Court B
Moat v Great Barn	Manor v Desmesne
High Hall v Gallery	Moat v Museum Road
Great Barn v Manor	Desmesne v High Hall
Gallery v Museum Road	Moat v Manor
Great Barn v Desmesne	High Hall v Museum Road
Gallery v Great Barn	Moat v Desmesne
Moat v High Hall	Manor v Museum Road
Manor v High Hall	Desmesne v Gallery
Moat v Gallery	Great Barn v Museum Road
Great Barn v High Hall	Desmesne v Museum Road
Manor v Gallery	
PLUS The Final	

With seven teams competing, there are 21 matches initially, plus the final – a total of 22 matches (7 × 6 = 42 divided by 2 = 21). Each team plays the other six teams once. Again, a matrix or other method should be used to assist in the timetabling and to check that no matches are left out or repeated. You can make sure that no team plays more than two matches without a break but the pattern becomes more irregular because of the uneven number. Similar thinking is used as in the six-school tournament but now there is a choice of two from three to make on each line to add back into the pool, or a choice of leaving one or two from the previous line in the next line.

Tournament

C   Eight Teams

With eight teams, there are 28 matches initially (8 × 7 = 56, divided by 2 = 28). This gives a total of 29 matches when the final is considered. A matrix or alternative again assists the planning and provides a check.

One possible timetable is as follows.

Court A	Court B
Moat v Great Barn	Manor v Desmesne
High Hall v Gallery	Museum Road v Courtyard
Moat v Manor	Great Barn v Desmesne
High Hall v Museum Road	Gallery v Courtyard
Moat v Desmesne	Great Barn v Manor
High Hall v Courtyard	Gallery v Museum Road
Moat v High Hall	Great Barn v Gallery
Manor v Museum Road	Desmesne v Courtyard
Moat v Gallery	Great Barn v Museum Road
Manor v Courtyard	Desmesne v High Hall
Moat v Museum Road	Great Barn v Courtyard
Manor v High Hall	Desmesne v Gallery
Moat v Courtyard	Great Barn v High Hall
Manor v Gallery	Desmesne v Museum Road
PLUS The Final	

Interesting patterns can be created here. You can start with two pools of four teams and get them to play each other once each. This gives the first 12 matches with each team playing a match and then resting for a match. At this point you need to start mixing the teams 1 to 4 with the teams 5 to 8. One way is to play 1 v 5 and therefore 2 v 6, 3 v 7, 4 v 8; followed by 1 v 6, 2 v 7, 3 v 8 and consequently 4 v 5; followed by 1 v 7, 2 v 8 and therefore 3 v 5 and 4 v 6; followed by 1 v 8 and therefore 2 v 5, 3 v 6 and 4 v 7. There are of course other routes. In any case, a matrix or alternative is a help, particularly as a check. Again, breaks after a maximum of two matches are timetabled. Some patterns are more regular than others.

QUESTION 2

It will be interesting to see which tournament the children think was hardest to organise. The author's own feeling is that the seven-team tournament is the most awkward because it is so irregular; the eight-school tournament was found easiest because setting up a model is simple. Some pupils might prefer to organise the six-school tournament – it is regular and there are fewer teams to worry about.

Tournament

QUESTION 3

There are likely to be great variations here, but two factors should be clear:

- the games must fit within the time span allocated
- the length of individual matches will reduce as the number of competing teams increases. The higher the number of matches the shorter they should be:

    a to fit them all in

    b to make the demands on the players reasonable.

A decision has to be taken on whether the final should be the same length as the other games or be longer because it is the final.

Here is one suggestion:

Six-team tournament

10 minutes each way gives 20 minute matches. Eight periods of time are needed to play 15 matches on two courts. Total playing time would be 160 minutes, or 2 h 40 min, before the final. With time to switch teams, a final and changing time at the end, there is some difficulty in finishing by 1.00 pm. The demands on players would be high – five matches at 20 minutes = 100 minutes. This has to be increased for children playing in the final. Some pupils might therefore suggest that seven minutes each way – therefore, 14 minutes per game – would be more suitable. A player now is on court for a maximum of 70 minutes prior to the final (less where players are substituted).

Seven-team tournament

With 21 matches plus a final to be timetabled, the match length should be less than the above. When using two courts, 11 'slots' are necessary. Seven minutes each way is perhaps now a maximum, as 2 h 34 min playing time is needed before the final (11 × 14) and with changeover time and a final, and a break before the final, plus time to clear up at the end, that runs the tournament close to 1.00 pm. Players would be on court for 84 minutes plus a possible final. As a consequence some pupils might suggest something less – perhaps five minutes each way – giving 60 minutes per player as a maximum before the final.

Eight-team tournament

28 matches necessitates 14 'slots' of time using two courts. Five minutes each way is now perhaps a realistic length. This gives 140 minutes or 2 h 20 min playing time before the final. With other additions still to be made as above, this would fit into the allocated period. Players would be on court for a maximum of 70 minutes before the final. Anything longer makes the demands on the players very high. It also gets increasingly difficult to fit in; for example, six minutes each way is 12 minutes per match with 14 'slots' needed. This is 168 minutes or 2 h 48 min. From 9.30 am we have now reached 12.18 pm without allowance for time as teams change over, a rest before the final, the final itself and clearing-up time at the end.

Tournament

QUESTION 4

This can only work where eight teams are involved. The four teachers of the teams playing watch and the other four teachers umpire the two games in progress. With seven teams, three 'spare' teachers are available and therefore one of the two matches at any one time could be umpired by two neutrals. With six teams, one of the two matches only could be umpired by neutrals. As consistency is required, it is perhaps most sensible that this idea is only used in the eight-team tournament. Even so there is a drawback as the teachers are always watching their own team or umpiring another game – this is very demanding for them and makes it impossible for them to discuss progress with their own players.

QUESTION 5

In an eight-team tournament there are 28 matches before the final with 56 points at stake. The seven teams quoted had scored 43 points between them. Therefore the other team, Moat, scored the rest; that is, 13 points. The two teams in the final were therefore Great Barn and Moat. Each had played seven matches for 13 points. They had each won six matches and drawn one. Their results must have been wins over the other six schools and a drawn game between them.

QUESTION 6

With 3 points for a win and 1 point for a draw, games can result in either 3 points or 2 points being allocated to the league table. A calculation shown in question 5 would therefore be impossible as the total number of points gained by all eight teams would not be known. A skilled mathematician might see a way of working out the points score of the eighth team by a much more complicated method than the one employed above. 'Answers on a postcard please …!'

Theme Five: Modern Foreign Languages

The learning of modern foreign languages can be made incredibly demanding and challenging by increasing the requirements in terms of grammar, sophistication, authenticism and breadth of vocabulary. In that sense, able pupils are already catered for and some teachers have taken the view that differentiation is in-built. Two other routes are to increase the number of languages learned, with some being more difficult to master than others, and to examine linguistics. Both of those routes have been explored in enrichment sessions organised by university departments. There have also been gatherings of able linguists brought together on special days so that they can 'fire off each other'. There is an interesting quote from actor John Cleese in the foreword to the modern foreign languages section of the National Curriculum (DfEE/QCA, 1999):

> *'Learning a language makes our minds stronger and more flexible.'*

Despite what is said above, there is a growing number of teachers who wish to exploit many of the methods used to engage able pupils in English lessons. Perhaps they have in mind another extract from the National Curriculum:

> *'… using the target language creatively and imaginatively.'*

In addition, the Scottish 5–14 Guidelines on Modern European Languages encourage the use of:

> *'… contexts which are within pupils' experience and engage their interest.'*

The problem seems to be that materials for word games, word play and other challenges are in short supply. On INSET days with linguists, the author has advised the acquisition of good collections of word games in English, for teachers to choose examples that interest them and then to see whether they work in the target language. It is this process that is examined in **Playing With Language** (page 159). Five examples are given to illustrate the process but until a suitable text appears (Is there one of which the author is unaware?) teachers will have to do some groundwork for themselves in the same manner.

Whether working in English or in a modern foreign language, curriculum guidelines always stress the use of dictionaries:

> *'Make use of word lists, glossaries and dictionaries with increasing accuracy and independence, to check the meaning of new words and phrases introduced in the context of a unit of work or personal reading activities.'*
>
> Scottish 5–14 Guidelines

> *'... how to use dictionaries and other reference materials appropriately and effectively.'*
>
> The National Curriculum (DfEE/QCA, 1999)

The homonyms section of *Playing With Language* provides one vehicle for practising use of dictionaries. *Hier sind* (page 161) gives practice in German with the letter 'G'. The piece is based upon publications in English such as *Animalia* by Graeme Base (Puffin, 1990) and *The Ultimate Alphabet* by Mike Wilkes (Pavilion, 1986).

Codes are a very profitable area to use with able pupils. *Adjectifs* (page 164) is based upon the correct and incorrect use of adjectives in French. Pupils get practice at an important skill but with an additional and interesting challenge.

Logical thought problems can be linked to any content. *J'Habite* (page 166) provides a logic problem while using a range of standard vocabulary.

The fifth piece, *Daylight Robbery* (page 169), has also been written to demonstrate the delivery of content in an enjoyable way. This is a short detective exercise in German. The piece was written in English by the author and then translated by a specialist, Kate Hannan, who also checked that the vocabulary used was suitable. If there are not enough materials in the target language to exploit areas like codes, logical thought and detective work, an answer may well be to translate pieces from English. At least that way the teacher does not also have to construct the original problem.

ATTENTION

See also the resources suggested below.

Book	Theme or Section	Activity
Elsewhere in this book	Theme One: English, Literacy	Tin Can
		A School Of Whales
		Tempting Titles
		Every Picture Tells A Story
	Theme Three: Science	Talking Science
Effective Provision For Able And Talented Children, Network Educational Press, 1997	Section Six	A Capital Idea
		What If?
	Section Seven	Words Are Magic, Words Are Fun
Effective Resources For Able And Talented Children, Network Educational Press, 1999	Theme One: Literacy	Carp
		Ant
	Theme Two: Language Across The Curriculum	Depict
	Theme Six: Science	Professor Malaprop
	Theme Eleven: Alternative Answers, Imagination ...	The Question Is

Playing With Language
Teaching Notes

There are no pupil sheets for **Playing With Language** as the work depends upon the teacher amending existing pieces in English where they fit the target language. That fit depends upon the vocabulary, conventions and structure of the individual language.

Word games abound in English and they are a valuable source of material for able pupils. Such activities do not appear to be as readily available for other languages. The teacher is advised to obtain copies of good word game books written in English, then to choose pieces that are interesting before considering whether they would work in the target language.

Below, some such examples are used to illustrate just a few possibilities.

Homonyms

The author included an exercise called **Carp** in *Effective Resources For Able And Talented Children* (Network Educational Press, 1999), where cryptic clues were given to a word with different meanings but the same spelling and pronunciation. The title ('Carp') was described as 'a freshwater fish complains'. For example:

- Something that went before is no longer young (adjective, French, 6 letters).
- The product of an artist makes an important person (noun, French, 5 letters).
- A silly person at the entrance to a field (noun, German, 3 letters).
- The person who is in charge has climbed the rungs of success (noun, German, 6 letters).

'*ancien*' meaning 'former' or 'old'

'*huile*' meaning 'oil painting' or 'bigwig'

'*Tor*' meaning 'fool' or 'gate'

'*Leiter*' meaning 'manager' or 'ladder'

The Butcher's Dog

In English, there is a famous word game called 'The Preacher's Cat'. Each child gives a line on the principle of:

> The preacher's cat is an <u>a</u>dventurous cat and his name is <u>A</u>rchimedes.

All the players in the group give their version using the letter 'A' to begin the adjective and the name, before play moves to 'B' and so on.

Playing With Language

In the target language, many variations are possible. Each child could take one letter in alphabetical order, putting the sentence into proper translation and working down a list of people and animals. For example:

- butcher   dog
- doctor   parrot
- teacher   horse

In this way a range of vocabulary can be covered.

Well Known For

A famous person's name is given and the initial letters are used for words, in the target language, that fit that person. For example:

- **C**eline **D**ion   **c**hanteuse **d**ramatique
- **D**ietmar **H**amann   **d**eutscher **H**eld

Butter, Bread, Head

In this game the first player says a word. Each subsequent player has to give a word that either fits by association or that rhymes with the last word. For example:

- beurre → pain → bain → savon   and so on
- Kaffee → Tee → See → Wasser   and so on

Three Steps

The English meaning of a first word and a fourth word are given. The pupil has to construct a four-word chain such that:

- one letter only is changed each time
- each link makes a proper word in the target language
- in the three steps allowed the transition is achieved.

For example:

- Go from hungry to wood in French.   faim → fais → fois → bois
- Go from shirt to gold in German.   Hemd → Held → Geld → Gold

These are just a few examples. Word games are fun to play but they also develop mental agility, give practice in vocabulary and stimulate word play so that pupils work in a challenging and interesting way.

Contexts

Such word games can be used:

- in normal classroom work
- within enrichment sessions
- as an activity for a French/German/Italian/Spanish Club.

HIER SIND

'Hier sind' or 'here are' a number of items that, in German, start with the letter 'G'.

Your Task

Look closely at the picture on the accompanying sheet.

Find thirty eight German words starting with the letter 'G' that are illustrated in the picture.

Some are shown as objects but some ideas are also illustrated.

Some parts of the picture represent more than one word.

Also be aware that some sections of the illustration are there to provide a 'framework' and do not refer to words beginning with 'G'.

Thirty eight words have been included deliberately but there may be others that are represented inadvertently.

Extension Tasks

- ▲ Create your own picture to illustrate various words that all begin, in German, with a particular letter (but not 'G').
- ▲ Look at Mike Wilkes' wonderful book *The Ultimate Alphabet* (Pavilion, 1986) and see how many words coincide in both English and German on the various pages.

Hier sind

Hier sind

Teaching Notes

Hier sind promotes use of the dictionary in an unusual way. Having completed this task, pupils could be asked to create a picture of their own but based on a different letter.

Contexts
Hier sind can be used in the following ways:

- as normal classroom work
- as extension material to vocabulary work
- as an enrichment activity for those ahead in standard tasks
- as differentiated homework
- as an activity within an enrichment session, summer school or cluster day
- as an activity for the German Club or Society
- as an open-access competition where the creation of a new picture based on another letter could act as 'discriminator'.

Answers
The following words beginning with the letter 'G' can be deduced from the picture.

English	German	English	German
baggage	das Gepäck	goose	die Gans
bell	die Glocke	grapefruit	die Grapefruit
birthday	der Geburtstag	grass	das Gras
border (frontier)	die Grenze	Greenhouse	das Gewächshaus
Britain	Grossbritannien	gun	das Gewehr
bulb (electric)	die Glühbirne	guitar	die Gitarre
cake (pastry)	das Gebäck	handle	der Griff
cucumber	die Gurke	happy	glücklich
dangerous	gefährlich	inn	das Gasthaus
drink	das Getränk	jar (container)	das Gefäss
face	das Gesicht	large	gross
fork (road)	die Gabelung	money	das Geld
fork (table)	die Gabel	poison	das Gift
gallery (art)	die Galerie	poisonous	giftig
garden	der Garten	same	gleich
gift	das Geschenk	speed	die Geschwindigkeit
glass	das Glas	thunderstorm	das Gewitter
golf	das Golf	vegetables	das Gemüse
good	gut	violin	die Geige

NOTE

- Some images may portray more than one word beginning with 'G'. Children may also spot other words that are unintentional.

Adjectifs

Polly, and her friend Kate, both love French at school. They are also fans of codes and puzzles. Recently both girls have learned about adjectives. Polly decided to send Kate a coded message by means of a follow-up to the work that they had been doing in the French lessons.

Your Task

Work out the coded message that Kate received by looking at the 'instructions' below in conjunction with the French exercise on adjectives.

THE INSTRUCTIONS FROM POLLY TO KATE

- Leave well alone and concentrate upon what is incorrect.
- In terms of the adjectives themselves think of gender, plural and position as being 'un, deux, trois'.

THE FRENCH EXERCISE

1	a loud voice	– une voix fort
2	the little cat	– le petit chat
3	the deceitful children	– les enfants trompeur
4	the old book	– le livre vieux
5	the long journeys	– les voyages longs
6	a grey shirt	– une chemise grise
7	a cruel remark	– une remarque cruel
8	a happy boy	– un garçon heureuse
9	an anxious look	– un regard inquiète
10	a young woman	– une jeune femme
11	a low ceiling	– un bas plafond
12	my favourite song	– ma chanson favori
13	the twin brothers	– les frères jumeau
14	the narrow streets	– les rues étroites
15	a good meal	– un repas bon

Extension Task

When you have worked out how the code works, and therefore what Polly's message said, construct your own exercise, based upon the same principles, spelling out a different message.

Adjectifs
Teaching Notes

Here we are combining standard content with a challenging and unusual method. The basic material involves adjectives in French – dealing with gender agreement, plurals and correct positioning (whether before or after the noun). It should be stressed that it is the normal position that we are concerned with as sometimes adjectives are deliberately placed wrongly to draw attention to them. The code is a vehicle providing a more demanding and interesting way of practising the rules for able pupils.

Solution

THE INSTRUCTIONS

- It is only what is wrong that will give parts of the code. Ignore any phrases translated correctly.
- When an adjective has been used incorrectly you take the first letter of the adjective for a gender error, the second letter for a plurals error and the third letter for a positional error.

THE FRENCH EXERCISE

1	gender error	first letter	F
2	correct	ignore	
3	plurals error	second letter	R
4	positional error	third letter	E
5	positional error	third letter	N
6	correct	ignore	
7	gender error	first letter	C
8	gender error	first letter	H
9	gender error	first letter	I
10	correct	ignore	
11	positional error	third letter	S
12	gender error	first letter	F
13	plurals error	second letter	U
14	correct	ignore	
15	positional error	third letter	N

The message is therefore:

French is fun

Extension Task

This is more testing, as pupils not only have to understand the adjectives but also select appropriate words to give the required letters for a message.

J'Habite

On a separate sheet you will find personal details about eight children (written in French).

Their names are Marie, Sylvie, Pierre, Monique, Paul, Juliette, Sophie and Maurice.

They live in different places – Dinan, Boulogne, Paris, Avignon, Calais, Rouen, Bordeaux and Marseilles.

Your Task

Read the clues below and the details about the children. Work out where each child lives.

NOTE
- Use only the information given. Ignore gaps in the information.

The Clues

1. The boy who doesn't get on with his sister, because they disagree about music, writes to a girl pen friend in Boulogne. She is one of the named children.

2. The oldest child visits her aunt in Paris sometimes but otherwise doesn't go to the capital.

3. The three children with blue eyes live in the capital city, Dinan and Bordeaux but not necessarily in that order.

4. The two children who wear glasses used to live in Rouen.

5. The girl who finds science interesting has only visited Dinan once and Bordeaux never.

6. Two children whose ages add up to 25 live in Calais and Boulogne. It is the child with black hair who lives in Boulogne.

7. The girl who has problems with her mother visits the girl who wants to be a teacher and who lives in Dinan.

8. An animal lover lives in Marseilles.

9. One child's brother plays football for a junior team in their home city of Rouen.

J'Habite

Les Enfants

MARIE
Chez moi, il y a seulement mes parents et moi. J'aime les sciences parce que je trouve ça intéressant. J'ai quatorze ans. J'ai les yeux bleus.

SYLVIE
J'habite une petite maison. J'ai un frère et une soeur. Ma soeur habite un village à la campagne. J'ai les yeux verts. J'aime les sports. J'ai treize ans.

PIERRE
J'ai dix ans. Je suis fils unique. J'adore les animaux. J'ai les yeux marron. L'année dernière, je suis allée en Italie. J'ai les cheveux courts.

MONIQUE
J'ai un frère et une soeur. Mon anniversaire est le 15 février. J'ai seize ans. Je ne m'entends pas avec ma mère. Elle est beaucoup trop stricte. J'ai les yeux bleus.

PAUL
J'ai une soeur. Je ne m'entends pas avec ma soeur. Nous n'aimons pas la même musique. J'ai treize ans. J'ai les yeux verts.

JULIETTE
J'ai dix-sept ans. Je suis fille unique. Il me faut travailler pour gagner mon argent de poche. J'ai les yeux bleus. Je veux devenir professeur.

SOPHIE
J'ai onze ans. Ma meilleure amie s'appelle Claudette. J'ai les cheveux noirs. J'adore les animaux. J'ai les yeux verts. J'ai deux frères et deux soeurs. Je porte des lunettes.

MAURICE
J'ai un frère. Mon frère est plus jeune que moi. Je porte des lunettes. J'aime le rugby. Je m'entends bien avec ma famille. Ma grand-mère habite chez nous. J'ai les yeux verts. J'ai quatorze ans.

More Effective Resources for Able and Talented Children © *Barry Teare (Network Educational Press, 2001)*

J'Habite
Teaching Notes

J'habite is a logical thought problem with much of the information in French. The section on the children uses vocabulary from standard units of work about the family, physical appearance, school, interests and so on. As a result pupils get practice on vocabulary but within a challenging and enjoyable task. The level of difficulty could be raised further by giving the clues also in the target language.

Contexts
J'habite can be used in a variety of ways:
- as extension material to the appropriate sections
- as an enrichment activity for those ahead in normal work
- as differentiated homework
- as an activity in an enrichment session, summer school or cluster day
- as an activity for the French Club or Society.

Solution
This problem can be solved by the matrix method as shown below. It is not essential to use this method, and pupils may well find another valid method.

Clue 1 This boy is Paul, who clearly does not live in Boulogne (one cross). It is a girl in Boulogne and therefore crosses can also be placed against Pierre and Maurice.

Clue 2 The oldest child is Juliette. She does not live in Paris (one cross).

Clue 3 The places are Paris, Bordeaux and Dinan and the children are Marie, Monique and Juliette but the pairings are not yet known. Crosses can be placed for those children for other places. You can also place crosses for the other five children against Paris, Bordeaux and Dinan.

Clue 4 The two children who wear glasses are Sophie and Maurice. Neither now lives in Rouen (two crosses).

Clue 5 This girl is Marie who doesn't live in Dinan or Bordeaux and therefore must live in Paris (one tick and three crosses).

Clue 6 Of the ages given, only 11 and 14 add up to 25. One fourteen-year old, Marie, has already been placed. This means that the two children are Sophie and Maurice. Sophie has black hair and therefore lives in Boulogne, with Maurice in Calais (two ticks and many crosses).

Clue 7 Monique visits Juliette in Dinan; therefore, Juliette lives in Dinan and Monique in Bordeaux.

Clue 8 Sophie has already been placed; therefore, the animal lover is Pierre who lives in Marseilles (one tick and four crosses).

Clue 9 Of the two children left only Sylvie has a brother; therefore, she lives in Rouen and Paul in Avignon.

	Dinan	Boulogne	Paris	Avignon	Calais	Rouen	Bordeaux	Marseilles
Marie	✗	✗	✔	✗	✗	✗	✗	✗
Sylvie	✗	✗	✗	✗	✗	✔	✗	✗
Pierre	✗	✗	✗	✗	✗	✗	✗	✔
Monique	✗	✗	✗	✗	✗	✗	✔	✗
Paul	✗	✗	✗	✔	✗	✗	✗	✗
Juliette	✔	✗	✗	✗	✗	✗	✗	✗
Sophie	✗	✔	✗	✗	✗	✗	✗	✗
Maurice	✗	✗	✗	✗	✔	✗	✗	✗

DAYLIGHT ROBBERY

THE CRIME

Despite many warnings, Frau Falke kept some valuable jewellery in a sideboard in the living room of her detached house. On Friday 10th October, while Frau Falke was out shopping, somebody broke into the house and stole her jewellery. Frau Falke knew that the jewellery was safe at 2 pm, as she had been examining it in order to choose what to wear for a family party the next day. When she returned at 4.15 pm the jewellery had gone.

When the police arrived they carried out a search of the house and garden. The contents of the sideboard were spread all over the floor but no other area of that room or any other room was disturbed. The burglar had entered through a small window on the ground floor. Outside footprints were discovered. They fitted the pattern of a training shoe and were size 42. Behind a large tree, other footprints were found together with a spent match and a cigarette end. (Frau Falke does not smoke.)

Your Task

After reading the information above, study the details of the five suspects on the next sheet. Imagine that you are the detective in charge of the case. From the evidence so far, state who would be your prime suspect, giving your reasons in detail for all the suspects.

Extension Task

Write a plan of further actions that you would take in this case to gather additional evidence and to bring your investigation to a successful conclusion.

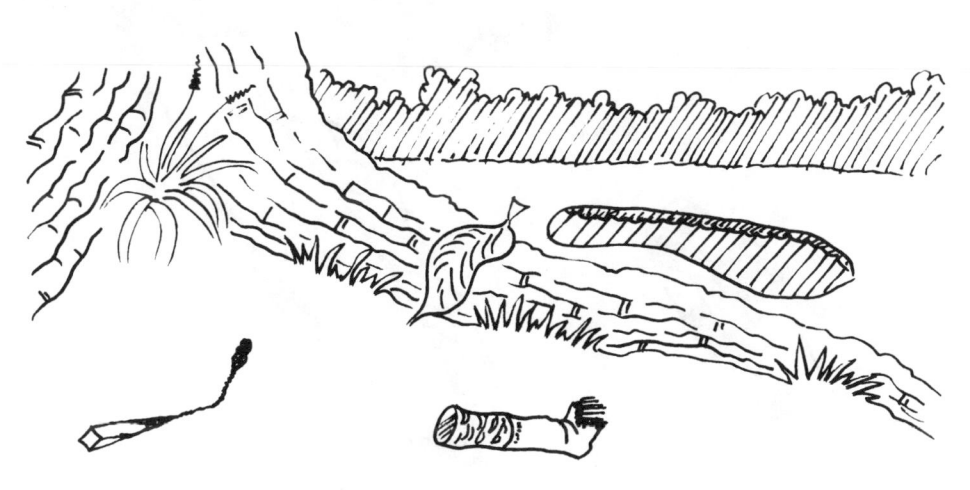

DAYLIGHT ROBBERY

DIE VERDÄCHTIGEN

HERR VOGT
65 Jahre alt. Gross und stämmig. Trägt Schuhgrösse 42. Nichtraucher. Kennt Frau Falke, denn er ist Mitglied desselben Lesezirkels wie sie, ist aber nie bei ihr zu Hause gewesen.

HERR SCHMITT
37 Jahre alt. Klein und dünn. Raucht Zigaretten. Trägt Schuhgrösse 41. Ist schon wegen Einbruchsdiebstahl vorbestraft. Hat Frau Falke nie kennengelernt.

HERR HESSLER
29 Jahre alt. Mittelgross, weder schlank noch dick. Raucht Zigaretten. Hat Reparaturarbeiten bei Frau Falke ausgeführt. Zur Verbesserung eines Fussproblems trägt er Sonderschuhe. Er behauptet, er arbeitete zur Zeit des Einbruchs im Garten. Dies kann aber niemand bestätigen.

HERR NEUMANN
30 Jahre alt. Nicht sehr gross und ziemlich dünn. Er behauptet, dass er an jenem Nachmittag allein im Lokalpark spazieren gegangen wäre. Trägt Schuhgrösse 42. Nichtraucher. Hat Frau Falke schon vielmals als Tapezierer besucht.

HERR DENZEL
Ein grosser aber schlanker 52jähriger, er trägt Schuhgrösse 42. Raucht Zigaretten. Am Freitag 10 Oktober hatte er um 15.00 Uhr einen Termin beim Zahnarzt. Er ist der Polizei als Kleinverbrecher bekannt aber Kontakt mit Frau Falke ist nicht bezeugt.

DAYLIGHT ROBBERY

Teaching Notes

Daylight Robbery looks to combine required vocabulary with a small detective case. This has been kept to a reasonable length so that the material is accessible but provides an interesting vehicle. The solution is not difficult when working in English but the target language adds to the challenge.

Solution

Reading 'The Crime' section leads us to believe that the burglar must be fairly small and agile and that he knows where the jewellery is kept so that only the sideboard is disturbed. There is a critical period of time when the suspects' movements are important. The other clues lead us to look for somebody who smokes cigarettes and who wears size 42 shoes.

No suspect fits every point.

- **Herr Vogt** looks too big to go through the window, does not know the house and does not smoke.
- **Herr Schmitt** is the right size and smokes but is unlikely to know about the jewellery.
- **Herr Hessler** fits the bill. He knows the property and has no alibi. The real doubts are the footwear and his build.
- **Herr Neumann** also fits the bill and has no alibi. He is likely to know the location of the jewellery. The one point that does not fit is that he does not smoke. Perhaps the match and cigarette end are unconnected with the crime and are there for some other reason.
- **Herr Denzel** may be too tall and he has no previous contact with the property. The dental appointment may also rule him out.

On balance Herr Neumann is the most likely suspect although Herr Hessler is worth further investigation.

Contexts

Daylight Robbery can be used in a variety of ways:

- as extension work
- as differentiated homework
- as an activity within an enrichment session
- as an activity for the German Club
- as a rather different method of revision.

Extension Task

Pupils are likely to write about a number of points in their plans for further action, including:

- investigating the suspects' lack of alibis
- finding possible witnesses to the crime
- finding out exact details of the dental appointment
- finding the trainer that made the footprints
- investigating smoking habits and brands of cigarette
- analysis of any other forensic evidence, such as fingerprints
- looking for possible outlets for the stolen jewellery
- interviewing neighbours of Frau Falke.

Theme Six: Young Children

This section is designated 'Young Children' but there is a wider application of these materials, as well as the need to recognise the possibility of able young pupils using materials from other sections. The items have been chosen for contexts that will make sense to younger pupils but they will still pose a real challenge to older children. Very few enrichment materials are produced commercially for Key Stage 1 in England and the equivalent age group in Scotland. This gap in provision does need to be addressed.

Providing successfully for able young children does have some difficulties associated with it. Some apparently able infants move farther and farther away from their peers, whereas other apparently able infants come back to the main body when others experience the same activities that they had 'ahead of time'. When identifying children as able, teachers do need to bear that point in mind. Even so, able youngsters should be provided for at their current level of attainment even though such precocious attainment is not maintained in all cases. Even traditional pointers, such as early talking and walking, have to be used with care as there are many instances of extremely able children not walking and/or talking until later than average.

Going to school for the first time can be a traumatic experience and it is not surprising that young children are treated gently. Again, there is a potential pitfall as such treatment could result in undemanding and unchallenging work that is aimed at a considerably lower level than a minority of children are capable of tackling.

Despite their lack of years, able young children are quite capable of getting benefit from logical thinking problems and from codes, provided that the context is appropriate and the presentation is suitable. Many practising teachers have amended examples for older children with great success. *The Bear's Name* (page 175) is likely to attract the attention of young children. It combines a short logical problem with information processing and literacy content. *A Is For Apple, Or Is It?* (page 177) takes a familiar context, that of pictures, to illustrate the letters of the alphabet, to pose a coded exercise involving synthesis. Very clear thinking is necessary.

Many able children, including able *young* children, have a pronounced sense of humour, delighting in the absurd and getting great enjoyment from word play, puns and other forms of word humour. Curriculum guidelines such as the Literacy Framework stress the importance of the extension of vocabulary. The origins of words and the creation of new words are included in such guidelines. The Scottish 5–14 Guidelines on English Language asks teachers to:

> *'... help pupils to develop confidence and pleasure in their own use of language.'*
>
> *'... provide a language environment which stimulates pupils' imaginations and their interest in and enjoyment of language in all its aspects.'*

Wondrous Words In The Woods (page 180) allows young pupils to be creative and imaginative and to have fun and enjoyment with made-up vocabulary. *Twice Upon A Time* (page 182) opens up exciting writing opportunities in response to unusual titles that give a new meaning to some traditional stories and situations. This follows upon work done some years ago by Doug Ross, a First School Adviser in Northumberland. The quirkiness of the suggestions will engage the attention of many able young writers and allow them to produce work of serious quality.

Teachers always need to have in mind the exact thinking skills required by particular tasks. *One Thing Leads To Another* (page 184) plays upon the important areas of classification and sequencing within a content dominated by science and geography. The task is carried out in a tactile way by using slips and should appeal especially to kinesthetic learners.

The final piece, *The Terrific Toyshop* (page 187), is a mathematical item. Synthesis of data is required. A number of linked operations are involved demanding a span of concentration – an important asset that has been promoted within the new National Curriculum Mathematics Guidelines. The Terrific Toyshop certainly plays to a theme within those guidelines:

> *'... break down a more complex problem or calculation into simple steps before attempting a solution: identifying the information needed to carry out the tasks.'*

All six pieces in this section use contexts that are appropriate for the age range – a teddy bear, an alphabet book, fantasy creatures, traditional tales, nursery rhymes and a toyshop. The work involved is challenging but fun and it does give scope in some items for imaginative and creative responses and in others for clear logical thinking.

ATTENTION

As indicated above, these six pieces can provide a very real challenge for older children. The themes within *Twice Upon A Time* have provided excellent responses from sixth-formers.

Able young children can gain great benefit from other materials by the author, especially perhaps the resources suggested below.

Book	Theme or Section	Activity
Elsewhere in this book	Theme One: English, Literacy	A School Of Whales
		Tempting Titles
	Theme Two: Mathematics, Numeracy	Fox, Rabbit, Rat
	Theme Three: Science	The Spider That Loves Mozart
	Theme Nine: Lateral Thinking	One Question, Many Answers
	Theme Ten: Competitions	The People Of Britain
		Snakes And Races, Square And Quotients
Effective Provision For Able And Talented Children, Network Educational Press, 1997	Section Six	A Capital Idea
		What If?
Effective Resources For Able And Talented Children, Network Educational Press, 1999	Theme One: Literacy	Carp
		Ant
	Theme Three: Reading	Mole, Rat, Badger, Toad And … Who?
	Theme Four: Writing	Straight From The Horse's Mouth
		The Man In The Van
	Theme Five: Numeracy, Mathematics	In The Balance
	Theme Six: Science	Property To Let
	Theme Eleven: Alternative Answers, Imagination …	The Question Is
		Or
		Now You See It
		Just Imagine

The Bear's Name

Your Task

Can you work out the bear's name from the following clues?

The Clues

1 The bear's name is five letters long.

2 The initial letter of his name is one of the letters in the colour of his bow. (This colour is an anagram of 'lube'.)

3 The name contains a consonant from that colour, used twice.

4 The bear has two of these on his head or face, but only one in his name.

5 The bear's name ends with a letter that sounds like a three-letter word asking a question.

The bear's name is _____

The Bear's Name

Teaching Notes

This is a short logical thinking puzzle for young children. The subject matter, a teddy bear, is designed to appeal. It would be best to actually display a small bear and to challenge the children to discover its name. If this is done, the bear needs to wear a *blue* bow. When the exercise is done from the book itself please note that the page will be in black and white. This is why an anagram has been given to identify the colour blue.

The Bear's Name can be tackled either by referring to the written sheet or by the teacher reading out the clues.

Young able children are both capable and willing to tackle logic problems as long as both the context and the presentation are appropriate. This particular piece combines some aspects of language with the logic. Synthesis of data is necessary as the clues have to be fitted together.

Solution

1. We are looking for a five-letter name.
2. It is a male bear. The name starts with either **l, u, b** or **e** and the more likely possibilities are **l** and **b**.
3. Either there is a double **l** or a double **b**.
4. There is one **i** in the name.
5. The fifth and final letter is **y**.

> The bear's name is Billy.

'A' Is For Apple, Or Is It?

Peter Roberts works for 'Little Acorns', a company that publishes books for young children. One of these books was an alphabet book with a suitable picture for each letter. During production, a number of mistakes were made so that many pictures were placed against the wrong letters. This gave Peter an interesting idea. He decided to produce a code for children to work out, where the message would use the wrongly-placed pictures.

Your Task

Work out the coded message below. Use the clues given by Peter on the movement of pictures against letters, and the separate sheet that shows how the pictures *should* have been used.

The Clues

Any numbers given refer to the correct order of the 26 letters of the alphabet. Remember that letters remain in their position – it is always the pictures that move. 'In correct order' for exchanges means that the lower of one pair interchanges with the lower of the second pair.

1. The first two domestic pets pictured exchanged places, in correct order, with the two animals that you would see in Africa.
2. A trip to Paris became a trip to Venice and vice-versa.
3. The two musical instruments moved on one place each.
4. The two creatures who live in water took the two spaces now left spare, in correct number order.
5. The two spaces left as a result of moves so far were filled by the two pictures made spare – again, in correct number order.
6. The remaining letters that can be divided by 5 without a remainder changed places.
7. The first odd number changed places with the fifth odd number and the first even number changed places with the fourth even number.
8. Any animals not moved so far stayed in their original places.
9. The three pictures not mentioned so far all changed places by moving to the next available space.

The Coded Picture Message

Extension Tasks

- Use the picture code sheet to set some messages of your own.
- Design your own picture code with new clues but the same original pictures.
- Design your own code with new pictures and new clues.

'A' Is For Apple, Or Is It?

How The Pictures And Letters Were Meant To Be

A Apple
B Banana
C Cat
D Dog
E Eiffel Tower

F Fish
G Gondola
H Horse
I Ice cream
J Jack-in-the-box

K Kangaroo
L Lion
M Mouse
N Net

O Octopus
P Pig
Q ?
R Rabbit

S Squirrel
T Teddy
U Umbrella
V Violin

W Windmill
X Xylophone
Y Yo-yo
Z Zebra

'A' Is For Apple, Or Is It?

Teaching Notes

This is a code with an appropriate context for younger children – that is, a picture alphabet book – but it is still a challenging task due to the number and complexity of instructions. It is very much a case of breaking down a problem into small, manageable steps as advocated in mathematics curriculum guidelines.

Key Elements

- abstract – as, in a code, something stands for something else
- alphabetical order
- following instructions
- breaking down a complex task
- good working habits, especially in the recording of data
- mathematical terminology

Solution

Children should make a new alphabet chart as the pictures change places, and remember that the letters stay put.

1. Cat (3) and lion (12) change places, as do dog (4) and zebra (26).
2. Eiffel Tower (5) and gondola (7) change places.
3. Violin (22) moves to represent W (23) and xylophone (24) moves to represent Y (25).
4. Fish (6) moves to V (22) and octopus (15) moves to X (24).
5. The two pictures displaced are windmill (23) and yoyo (25) and they go to F (6) and O (15) respectively.
6. Letters (5), (15) and (25) have already been dealt with so this clue refers to jack-in-the-box (10) and teddy (20), which change places.
7. Apple (1) and ice cream (9) change places, as do banana (2) and horse (8).
8. The remaining animals are kangaroo (11), mouse (13), pig (16), rabbit (18) and squirrel (19) and they stay in their original places.
9. The last three pictures are net (14), question (17) and umbrella (21). They move to the next vacant space, with net going to (17), question to (21) and therefore umbrella to (14).

This gives a new picture alphabet as follows.

A – ice cream	**H** – banana	**O** – yoyo	**V** – fish
B – horse	**I** – apple	**P** – pig	**W** – violin
C – lion	**J** – teddy	**Q** – net	**X** – octopus
D – zebra	**K** – kangaroo	**R** – rabbit	**Y** – xylophone
E – gondola	**L** – cat	**S** – squirrel	**Z** – dog
F – windmill	**M** – mouse	**T** – jack-in-the-box	
G – Eiffel Tower	**N** – umbrella	**U** – question	

The picture code message says, therefore:

Do you get the picture

Extension Tasks

Children can use other connections in the pictures to devise clues, or create their own original pictures. If it becomes too tedious to draw out the pictures, words can be used instead; for example, 'gondola', 'Eiffel Tower'.

More Effective Resources for Able and Talented Children © Barry Teare (Network Educational Press, 2001)

WONDROUS WORDS IN THE WOODS

When he was even smaller than he is now, Ian The Imp read Roald Dahl's *The BFG* and enjoyed the words made up by the giant. What Ian The Imp thought was really clever was that you could understand what the BFG meant even though the words do not really exist. Being mischievous by nature, Ian The Imp decided to make up some words of his own. Below is some of his writing about the woods where he lives.

Your Tasks

1. Read the section from Ian The Imp's notebook.
2. Find fourteen words made up by the imp that do not exist in our language.
3. Some of these are based upon onomatopoeia, where the sound tells you the meaning. Write down these words and what the sound suggests they mean.
4. Describe what sort of creatures the following are by reference to the made-up words about them: **a** goblins, **b** giants, **c** sprites.
5. Why do people not normally get bothered by the giants described in Ian The Imp's notebook?
6. Explain why you would prefer to deal with the oldtimers rather than the newcomers.

IAN THE IMP'S NOTEBOOK

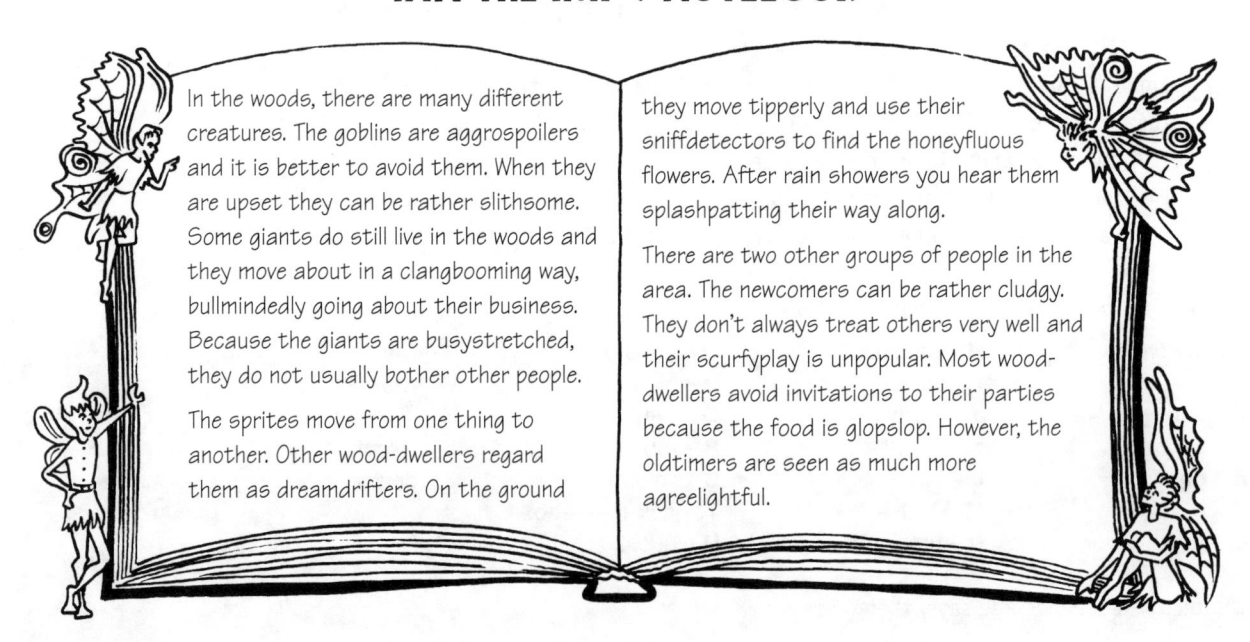

In the woods, there are many different creatures. The goblins are aggrospoilers and it is better to avoid them. When they are upset they can be rather slithsome. Some giants do still live in the woods and they move about in a clangbooming way, bullmindedly going about their business. Because the giants are busystretched, they do not usually bother other people.

The sprites move from one thing to another. Other wood-dwellers regard them as dreamdrifters. On the ground they move tipperly and use their sniffdetectors to find the honeyfluous flowers. After rain showers you hear them splashpatting their way along.

There are two other groups of people in the area. The newcomers can be rather cludgy. They don't always treat others very well and their scurfyplay is unpopular. Most wood-dwellers avoid invitations to their parties because the food is glopslop. However, the oldtimers are seen as much more agreelightful.

Extension Tasks

1. Create some words of your own to indicate pleasant things and not-so-pleasant things.
2. Design new words based upon a combination of existing words.
3. Add two new sets of creatures to Ian The Imp's woods and use made-up words that make it clear how the creatures behave.
4. If you have not already done so, read *The BFG* by Roald Dahl.

WONDROUS WORDS IN THE WOODS

Teaching Notes

Curriculum guidelines, including the Literacy Framework, advocate the imaginative, original and diverse uses of language, the origin of words and inventing words using known roots, prefixes and suffixes. ***Wondrous Words In The Woods*** incorporates these ideas in a fun way. Word humour is one of the characteristics of many able children.

Answers

2   The fourteen made-up words in the notebook are:

aggrospoilers	slithsome	clangbooming	bullmindedly	
busystretched	dreamdrifters	tipperly	sniffdetectors	honeyfluous
splashpatting	cludgy	scurfyplay	glopslop	agreelightful

3   'Splashpatting' sound like moving in a regular way through water; 'glopslop' clearly sounds very loose and unappetising. (Note that, as these words are inventions, the definitions given here are indicative only.)

4 a   The goblins are troublemakers ('aggrospoilers') and can be sly and difficult ('slithsome').

  b   The giants are noisy ('clangbooming') and move about clumsily and directly ('bullmindedly').

  c   The sprites flit from one thing to another in a daydreaming, flippant way ('dreamdrifters'). They move gingerly, perhaps on tiptoes ('tipperly') using their noses ('sniffdetectors') to find sweet or full-of-nectar flowers ('honeyfluous').

5   The giants are overworked or have too much else to occupy them ('busystretched').

6   The oldtimers are agreeable and delightful ('agreelightful') whereas the newcomers are 'cludgy' (clumsy, dour, stodgy?), get up to dirty tricks ('scurfyplay') and serve food which is 'glopslop' (how unappetising that sounds, like poor quality gruel!).

Key Elements

- word play
- word humour
- engaging with text
- creativity and imagination
- inference and deduction

Contexts

Wondrous Words In The Woods can be used in a variety of ways:

- as extension work to other exercises on words
- within the Literacy Hour
- as enrichment work for able children who have completed set tasks early
- as differentiated homework
- as part of an enrichment activity
- as an activity for an English Club
- in conjunction with reading of *The BFG* by Roald Dahl.

Twice Upon A Time

Many traditional tales, fairy stories and nursery rhymes are well known to us all. The characters and storylines are very familiar indeed – perhaps too familiar. Here is your chance to give them a twist and to use your sense of humour at the same time.

Try writing a 'twice upon a time' tale to one, or more, of the following titles or themes.

1. Rewrite the story of Cinderella where the Prince was not Charming but Obnoxious.

2. Create a new version of 'As I was going to St. Ives' by visiting instead either St. Just or St. Brides.

3. You are the detective in charge of the cases of Peter Rabbit and Benjamin Bunny. Write about your investigations.

4. Imagine that the wolf had very bad teeth and had just visited the dentist before meeting Little Red Riding Hood.

5. Send a doctor other than Foster to a place other than Gloucester and explain why he or she never returned.

6. Write an alternative version of Peter Pan where his magical property was not to be able to fly but instead to be able to swim long distances under water.

7. Help the Prince to solve his problems in a story where Rapunzel had short hair.

8. Rewrite the trial scene in *Alice's Adventures In Wonderland* where the pack of cards is replaced as characters by a box of dominoes.

Twice Upon A Time

Teaching Notes

Although this has been placed in the section for younger children, the titles can be used profitably with children of all ages. The author has used other suggestions by Doug Ross (who was a first-school adviser in Northumberland) for sixth-form writing competitions with excellent results.

Before writing their new versions it would be helpful for children to research the original situations or for the teacher to hold a class discussion on the original storylines.

Key Elements

- a keen sense of humour
- appreciation of the absurd (these two being characteristics of many able children)
- creativity and imagination
- analysis of original data
- synthesis of original and new data

Contexts

Twice Upon A Time can be used in the following ways:

- as a piece of enrichment work in the normal classroom
- as a differentiated piece of homework
- as part of an enrichment session or cluster activity
- during a writing summer school
- as an open-access competition.

One Thing Leads To Another

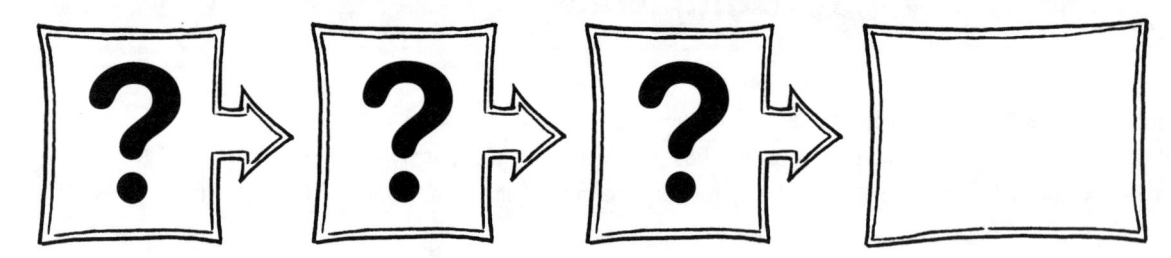

Many items are connected either because they are about the same subject or because they follow each other. This piece of work uses both types of link.

You will use two important ways of thinking.

1 GROUPING OR CLASSIFICATION

Items can be placed in groups when they are linked in terms of use or subject. For example:

- saw   hammer   chisel   screwdriver   (tools)
- page   chapter   cover   index   (books)

2 SEQUENCING OR ORDERING

A story follows a sequence as one event leads to another. Cause and effect is another type of sequencing. Living things follow a pattern of growth and development. For example:

- seed → seedling → plant   (natural development)
- over-eating → getting fat → need for larger clothes   (cause and effect)

Your Tasks

1. On a separate sheet you will find 42 items that can be cut out to make separate slips.
2. Divide the items into eight groups of four, and two groups of five so that they fit together by subject. Sometimes the same item is repeated and both fit into the one group. Sometimes repeated items fit into separate groups.
3. At the same time, place the items in each group in order or sequence, from what comes first to what comes last. Some groups start and end with the same item because of the lifecycle of a living thing.

Extension Task

For the ten groups with items placed in order, carry out a further grouping or classification activity. Put each group into one of the following categories:

- cause and effect, where the first action leads to the others in turn
- metamorphosis, where a living creature goes through very different forms before becoming an adult
- stages of development of a living item
- stages of development for items that have never been alive
- stages of development for an item once living, then dead.

One Thing Leads To Another

frog	egg
mine	bluebottle
dead seabirds	log
butterfly	sapling
tadpole	air cooling
can	frogspawn
oak tree	bird
maggot	tanker aground
egg	frog
polluted beaches	butterfly
river	chrysalis
chick	oil spillage
bluebottle	oak tree
egg	estuary
tin	rain
pupa	stream
caterpillar	ore
chair	acorn
spring	plank
bird	condensation
tree	air rising

More Effective Resources for Able and Talented Children © Barry Teare (Network Educational Press, 2001)

One Thing Leads To Another

Teaching Notes

One Thing Leads To Another has elements of science and geography as well as the important thinking skills of classification and sequencing. Children may need some help interpreting the instructions but once they are working physically with the slips the task will become clearer. It would be sensible to photocopy the 42 items onto card rather than paper.

There are three practical hints.
1. Children will find it easier to deal with both grouping and sequencing at the same time.
2. They need to be encouraged to take into account the fact that duplicated items can appear at the start and end of a sequence or that they might be part of more than one sequence.
3. Some apparently sensible alternative groups may prevent all the cards being used as they need to be.

Key Elements

- classification or grouping
- sequencing or ordering
- following instructions
- life processes
- development
- specific vocabulary
- cause and effect

Contexts

One Thing Leads To Another can be used in a variety of ways:
- as teacher-led classwork with differentiation by support and dialogue
- as extension work in the classroom for able young children
- as differentiated homework
- as part of an enrichment activity
- for groups, involving discussion work.

Solution

Group 1:	frog	→ frogspawn	→ tadpole	→ frog	
Group 2:	bird	→ egg	→ chick	→ bird	
Group 3:	oak tree	→ acorn	→ sapling	→ oak tree	
Group 4:	butterfly	→ egg	→ caterpillar	→ chrysalis	→ butterfly
Group 5:	bluebottle	→ egg	→ maggot	→ pupa	→ bluebottle
Group 6:	air rising	→ air cooling	→ condensation	→ rain	
Group 7:	tanker aground	→ oil spillage	→ polluted beaches	→ dead seabirds	
Group 8:	tree	→ log	→ plank	→ chair	
Group 9:	spring	→ stream	→ river	→ estuary	
Group 10:	mine	→ ore	→ tin	→ can	

Extension Task

- cause and effect – groups 6 and 7
- metamorphosis – groups 1, 4 and 5
- stages of development of a living item – groups 2 and 3
- stages of development for items that have never been alive – groups 9 and 10
- stages of development for an item once living then dead – group 8

The Terrific Toyshop

Lucy, Laura and Linda are great friends. They like to visit The Terrific Toyshop where the owner keeps his prices low. On this particular day prices were even lower for nine items in a sale.

The three girls took a different sum of money and bought three toys each from the sale.

Your Task

Work out the toys bought by each girl by using the different pieces of information given below.

Information On The Money

1. There are eight different coins in normal use – 1p, 2p, 5p, 10p, 20p, 50p, £1 and £2.

2. On the day, Lucy, Laura and Linda each had four coins. The 12 coins were one each of the eight in use with four added, as the two smallest value coins were repeated and the two highest value were repeated.

You should now know the 12 coins – write a list.

3. The girl with the shortest name had the four coins involving the lowest number but not always the lowest value.

4. The girl with the most vowels in her name had four coins, each involving the lowest even number somewhere. Only one of them was a coin of the highest value.

5. The other girl had the remaining four coins that gave her more money than her two friends.

You now know which four coins each girl had and the total of their money – make a note of this.

The Terrific Toyshop

Information On The Toys In The Sale

1 The top shelf had:
  a a set of colouring pencils priced £1.44
  b a zoo animal set priced £1.88
  c a puppet priced £2.00.
2 In the sale these three toys were being sold at half the marked price.

You know the actual prices of the toys on the top shelf.

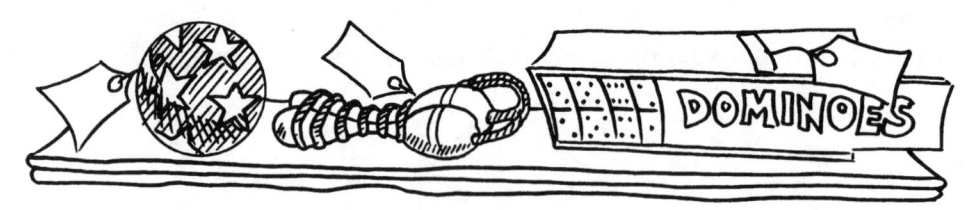

3 The middle shelf had:
  a a skipping rope priced £1.20
  b a set of dominoes priced £1.00
  c a ball priced 90p.
4 In the sale these three toys were being sold at 20p off the marked price.

You know the actual prices of the toys on the middle shelf.

5 The bottom shelf had:
  a a pack of playing cards priced 70p
  b a face mask priced 60p
  c a bag of marbles priced 75p.
6 In the sale these three toys were being sold at 10p off the marked price.

You know the actual prices of the toys on the bottom shelf.

Information On What Was Bought

1 Each girl bought one toy from each of the three shelves.
2 Each girl spent exactly the sum of money she had.

You can work out the three toys bought by each girl.

The Terrific Toyshop

Teaching Notes

Key Elements
- answers requirements of the Mathematics Guidelines in the new National Curriculum (DfEE/QCA, 1999) for children to:

> *'... approach problems involving number, and data presented in a variety of forms, in order to identify what they need to do.'*
>
> *'... explore and record patterns.'*
>
> *'... break down a more complex problem or calculation into simpler steps before attempting a solution: identify the information needed to carry out the tasks.'*
>
> *'... use the correct language, symbols and vocabulary associated with number and data.'*

- synthesis of various data
- developing a span of concentration
- work on different mathematical operations within the same piece

Contexts
The Terrific Toyshop can be used in a number of ways:
- as a differentiated homework
- as extension work on calculations, money, mathematical vocabulary and so on
- as part of an enrichment activity for mathematically able young children
- as part of a team activity in a cluster enrichment session.

Solution
→ The 12 coins are 1p, 1p, 2p, 2p, 5p, 10p, 20p, 50p, £1, £1, £2, £2.
→ The girl with the shortest name is Lucy. Her four coins involve 1, therefore they are 1p, 1p, £1, £1 with a total value of £2.02.
→ The girl with the most vowels in her name is Laura. Her four coins are 2p, 2p, 20p, £2 with a total value of £2.24.
→ The third girl is Linda. The remaining four coins are 5p, 10p, 50p, £2 with a total value of £2.65.
→ The actual prices of the toys on the top shelf are: colouring pencils 72p, zoo animal set 94p, puppet £1.
→ The actual prices of the toys on the middle shelf are: skipping rope £1, dominoes 80p, ball 70p.
→ The actual prices of the toys on the bottom shelf are: cards 60p, mask 50p, marbles 65p.
→ One combination that works is as follows.
   - Lucy bought the colouring pencils at 72p, the dominoes at 80p and the mask at 50p. Total £2.02.
   - Laura bought the zoo set at 94p, the ball at 70p and the pack of cards at 60p. Total £2.24.
   - Linda bought the puppet at £1, the skipping rope at £1 and the marbles at 65p. Total £2.65.

(Are there any other combinations that work?)

NOTE
- Children can look for clues. 'Half price' on the top shelf points to a 2 or a 4 as the last digit. The price of only one toy (the marbles) ends with a 5.

Theme Seven: Logical Thought

The Concise Oxford Dictionary defines 'logic' as *'the science of reasoning, proof, thinking or inference'* and as *'a chain of reasoning'*. The same dictionary defines 'logical' as *'not contravening the laws of thought, correctly reasoned'* and *'deductible or defensible on the ground of consistency; reasonably to be believed or done.'*

A whole range of vital skills are included within those definitions – deduction, inference, sequencing, chronology, cause and effect, classification, hypothesising, evaluating, prioritising, recommending, analysis, synthesis and so on.

Edward de Bono warns us of the potential limitations of point-to-point thinking and he is a strong supporter of lateral thinking. Pupils need to build up an armoury of contrasting methods of thinking to deal appropriately with different situations. However, in *Teaching Thinking* (Penguin Books, 1976) de Bono does recognise the place of logical thought:

> *'The role of logic is to show what is implicit in the concept used and to expose contradictions. Logic has a similar role in disputes and arguments where it is used in an attempt to show the contradictory nature of the opposing argument.'*

Contradictions and disputes are important elements in various parts of the curriculum. In mathematics one looks for patterns but also exceptions and contradictions. Logical thought is a key feature of the subject.

> *'Mathematics is not just a collection of skills, it is a way of thinking. It lies at the core of scientific understanding, and of rational and logical argument.'*

Dr Colin Sparrow

> *'... show step-by-step deduction in solving a problem: explain and justify how they arrive at a conclusion.'*
>
> *'... search for pattern in their results; develop logical thinking and explain their reasoning.'*

The National Curriculum (DfEE/QCA, 1999)

Logical thinking is also a strong feature of the Science Guidelines of the National Curriculum:

> *'They evaluate their work, in particular the strength of the evidence they and others have collected.'*
>
> *'... that it is important to test explanations by using them to make predictions and by seeing if evidence matches the predictions.'*

Clearly, this does not deny the importance of using lateral thinking as well. Many major scientific discoveries have been made accidentally, where the discoverer thought laterally (for example, see *Eureka*, page 253).

Logic within disputes, arguments, discussions and debates plays a major role elsewhere in the curriculum, even if side-by-side with alternative ways of thinking. The following references to the National Curriculum (DfEE/QCA, 1999) illustrate the point.

> *'... think about topical political, spiritual, moral, social and cultural issues, problems and events by analysing information and its sources.'*
>
> *'... use their imagination to consider other people's experiences and be able to think about, express, explain and critically evaluate views that are not their own.'*

Citizenship

> *'... evaluating critically what they hear, read and view, with attention to explicit and implied meanings, bias and objectivity, and fact and opinion.'*
>
> *'... develop logical arguments and cite evidence.'*

English

> *'... analyse evidence and draw conclusions.'*
>
> *'... explain why places are like they are.'*

Geography

> *'... how and why historical events, people, situations and changes have been interpreted in different ways.'*

History

> *'... plan what they have to do, suggesting a sequence of actions and alternatives, if needed.'*

Design and Technology

Most of the pieces in this Theme have not been designed to deliver content but rather to make able pupils think and be challenged in an enjoyable way. The processes involved are concerned with a range of generic skills – understanding the problem, making sense of the data, recording progress clearly and reaching a conclusion. These generic skills are transferable and they are in great demand in society. The CBI (Confederation of British Industry) regards very highly the ability to solve problems through thinking skills.

The Votewell Election (page 194) is one of many variants on the theme of true and false statements. Strong synthesis and clear thinking are required to sort out the finishing positions of the racehorses in *First Past The Post* (page 196). The logic in *Take Any Five From Fifty Two* (page 198) is based upon playing cards and involves number and space.

The matrix method is a popular way of tackling a certain type of logic problem where one set of variables is linked uniquely with another set of variables. Although matrix solutions have been given, pupils should be encouraged to use any method that suits them personally, providing that it is not grossly inefficient in terms of time and effort. *Just The Job* (page 200) is a small, easy example with which to start. *Case Histories* (page 202) is rather more complicated and uses the popular vehicle of detective work. *Detective Case Clues* (page 204) is an extension of *Case Histories* with the added complication that there are now three sets of variables. Getting children to write their own quality problems is a very useful extension as well.

The final piece, *Birds Of A Feather* (page 207), is rather different. It delivers some strong content in terms of living processes, mathematics and word play. *Birds Of A Feather* demonstrates the point that any content can be delivered in this way. Elsewhere in this book, *Running Rings Round Saturn* (Theme Three: Science, page 94) has strong content relating to astronomy and elements of physical processes.

The other major difference between *Birds Of A Feather* and the other pieces in this Theme is in terms of length. There are many sheets of information to use (pages 209 to 216). This increases the complexity of the task, extends the degree of synthesis and helps to increase the span of concentration – a vital need in our 'soundbite society'.

ATTENTION

See also the resources suggested below.

Book	Theme or Section	Activity
Elsewhere in this book	Theme One: English, Literacy	The Mystery Unfolds
		Every Picture Tells A Story
		Tempting Titles
	Theme Two: Mathematics, Numeracy	Make A Date
		Running Total
		Watch Carefully
	Theme Three: Science	Running Rings Round Saturn
	Theme Four: Humanities, Citizenship …	Shipping Forecast
		Finders Keepers … Sometimes
		Tournament
		Silence In Court
	Theme Five: Modern Foreign Languages	J'Habite
	Theme Six: Young Children	The Bear's Name
		One Thing Leads To Another
	Theme Eight: Detective Work, Codes	Cliffhanger
		Critical Clues
Effective Resources For Able And Talented Children, Network Educational Press, 1999	Theme Four: Writing	… And That's The End Of The Story
		Opening Up A New Chapter
	Theme Five: Numeracy, Mathematics	A Calculated Risk
	Theme Six: Science	In The Swim
		Ruby Red
	Theme Seven: Logical Thought	Field And Track
		Food For Thought
		According To The Book
		Radio Six
	Theme Ten: Detective Work	Seeing Is Believing
		According To The Evidence
		An Arresting Problem
		Vital Evidence

The Votewell Election

There were seven candidates in the Votewell election. The political reporters were given confused information about the result. Each sent a report to his or her newspaper in which one statement was correct and the other was incorrect.

Report A
Shower was third and Snow was fourth.

Report B
Rain was last and Breeze was first.

Report C
Thunder was first and Sun was second.

Report D
Lightning was fifth and Sun was sixth.

Report E
Snow beat Lightning and Breeze was second.

Report F
Thunder was third and Sun was fifth.

Report G
Snow was second and Breeze was sixth.

Can you work out the correct election result?

The Votewell Election

Teaching Notes

Solution

The result of the Votewell Election was:

First: Shower

Second: Sun

Third: Thunder

Fourth: Snow

Fifth: Lightning

Sixth: Breeze

Seventh: Rain

It is possible to get the solution by trial-and-error but it is better to use a method. Try Report A. Assume Shower was third and therefore in Report F Thunder could not be third so that Sun was fifth. However, in Report D Lightning could not be fifth nor could Sun be sixth. Both parts cannot be incorrect. In Report A, the other part must have been correct; that is, that Snow was fourth. Therefore, in G Snow was not second and Breeze must have been sixth; in B Breeze was not first and Rain must have been last (seventh); in E Breeze was not second and Snow must have beaten Lightning, thus meaning that Lightning must have been fifth; in F Sun was not fifth and therefore Thunder was third; in C Thunder was not first and therefore Sun was second. This leaves Shower in first place.

FIRST PAST THE POST

After the 22nd running of the Classic Bowl the following observations could be made about the result. Can you work out the finishing positions of the ten horses?

THE RUNNERS

- Autumn
- Grey Tower
- Penny Farthing
- Sea Mist
- Totem Pole
- Drainpipe
- High and Low
- Queen B
- Sweet Biscuit
- Trolley

THE CLUES

1. The horse in seventh place has the same number of letters in its name as its position in the race.

2. Penny Farthing finished one place behind Autumn.

3. Drainpipe finished four places behind Sea Mist.

4. Queen B had twice as many horses behind her as were in front of her.

5. High and Low finished two places behind Grey Tower, who in turn finished three places behind Drainpipe.

6. Totem Pole finished three places in front of Sweet Biscuit.

7. Autumn's finishing position was an even number.

FIRST PAST THE POST

Teaching notes

Solution

1. Seventh was either Sea Mist or Trolley (the only two horses whose names have seven letters).

2. This gives the relative positions of Penny Farthing and Autumn but no more at this stage.

3. This gives the relative positions of Sea Mist and Drainpipe but it also means that Sea Mist could not have been seventh as there would only be three horses behind that position. Therefore Trolley was seventh (clue 1).

4. The only combination of numbers that will work is to have three in front of Queen B and six behind her. Therefore Queen B was fourth.

5. A combination of this clue and clue 3 shows High and Low to be nine places behind Sea Mist. (High and Low was two places behind Grey Tower, who was three places behind Drainpipe, who was four places behind Sea Mist; 2 + 3 + 4 = 9). The only way that could be true is for Sea Mist to be first and High and Low to be last. This also places Drainpipe at fifth and Grey Tower at eighth.

6. With places two, three, six and nine left to be decided, Totem Pole and Sweet Biscuit must be placed at third and sixth or sixth and ninth.

7. The only two even places left are two and six, but six is taken by either Totem Pole or Sweet Biscuit and therefore Autumn finished second. This means that Penny Farthing was third (from clue 2). Therefore Totem Pole was sixth and Sweet Biscuit was ninth.

The placings were therefore:

First:	Sea Mist
Second:	Autumn
Third:	Penny Farthing
Fourth:	Queen B
Fifth:	Drainpipe
Sixth:	Totem Pole
Seventh:	Trolley
Eighth:	Grey Tower
Ninth:	Sweet Biscuit
Tenth:	High and Low

Take Any Five From Fifty Two

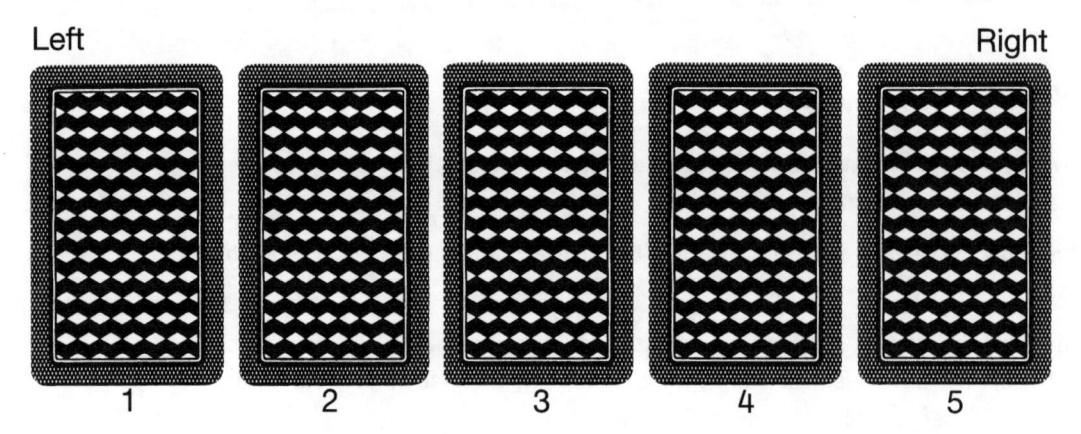

Left   **Right**

   1   2   3   4   5

There are five playing cards face-down on the table.

Can you identify them in their correct positions from the information below?

Introduction

A pack consists of 52 playing cards divided into four suits. The two red suits are hearts and diamonds; the two black suits are clubs and spades. For the purposes of this puzzle the picture cards are regarded as being the ace (value 1 point), the jack (value 11 points), the queen (value 12 points) and the king (value 13 points). The other cards in each suit – that is, 2 to 10 inclusive – have the points value that equals their number. Thus, the eight of spades is valued at 8 points. Left and right are taken from the viewer's position, as indicated in the diagram above.

The Clues

a All four suits are represented.

b The total value of the points is 27.

c One of the picture cards is on the extreme left, the other is in the middle position.

d The three cards occupying the middle position and those to the right of middle have a points total of 12. The middle card and the card to its immediate right together add up to the value of the card on the extreme right.

e The two is to the immediate left of the spade.

f The club is the card of highest points value.

g The suit with the longest name is represented by two cards that are next to each other.

Take Any Five From Fifty Two

Teaching notes

Solution

Clues **a**, **b** and **c** cannot be used immediately.

d Cards 3, 4 and 5 add up to 12 points and Card 3 is a picture card (Clue **c**). Neither cards 4 nor 5 are picture cards. Card 3 must be an ace, scoring 1 point or the total of 3, 4 and 5 would be greater than 12. Cards 4 and 5 add up to 11 points. The value of cards 3 and 4 equals Card 5. Therefore Card 4 is a five and Card 5 is a six.

The remaining two cards add up to 15 points (Clue **b**) and Card 1 is a picture card (Clue **c**). Therefore, Card 1 cannot be an ace, scoring 1 point.

If Card 1 is a king (13 points), then Card 2 is a two.

If Card 1 is a queen (12 points), then Card 2 is a three.

If Card 1 is a jack (11 points), then Card 2 is a four.

e Only Card 2 can be the two (picture card, ace, five and six are Cards 1, 3, 4, 5 respectively). Therefore Card 3 is the ace of spades and Card 1 must be a king.

f Card 1 is the king of clubs.

g The longest name belongs to diamonds and the two cards must be Card 4 and Card 5, which are the five of diamonds and the six of diamonds respectively. As all suits are represented (Clue **a**), Card 2 is the two of hearts.

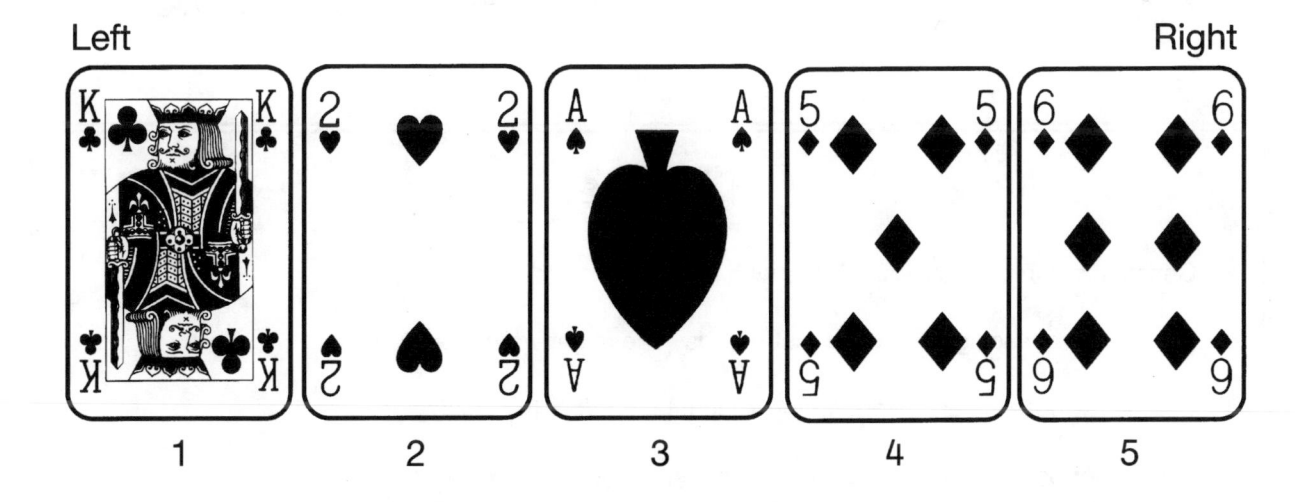

Left   Right

1	2	3	4	5
K♣	2♥	A♠	5♦	6♦

Just The Job

Christine, Dorothy, Sally and Karen became friends during a holiday in Italy. In conversation they discovered that their four careers were engineer, teacher, accountant and author. They also learned that of the four one was an only child, one had a brother but no sister and two had a sister but no brother. Can you place the four women with their respective professions from the following clues?

The Clues

a Christine had previously visited Italy with her sister.

b Karen enjoys reading and hopes that one day she might write a book herself.

c Sally knew both the engineer and the accountant before the holiday.

d The author based one of her books on her experience as an only child.

e The teacher taught Dorothy's sister last year (this was not her own sister).

f The engineer enjoys discussing her job with her brother.

Just The Job

Teaching notes

Solution

	Engineer	Teacher	Accountant	Author	Family
Christine	✗	✓	✗	✗	sister
Dorothy	✗	✗	✓	✗	sister
Sally	✗	✗	✗	✓	only
Karen	✓	✗	✗	✗	brother

- From clue **a** we know that Christine has a sister.
- From clue **b** we know that at the present time Karen is not the author.
- From clue **c** we can rule out engineer and accountant against Sally.
- From clue **d** we know that the author is an only child; therefore, Karen is not an only child.
- From clue **e** we know that Dorothy has a sister and therefore Sally is the only child and Karen has a brother.
- The author must be Sally, from **d**.
- Also in **e**, Dorothy is not the teacher.
- The final clue **f** combined with the information already worked out on the families, means that Karen is the engineer.
- From the matrix, Christine now has to be the teacher and therefore Dorothy is the accountant.

CASE HISTORIES

A group of detectives at a conference discussed important cases in their careers, one case for each of the eight detectives. When they considered the dates of the cases they realised just how time had passed.

Given the information below, can you match the cases to the years – no year is repeated.

The cases, in no particular order, were:

- 'Train Vandals',
- 'Missing Racehorse',
- 'Bristol Mugging',
- 'Birmingham Stabbing',
- 'Doped Greyhound',
- 'Manchester Murder',
- 'Threatening Letters'
- 'Brighton Blackmail'.

The dates, in chronological order, were 1977, 1979, 1980, 1984, 1985, 1991, 1997, 1998.

THE CLUES

1. The only two cases from one decade both involved a named place.

2. The murder case took place in a leap year.

3. Two cases set in particular places were in years where the sum of the digits was the same.

4. It was in a palindromic year that the 'Train Vandals' case took place, some years before the knifing incident in Birmingham.

5. The detective who solved the 'Doped Greyhound' case did not begin his career until 1986.

6. There was only one year difference between the Bristol case and that involving the missing racehorse.

CASE HISTORIES

Teaching notes

Solution

This is a short logical thought problem with two variables. It can be solved by the matrix method or by a written route. The content holds interest for many children. Careful deduction and recording are key elements. A slight variation from similar problems is noting how many gaps are left for particular cases. Other features involved are leap years, palindromic numbers, word play and simple numeracy.

Clue 1 1977 and 1979 were the dates of two out of the following four possible cases: from 'Bristol Mugging', 'Birmingham Stabbing', 'Manchester Murder' and 'Brighton Blackmail'. Crosses for these years can be placed against the other cases.

Clue 2 1980 and 1984 are the only leap years (divide exactly by 4) and therefore crosses can be placed against other years for 'Manchester Murder'.

Clue 3 For 1979 and 1997 the sum of the digits is 26. This does not add to the data for 1979 but does place crosses against the other cases for 1997.

Clue 4 1991 is the palindromic year, so a tick can therefore be placed against 'Train Vandals' and crosses placed against the other cases for this year. 'Birmingham Stabbing' has to be either 1997 or 1998. As there are three named-place cases and three years to be filled – 1977, 1979 and 1997 – 'Birmingham Stabbing' is definitely 1997 (one tick, plus crosses elsewhere).

Clue 5 'Doped Greyhound' is post-1986 and only 1998 remains (one tick, plus crosses elsewhere).

Clue 6 'Bristol Mugging' and 'Missing Racehorse' must be 1979 and 1980 respectively (Bristol and Brighton are the only ones that can fill 1997 and 1999), which leads to two ticks and a number of crosses immediately. Then 'Manchester Murder' has to be 1984, 'Brighton Blackmail' 1977 and 'Threatening Letters' 1985.

	1977	1979	1980	1984	1985	1991	1997	1998
Train Vandals	✗	✗	✗	✗	✗	✔	✗	✗
Missing Racehorse	✗	✗	✔	✗	✗	✗	✗	✗
Bristol Mugging	✗	✔	✗	✗	✗	✗	✗	✗
Birmingham Stabbing	✗	✗	✗	✗	✗	✗	✔	✗
Doped Greyhound	✗	✗	✗	✗	✗	✗	✗	✔
Manchester Murder	✗	✗	✗	✔	✗	✗	✗	✗
Threatening Letters	✗	✗	✗	✗	✔	✗	✗	✗
Brighton Blackmail	✔	✗	✗	✗	✗	✗	✗	✗

DETECTIVE CASE CLUES

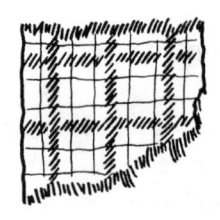

At a conference of detectives, not surprisingly, talk came round to past cases in which various inspectors had been involved. Each of the eight detectives spoke about a particular case and the clue that had been crucial in solving the case.

Below are miscellaneous pieces of information that should allow you to match the detective with the case and also with the important clue. (Note: for ease, the cases are described by two main words, rather than 'The Case of the ...'.)

The detectives' surnames, in alphabetical order, were Archer, Denton, Finch, French, Gates, Hardaker, Hardiman and Harrison.

The case names, in no particular order, were 'Train Vandals', 'Missing Racehorse', 'Bristol Mugging', 'Birmingham Stabbing', 'Doped Greyhound', 'Manchester Murder', 'Threatening Letters' and 'Brighton Blackmail'.

The clues associated with the cases, but out of order, were a footprint, a fingerprint, some thread, a torn piece of cloth, a button, a spent match, a cigarette end and a torn message.

INFORMATION

1. The two detectives whose names end with the same three letters handled cases with place names involved and the initial letter of those place names could be described as the mode.

2. The detective whose surname suggests incorrectly that he is not English, handled an unpleasant blackmail case with one of the two 'damaged' clues.

3. The second 'alliterative' case (in alphabetical order) was solved by a detective with a surname whose initial letter is not the initial letter for any of the other detectives. The critical clue made her joke that the case had been 'hanging by a ...'

4. Two cases could be said to be linked by their clues in that the end of one could have been produced by the action of the other before it was 'finished'. These cases were handled by detectives Archer and Hardiman.

5. The two animal cases ironically were looked after by animal-lovers – detectives Hardaker and Archer. A print was the clue in one of them.

6. A detective, whose name is the joint longest, found that a torn piece of cloth helped her to solve the 'Birmingham Stabbing'.

7. The 'Missing Racehorse' case was difficult to sort out, as might be suggested by the name of the detective in charge. However, ultimately it proved less complicated than the case of detective Gates, solved by the evidence of a thread, or the 'Train Vandals' and its cigarette end clue, handled by another detective whose name did not indicate an 'easy' answer.

8. The footprint in an animal case was easier to detect than the fingerprint in the case with a place name whose initial letter follows immediately in the alphabet the initial letter of the detective who brought the 'Doped Greyhound' case to a successful conclusion.

DETECTIVE CASE CLUES

Teaching Notes

This piece offers an extension to *Case Histories* (page 202), as the number of variables is increased. Care has to be taken to transfer relevant information from one grid to another.

Solution

	footprint	fingerprint	thread	torn piece of cloth	button	spent match	cigarette end	torn message	Train Vandals	Missing Racehorse	Bristol Mugging	Birmingham Stabbing	Doped Greyhound	Manchester Murder	Threatening Letters	Brighton Blackmail
Archer	✗	✗	✗	✗	✗	✓	✗	✗	✗	✗	✗	✗	✓	✗	✗	✗
Denton	✗	✗	✗	✗	✓	✗	✗	✗	✗	✗	✗	✗	✗	✗	✓	✗
Finch	✗	✓	✗	✗	✗	✗	✗	✗	✗	✗	✓	✗	✗	✗	✗	✗
French	✗	✗	✗	✗	✗	✗	✗	✓	✗	✗	✗	✗	✗	✗	✗	✓
Gates	✗	✗	✓	✗	✗	✗	✗	✗	✗	✗	✗	✗	✗	✓	✗	✗
Hardaker	✓	✗	✗	✗	✗	✗	✗	✗	✗	✓	✗	✗	✗	✗	✗	✗
Hardiman	✗	✗	✗	✗	✗	✗	✓	✗	✓	✗	✗	✗	✗	✗	✗	✗
Harrison	✗	✗	✗	✓	✗	✗	✗	✗	✗	✗	✗	✓	✗	✗	✗	✗
Train Vandals	✗	✗	✗	✗	✗	✗	✓	✗								
Missing Racehorse	✓	✗	✗	✗	✗	✗	✗	✗								
Bristol Mugging	✗	✓	✗	✗	✗	✗	✗	✗								
Birmingham Stabbing	✗	✗	✗	✓	✗	✗	✗	✗								
Doped Greyhound	✗	✗	✗	✗	✗	✓	✗	✗								
Manchester Murder	✗	✗	✓	✗	✗	✗	✗	✗								
Threatening Letters	✗	✗	✗	✗	✓	✗	✗	✗								
Brighton Blackmail	✗	✗	✗	✗	✗	✗	✗	✓								

DETECTIVE CASE CLUES

1. French and Finch are the detectives identified. 'Mode' means 'the most used' and this letter is B. Therefore, the cases linked with French and Finch are two out of the 'Bristol Mugging', 'Birmingham Stabbing' and 'Brighton Blackmail'. Crosses can be put against those two detectives for all other cases.

2. The detective identified is French, linked with the 'Brighton Blackmail' and either the torn piece of cloth or torn message. So we can enter one tick plus crosses in the Detectives/Cases grid, and transfer the data into the Detective/Clues grid and the Cases/Clues grid.

3. The case is the 'Manchester Murder', solved by Archer, Denton or Gates and the clue was thread. place a tick for 'Manchester Murder' and thread, plus crosses elsewhere.

4. The clues are the spent match and the cigarette end and the detectives are Archer and Hardiman. Place crosses against other clues for those two detectives, and for the other detectives for those clues.

5. The cases are the 'Missing Racehorse' and 'Doped Greyhound'; the detectives are Hardaker and Archer. One of them is involved with either the fingerprint or the footprint. From 4, this cannot be Archer and therefore Hardaker's case involved a fingerprint or a footprint.

6. Detective Hardaker or Hardiman or Harrison is linked with the torn piece of cloth and the 'Birmingham Stabbing' (definite tick in that grid); therefore, the 'Brighton Blackmail' is linked with the torn message, and thus with French.

Keep checking ticks and transferring, where possible, to the other grids.

Only Harrison can be the case with the torn piece of cloth (enter ticks and crosses accordingly) and therefore the 'Birmingham Stabbing'. This means that Finch is linked with the 'Bristol Mugging' (enter ticks and crosses).

7. The 'Missing Racehorse' detective is Hardaker or Hardiman. Gates is linked with the thread. 'Train Vandals' is linked with the cigarette end and either Hardaker or Hardiman. This means Archer is linked with the 'Doped Greyhound' case. Enter ticks for Gates and thread, which we know was linked to the 'Manchester Murder' (enter ticks and crosses). This means Hardaker is linked with the 'Missing Racehorse' (enter ticks and crosses). 'Train Vandals' goes with the cigarette end (place other ticks and crosses). This can only be Hardiman (not Hardaker); therefore, ticks and crosses can be placed (and also in the Detectives/Cases grid). This means Denton is linked to the 'Threatening Letter' case (enter tick).

8. The footprint goes with 'Missing Racehorse' or 'Doped Greyhound', so enter crosses against the other cases and the footprint. The fingerprint is linked to a 'B' place name – only 'Bristol Mugging' fits (place ticks and crosses elsewhere). This we know was Finch; therefore, tick against the fingerprint. Consequently, Hardaker is linked to footprint (place tick and crosses), which is linked with the 'Missing Racehorse' case – enter a tick in the other grid. Archer goes with the spent match (tick) and therefore 'Doped Greyhound'. This places Denton with the button (tick) and the 'Threatening Letter' case.

BIRDS OF A FEATHER

The 600 members of the Dinley Ornithologists' Society have just held a poll to choose the most popular British bird. By reference to the information and the clues below, you should be able to draw up a 'Top Twenty-Five' in order of popularity of the following birds.

- barn owl
- blackbird
- blue tit
- carrion crow
- chaffinch
- cuckoo
- golden eagle
- green woodpecker
- house sparrow
- jackdaw
- jay
- kestrel
- kingfisher
- lapwing
- magpie
- nightingale
- pied wagtail
- raven
- robin
- skylark
- song thrush
- starling
- swallow
- wren
- yellowhammer

NOTES

1. No two birds received the same number of votes.
2. Each member of the Society cast one vote.

Your Task

Draw up a table of the 25 birds in order of preference, showing the number of votes cast for each. (Perhaps you could also carry out your own poll to see whether your group has the same views as the Dinley Ornithologists' Society.)

THE CLUES

1. The longest bird received votes equivalent to the minimum voting age in a General Election.
2. The three summer visitors received 8, 28 and 35 votes.
3. One does not make a summer, but it did attract 28 votes.
4. Two dozen votes were attracted by a bird that tunnels with its beak through a decayed area of a tree to make its nest.
5. 5% of the votes were cast in favour of *Fringilla coelebs*
6. The bird that lays eggs in other birds' nests received 8 votes.
7. The bird who sang for 'a little bit of bread and no cheese' scored a score.
8. The little bird who performs acrobatics for nuts and fat got one more vote than the nightingale.
9. The two birds most likely to be on a police wanted list scored 19 votes in total. There was only a single vote difference between them.
10. The shortest bird received 3^3 votes.
11. Two birds use a stone as a tool. They gained 37 and 40 votes.
12. The bird who gained 10 votes is black and white with a glossy sheen of blue, green or purple.
13. One quarter of a century votes were for the night hunter with the large white face.
14. The bird that has inadvertently been helped by Britain's road-building programme gained three fewer votes than the golden eagle.
15. Despite imitating other birds, this particular bird came bottom of the poll with only 5 votes.
16. The bird with 40 votes lays bright turquoise-blue eggs, which are spotted with black.
17. The large bird that finished next to bottom of the poll, with only two more votes than the least popular bird, got part of its name from one part of its diet.
18. 13 and 34 were the votes cast for the remaining two birds where the nest is constructed with sticks or twigs.
19. This 'chirpy' bird gained as many votes as the jackdaw and the starling added together. It has two styles of nest-building – a loose construction in a building or a neat, domed nest in a bush.
20. Two crested birds gained 54 votes between them. The difference between them was 10 votes.
21. Britain's National Bird confirmed its popularity by topping the poll with exactly one-twelfth of the total votes cast.
22. There were 13 votes for the largest member of the crow family.
23. The name of this bird is contradicted by the colouring of the female. Its popularity was shown by it gaining third place, two votes behind the second choice.
24. The bird with 22 votes lays olive eggs blotched with dark brown.
25. The only bird not yet discussed, finished in 14th place.

INFORMATION

CARRION CROW

Corvus corone corone
Length 47 cm

The carrion crow is a widespread resident frequent in farmland, moorland, sea cliffs, town parks and suburbs.

It is an all-black bird but there is a greenish gloss on the plumage. Almost anything is eaten. The main items are small birds and animals, eggs, carrion, grubs, insects, worms, grain and berries. The call is a deep croak.

The nest is mostly of twigs and it is built on a cliff ledge or high in a tree. Carrion crows do not congregate in such large colonies as rooks. There are often family groups but at other times they may be solitary. Four or five eggs are laid. These are bluish-green, blotched with brown.

PIED WAGTAIL

Motacilla alba yarrellii
Length 18 cm

Pied wagtails are present all the year. They are often found near water but they are also seen in gardens and on farms.

This is the only small black and white bird with such a long tail. On the ground it runs very quickly in short rushes. A great number of insects, chiefly flies, are eaten. The call is a distinctive high-pitched 'tschizzick'. There is also a low song.

The nest is built in walls, among creepers and in greenhouses. It consists of dried grass, roots, hair and wool. The eggs are whitish, covered with grey speckles. There are normally between four and six.

CUCKOO

Cuculus canorus
Length 33 cm

Cuckoos are summer visitors from Central and South Africa and Southern Arabia. They arrive in April. Distribution is very widespread and habitat varies from moors, heaths and forests to farmland, town parks and coastal marshes.

The plumage is slate-grey and the white underparts are strongly barred. Cuckoos feed on insects and caterpillars including the hairy ones that most birds ignore. As well as the 'cuckoo' song there are low, harsh calls like coughing or clearing the throat.

Normally ten to twelve eggs are laid, one at a time, in the nests of other birds. When the young cuckoo is hatched, it turns out the other eggs and fledglings.

KINGFISHER

Alcedo atthis
Length 16.5 cm

The kingfisher is a resident of the British Isles. Its haunt is by water of one type or another – lakes, rivers, streams and sometimes the coast.

The colouring is so brilliant as to almost dazzle the eye. The back, head, wings and short tail are a metallic blue-green. The underparts are rich chestnut and the small feet are bright red. The diet consists of water insects, shellfish, tadpoles, frogs and small fish. When the kingfisher catches a fish it beats it against a stone. The bird is often seen diving into the water from a branch. The call is a loud shrill 'chee' or 'chikee'.

The nesting-hole is usually in a sandy river bank. Six or eight white eggs are laid.

RAVEN

Corvus corax
Length 64 cm

A resident, the raven is found mainly in the hills and sea cliffs of the north and west of Britain. Sometimes it is found in woods.

The colouring is glossy black. The raven is the largest member of the crow family. The diet is varied, with carrion, small animals and birds, eggs, grubs, worms, grain and fruit all eaten. The call is a deep, croaking 'pruk'.

A large nest of sticks, lined with grass and wool, is built on a high ledge or sometimes in a tree. Between three and seven eggs are laid. They are greenish, with dark brown blotches.

ROBIN

Erithacus rubecula
Length 14 cm

This popular resident is Britain's National Bird. The haunts are now very general. Once a woodland bird, the robin is now seen regularly in suburban gardens.

The cock and hen are alike. The red face distinguishes the robin from all other red-breasted birds. The young are brown and speckled. The natural food consists of insects, spiders, worms, seeds, fruit and berries but the robin also enjoys crumbs and other scraps. The calls include 'tic, tic', 'tsit' and 'tswee'. The song is clear, high and very varied.

The nest is made of grass, wool, moss and hair. It might be almost anywhere – in a hole in a wall, tree or bank or even in an old can or bucket. The eggs are white, speckled with light red. Five or six are laid, and there are two broods, sometimes three.

KESTREL

Falco tinnunculus
Length 34 cm

This resident is the best known of British birds of prey. In the country, the kestrel may be seen on moors, coasts, farmland and in open woodland. It is attracted to motorway verges where there is undisturbed wildlife on which to feed.

The plumage of the male is slate-grey on the head, rump and tail. The back is light chestnut-brown, spotted with black. The female is barred across the tail. When the bird is in search of prey, its hovering flight is very distinctive. Food consists chiefly of mice and insects and occasionally small birds. In the cities sparrows are plentiful as prey. The call is a loud shrill 'kee-kee-kee'.

Kestrels do not build nests of their own. Instead they use the abandoned nests of other birds or ledges on cliffs or high buildings. There are between three and five eggs, which are buff coloured, thickly mottled with red-brown.

YELLOWHAMMER

Emberiza citrinella
Length 16.5 cm

The yellowhammer is present all the year in the British Isles. The distribution is widespread but the bird is found chiefly in open country and hedgerows.

The male has a bright yellow head and underparts and chestnut brown upper parts streaked with black. The female is browner and less yellow. Both sexes have a chestnut rump and white outer tail feathers. The diet consists of corn, weed seeds, wild fruits and insects. The high-pitched song has an unmistakable pattern and it is said to resemble the phrase 'a little bit of bread and no cheese'.

The nest is made of grass, moss and hair and is situated in hedges, by roadsides or in young trees, usually on or near the ground. Between three and five eggs are laid. The colour is white but there are dark purplish-brown markings.

JACKDAW

Corvus monedula
Length 33 cm

This resident is smaller than the crow and the rook. The jackdaw is often seen on sea cliffs, and around church towers, ruins or old trees.

The colouring is generally black but there is grey on the back and sides of the head. The main items in the diet are grubs and insects but the jackdaw also eats eggs, young birds and mice, and a small quantity of grain and fruit. One strange habit is the bird's theft of bright objects. The main call is 'chack'.

The nest is made of twigs lined with grass and wool. The birds normally gather in colonies. The eggs are bluish, spotted with brown. There are normally between three and six laid.

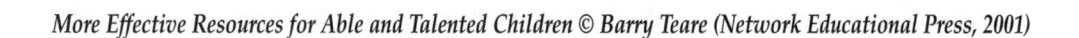

BIRDS OF A FEATHER

GREEN WOODPECKER

Picus viridis
Length 32 cm

This resident is the largest of the three British woodpeckers. It is seen in woods, parks and gardens.

The green woodpecker is a beautiful bird. The plumage is green above with a yellow rump and a red crown and nape. The favourite foods are insects. The bird also eats nuts, berries and fruit. Ants are regarded as a delicacy and the green woodpecker raids their nests with its long sticky-ended tongue. The call is a loud echoing laugh.

The nest is in a hole in a tree usually drilled in decayed wood. Between four and seven white eggs are laid.

BLUE TIT

Parus caeruleus
Length 11.5 cm

The blue tit, which is a popular resident bird, is seen in a great variety of locations.

The plumage is primrose-yellow on the underparts and a greyish-blue and green above. The distinctive head is blue and white. Many insects are eaten and the birds help gardeners by eating aphids and other pests. The blue tit performs acrobatics to eat nuts, fat and scraps that are hung up. The most typical of many calls is a scolding 'tsee-tsee-tsee-tsit'.

The nest is made of moss, wool and feathers in a hole in a tree or wall and sometimes in most unlikely locations such as street lamp standards and letterboxes. The eggs are white, spotted with light red. Many are laid – in excess of seven or eight.

BARN OWL

Tyto alba
Length 34 cm

Barn owls are present all the year in the British Isles. Favourite haunts are barns, towers, ruins, woods and farm buildings although the bird normally remains hidden during the day.

In colour, barn owls are orange-buff above, faintly speckled, and white below. The face is white with black eyes. The main foods are rats, moles, all kinds of mice, small birds and beetles. The indigestible parts are brought up as pellets. The call is a prolonged, strangled screech. There are also hisses, snores and barks.

There is no nest in the accepted sense. The three to eight eggs are laid in a few feathers on a ledge. They are coloured white.

STARLING

Sturnus vulgaris
Length 21.5 cm

This resident is very common and general in distribution. There are large numbers even in the centres of cities.

At first sight, the starling looks black but in fact the plumage is glossed with green and purple. Insects and grubs are the mainstays of the diet but fruit is also eaten. The song is very varied with chatters, twitters, clicks and whistles. An interesting feature is the habit of the starling of imitating the songs of other birds, and other sounds.

A nest made from straw, grass and feathers is built in a hole in a variety of locations – in masonry, under the eaves of buildings or in trees and creepers. Four to seven pale blue eggs are laid.

GOLDEN EAGLE

Aquila chrysaetus
Length 75–88 cm

The golden eagle is a resident of the British Isles but the numbers are not great. It is seldom seen outside Scotland. Favourite haunts are mountains and crags.

The plumage is dark brown with golden feathers on the head and under the wings. The golden eagle has a majestic soaring and gliding flight. It eats animal food entirely, especially rabbits, hares, rats, grouse, small lambs and carrion. The typical calls are a shrill yelp or bark.

A large nest of branches and sticks is lined with grass. Sometimes the same nest is used for years. Usually two eggs are laid. They are whitish, blotched all over with red-brown.

SONG THRUSH

Turdus philomelos
Length 23 cm

Song thrushes are present all the year and their distribution is very general, including fields, woods, parks and gardens.

The plumage is brown above and buffish-white below, with very dark brown spots on the breast. Favourite foods are worms, slugs, snails, grubs, insects and berries. A stone is used as an anvil against which snails are beaten to crack the shell. The song thrush is well known for its call and songs. Each phrase is repeated twice and sometimes up to five times. It is said that a careful listener can distinguish 'did he do it, did he do it, Judy did' and 'come out, come out'.

The nest is made of grasses, roots, moss, leaves and soil. The four or five eggs are bright turquoise-blue, spotted with black.

BIRDS OF A FEATHER

LAPWING

Vanellus vanellus
Length 30 cm

This resident is sometimes known as the peewit. Typical haunts are fields, pastures, marshes, tidal mudflats and moors.

The lapwing is a handsome bird. It is easily recognised by the elegant thin crest, black breast above white underparts and metallic green back. Wireworms, leatherjackets, snails, slugs and worms are eaten. The diet also includes vegetable matter, seeds and grass. Calls and the song are all variations on the 'pee-wit' theme.

The nest is a slight depression in the ground, in a field or any open place. There are usually four eggs. They are olive in colour, heavily blotched with very dark brown.

HOUSE SPARROW

Passer domesticus
Length 14.5 cm

House sparrows are present all the year round. They are seen in great numbers close to human habitations. In autumn many move to farmland to feed on the grain.

The female is all brown but the male has a black bib and a dark grey crown. Grain, seed and insects are eaten. The house sparrow does not have a real song but the typical call is a loud and aggressive 'chirp'.

The nest is loosely made with straw and feathers in a hole in a building or wall or under the eaves. If it is built in a bush it tends to be neat and domed. Five or six eggs are laid. They are grey or brown but are heavily marked with speckles and blotches.

CHAFFINCH

Fringilla coelebs
Length 15 cm

The chaffinch is a familiar resident. Its distribution is very general although it does not thrive in the centres of cities. Numbers have declined, perhaps due to toxic seed dressings.

The breast and cheeks of the adult male are pinkish-brown and the underparts pink. The female is duller in colour. Chaffinches are mainly seed-eaters but they also take fruit, corn and many insects. The most common call-note is 'pink, pink' but other sounds include 'tsup', 'tsit', and 'wheet'.

The nest is beautifully made. It is very neat and round and it is constructed of moss, lichen, wool, feathers and hair. The most common location is in the fork of a branch. Between four and six eggs are laid. They are grey, tinged with pink, and with brown blotches.

SWALLOW

Hirundo rustica
Length 19 cm

The swallow is a summer visitor to the British Isles. The distribution is general but they are often seen skimming low over a pond.

The swallow can be identified by the continuous dark blue upper parts and long tail streamers. The throat is dull chestnut with a dark blue band below it. The forehead is also dark chestnut. Swallows eat insects, which are caught in flight. The song is a continuous warbling and twittering.

The nest is rather open and saucer-shaped. It is made of mud, grass and feathers. The typical position is on rafters in buildings. Quite often the same nest is used year after year. The eggs are white, spotted with brown. Normally four to six eggs are laid.

NIGHTINGALE

Luscinia megarhynchos
Length 16.5 cm

The nightingale is a summer visitor from Africa. Favourite haunts are woods and thickets.

The appearance of the bird is quite undistinguished. The plumage is smooth brown with paler underparts and chestnut tail. The main foods are insects, grubs, worms and berries. The nightingale's fame is due to its song, which is rich in volume and range of notes. Surprisingly it sings as much in the daytime as at night.

The nest is made of dead leaves and grass and it is positioned close to the ground in thick undergrowth. The four to six eggs are olive-blue or olive-brown.

JAY

Garrulus glandarius
Length 34 cm

The jay is a resident of the British Isles. It is normally found in woods and copses.

It is one of our most brightly coloured birds. The plumage is pinkish-brown. There are black and white markings on the head. There is also a bright blue patch on the wings, finely barred black and white.

In autumn the jay buries acorns ready for the hard weather. Other foods include small animals and birds, eggs, insects, grubs, snails and fruit. There is no proper song. A harsh call is repeated two or three times.

The nest, which consists of twigs and soil lined with roots, is normally found in a bush or small tree. Between five and seven eggs are laid. They are pale greenish or buff, speckled with light brown.

SKYLARK

Alauda arvensis
Length 18 cm

Skylarks are present all the year in the British Isles. Favourite haunts are open country, fields and downs.

The upper parts are brown, streaked with black but the underparts are paler. The outer tail feathers are white. The small brown crest is raised in excitement. The diet consists of weed seeds, corn, leaves, worms and insects. The skylark is famous for its beautiful and joyous song. It is high-pitched, loud and clear. Its call is a 'chirrup'.

The nest is on the ground and it is lined with grass and hair. The eggs are heavily marked with brown specks and freckles. The normal number is between three and five.

MAGPIE

Pica pica
Length 46 cm

The magpie is present in the British Isles all year. The haunts are general. In recent years the bird has spread into towns and city parks.

This is one of the most distinctive birds as it is the only large black and white land bird with a long graduated tail. Close to, the magpie is seen to have a glossy sheen of blue, green or purple. The diet consists of small animals and birds, eggs, insects, snails, worms, fruit, grain and acorns. The magpie is attracted to bright things, and it steals rings and other objects. There is no true song but the call is a harsh chatter.

The nest is built in a tree or tall bush and it is made of sticks, roots and mud. It is shaped like a dome. Five to eight eggs are laid. They are pale bluish-green, speckled with brown.

BLACKBIRD

Turdus merula
Length 25 cm

The blackbird is a very popular and common resident. It is seen in many surroundings – forest, scrub, parks, gardens, orchards and towns.

The male is jet-black with a bright orange-yellow bill, whereas the female is dark brown, darkest on the tail and wings. The food consists of fruit, seeds, insects and worms. Calls include 'tchook, tchook', 'pink, pink' and 'tsee'. When it is alarmed the blackbird gives a hysterical cackle.
The nest consists of mud, moss and grass and it is built in a bush, creeper or tree. There are usually four or five eggs. They are greenish-blue, speckled with brown.

WREN

Troglodytes troglodytes
Length 9.5 cm

The wren is one of the smallest British residents. There is a wide range of habitats from rocky mountains, sea cliffs and moors to forests, scrub, parks and gardens.

The brown plumage is closely barred. The tiny cocked tail is very distinctive. The wren has a mouse-like way of creeping about. Caterpillars, spiders and all kinds of insects are the mainstay of the diet. The call is 'tic-tic-tic' and the song is very loud for so small a bird. It is clear and sweet.

The nest is situated in a bank, wall or bush. The cock builds several beautifully-constructed domed nests of moss and grass. The hen chooses the one she likes the best and lines it with feathers. Five to twelve eggs are laid. They are white, faintly speckled with red-brown.

BIRDS OF A FEATHER
Teaching Notes

Long logical thought problems such as **Birds Of A Feather** combine important content with thinking skills. The two can be delivered together.

Key Elements

- information processing
- synthesis of data
- mathematical operations
- word play
- science content (living processes)
- construction of a league table
- logical thinking

Contexts

Birds Of A Feather can be used in a variety of ways:

- as extension work
- as an enrichment item for those ahead in normal work
- as an activity in an enrichment session, summer school or cluster day
- as differentiated homework.

Solution

1. The golden eagle gained 18 votes.
2. The cuckoo, the swallow and the nightingale scored 8, 28 and 35 votes but we do not know which scored which.
3. The swallow got 28 votes. ('*One swallow does not make a summer.*')
4. Two dozen votes = 24 for the green woodpecker.
5. 5% = 30 votes for the chaffinch.
6. The cuckoo got 8 votes and therefore from Clues **2** and **3** the nightingale received 35 votes.
7. The yellowhammer had the votes of 20 members.
8. The blue tit scored 35 + 1 = 36 votes.
9. The jackdaw and the magpie (both 'thieves') got 19 votes between them, split as 10 and 9. At this stage we do not know which is which.
10. The wren got 3 × 3 × 3 = 27 votes.
11. The song thrush and the kingfisher got 37 and 40 votes but we do not know which way round.
12. From Clue **9**, the magpie got 10 votes and therefore the jackdaw received 9.
13. 25 members supported the barn owl (¼ × 100).
14. The kestrel (which catches prey on motorway verges) got 18 − 3 = 15 votes.
15. The starling was in bottom place with 5 votes.

BIRDS OF A FEATHER

16. From Clue **11**, the song thrush got 40 votes and therefore the kingfisher 37.
17. In 24th place with 5 + 2 = 7 votes was the carrion crow.
18. The raven and the jay are the only two birds left with nests of twigs or sticks. They got 13 and 34 votes but we do not know which scored which.
19. The house sparrow got 9 + 5 = 14 votes.
20. The skylark and the lapwing got 54 votes between them. These are split 32 and 22 but we do not know which way round.
21. The robin finished in first place with one-twelfth of 600 = 50 votes.
22. From Clue **18**, 13 votes were for the raven and therefore 34 were for the jay.
23. The blackbird finished in third place with 40 − 2 = 38 (the place can be used – the actual votes need to be calculated when all the clues are solved and it is seen that the song thrush is in second place with 40 votes).
24. From Clue **20**, the lapwing got 22 votes and therefore the skylark received 32.
25. The pied wagtail is the one left. That finished in 14th place. The votes can only be calculated by the construction of the table. This will show that the pied wagtail is between the green woodpecker with 24 and the lapwing with 22. As a result the pied wagtail gained 23 votes, remembering that every bird received a different number of votes.

Final 'League Table'

Place	Bird	Votes	Place	Bird	Votes
1st	robin	50	14th	pied wagtail	23
2nd	song thrush	40	15th	lapwing	22
3rd	blackbird	38	16th	yellowhammer	20
4th	kingfisher	37	17th	golden eagle	18
5th	blue tit	36	18th	kestrel	15
6th	nightingale	35	19th	house sparrow	14
7th	jay	34	20th	raven	13
8th	skylark	32	21st	magpie	10
9th	chaffinch	30	22nd	jackdaw	9
10th	swallow	28	23rd	cuckoo	8
11th	wren	27	24th	carrion crow	7
12th	barn owl	25	25th	starling	5
13th	green woodpecker	24		**TOTAL VOTES**	**600**

Theme Eight: Detective Work, Codes

Detective work is a very useful vehicle for work with children for the following reasons:

- it has an intrinsic interest that attracts a large number of people
- there is a strong element of logical thinking
- some solutions also involve lateral thinking
- synthesis of data is important
- analysis and evaluation of evidence plays a key part
- English and literacy are involved through emphasis on words and statements and via the genre of detective fiction
- the forensic element is closely associated with science
- skills involved in the study of history apply; for example, the weighting of evidence
- a mapping element – looking at how things relate to each other in terms of position – is a feature of some cases
- organisational skills are very important.

Critical Clues (page 221) presents five very varied cases for pupils to interpret. The data has to be used carefully and logically but there is also scope for lateral thinking and the production of alternative answers, provided that the explanations fit the given facts. Children come up with a fascinating range of responses.

Cliffhanger (page 228) is strong on analysis and synthesis. Interpretation of evidence is linked to use of a protractor and a map. It can be handled 'straight' or be dramatised into a race against time by rival crime squads.

Codes also give opportunities for content to be delivered in an unusual and challenging way. Codes can be of varying difficulty and those that are taxing have particular advantages in the teaching of able pupils. Many forms of entertainment for the young use fast movement from one focus to another, requiring very little sustained attention or concentration. Lengthy, demanding codes help to build up a span of concentration. Additional clues can be given gradually on a board or flipchart but not until pupils have grappled properly with each stage. It is important that able children have to work hard for success on some occasions.

Codes are of course abstract – where something stands for something else. Some pupils need to work in the concrete for longer than others but many able children thrive by more rapid progress to the abstract. In *Improving Science Education 5–14* (Schools Scottish Executive Department, 1999) the following is said:

> *'Science, like Mathematics, has a significant component of knowledge and understanding, built around a number of key concepts or ideas. Some pupils grasp these ideas quite quickly, whereas others need more support from their teacher or more opportunities to explore and develop their understanding through working with concrete materials.'*

Making predictions and hypothesising are key elements in both the science and mathematics sections of the National Curriculum (DfEE/QCA, 1999). Decoding is very much about these elements. The mathematics document includes the line:

> *'... develop logical thinking and explain their reasoning.'*

Content of all sorts can be delivered through the exciting medium of codes, which – like detective work – has an intrinsic interest for many able pupils. *Mrs Pascal's Proposition* (page 232), as the title would imply, is a mathematical code based upon simple equations. *The Shapes* (page 234) is a number code. Basic calculations are involved but the piece also contains a visual stimulus in the form of a child's comic strip and deduction of what is conveyed through a rhyme.

The Hidden Will Of Gresham Grange (page 237) also has a link with numbers but here much more is to do with positioning. Synthesis of data is required – the basic scenario, cryptic messages, a list of book titles and a map (quite a mixed bag!).

Searching For Words (page 241) places much greater emphasis upon language. Again, synthesis of information is important. On this occasion the components are a pithy saying, cryptic directions and a wordsearch grid containing words or phrases associated with detective stories and cases, thus linking neatly the two elements in this Theme of the book.

ATTENTION

See also the resources suggested below.

Book	Theme or Section	Activity
Elsewhere in this book	Theme One: English, Literacy	The Mystery Unfolds
	Theme Three: Science	Carol Catalyst The Cryptic Chemist
	Theme Four: Humanities, Citizenship …	Silence In Court
	Theme Five: Modern Foreign Languages	Adjectifs Daylight Robbery
	Theme Six: Young Children	A Is For Apple, Or Is It?
	Theme Seven: Logical Thought	Case Histories Detective Case Clues
Effective Provision For Able And Talented Children, Network Educational Press, 1997	Section Six	A Capital Idea
Effective Resources For Able And Talented Children, Network Educational Press, 1999	Theme Eight: Codes	Lucky The Cat Mosaic Crossedwords The Way The Wind Blows
	Theme Ten: Detective Work	Seeing Is Believing According To The Evidence An Arresting Problem Vital Evidence

Critical Clues

Some detective cases rely on a combination of evidence, some are solved by routine investigative methods, but there are cases where one or two critical clues prove to be all-important. The five cases below fall into that last category. Can you recognise the significance of the 'Critical Clues'?

Case One: Lady In Red

When questioned by the police, the attendant at Victoria tube station had no problem in remembering his encounter with the woman believed to be Judith James. He described her striking appearance, which was dominated by a brilliant red coat and a stunning scarlet hat – topped with feathers and with a very wide brim, which shaded her face considerably. Indeed, the attendant was so taken by her appearance that he thought of her as the 'Lady In Red', a song from a favourite singer of his, Chris de Burgh.

There had been other things too about their meeting that stuck in his mind. The woman had made quite a fuss about asking for assistance in going through the special gate for those with large suitcases or other luggage, when in fact she herself was carrying only a medium-sized bag. Her loud and prolonged insistence had led the attendant to open the gate even though such a move seemed very unnecessary.

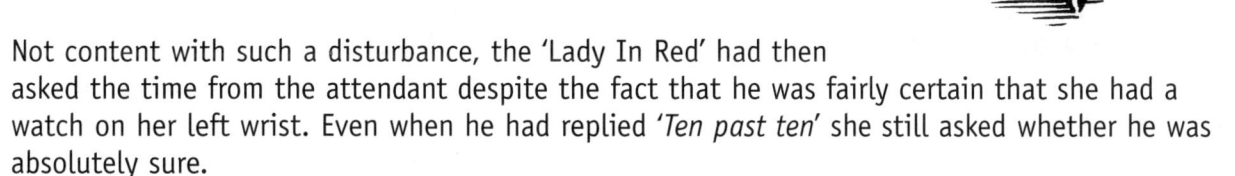

Not content with such a disturbance, the 'Lady In Red' had then asked the time from the attendant despite the fact that he was fairly certain that she had a watch on her left wrist. Even when he had replied *'Ten past ten'* she still asked whether he was absolutely sure.

All in all, the attendant had no problem in answering the police questions about the woman's movements but he could not give much of a description of her face due to the large brim of the hat.

Your Tasks

The interview with the tube station attendant was of great importance in the 'Lady In Red' case. Come to your own conclusions on the case with particular reference to:

1 the significance of the woman's appearance

2 an explanation of her rather 'showy' behaviour

3 how the encounter at Victoria tube station fitted into the case as a whole.

Case Two: Suspected Suicide

When Inspector Leyland arrived at the home of Graham Digby, he was met by Sergeant Train who told him that it looked as though the owner of the house had committed suicide. In support of this theory, Sergeant Train explained that Graham Digby's body had been found slumped face forward onto his desk in the study. There was a bullet through his forehead and a revolver lay on the desk by the dead man's right hand. Sergeant Train said that there was no other sign of violence in the room, no indication of anyone else's presence and the suicide was confirmed by a tiny slip of paper, reproduced below.

I can't go on

This matched the handwriting of the dead man, as seen from his diary.

On further investigation of the room, nothing unusual was to be found. Other objects on the desk included a letter rack, a tidy for pens, pencils and other items of stationery and a copy of that day's *Guardian* newspaper. The paper was open at the page containing the crossword, which was almost completed. Further evidence of the crossword activity was a dictionary on a nearby table. The dictionary was open at the page that included 'paradigm' – one of the answers filled out in pen on the crossword grid.

The right-hand side of the desk was covered with an in-tray, a stand-up calendar and a number of books. Very much to the left and front of the desk was a blotting pad. Graham Digby was slumped in a chair, which seemed to be in its normal position as his knees fitted into the space left for such a purpose beneath the desk and to the right of a set of built-in drawers. His body lay forward so that his outstretched left arm rested on the right end of the blotting pad. The forefinger of the left hand was stained with ink.

Sergeant Train watched his senior colleague look carefully at the scene, a frown on his face. Eventually Inspector Leyland turned to his colleague. *'I am not so sure that this is a suicide,'* he said.

Your Tasks

1. From the information above, find three reasons, with supporting evidence, for the inspector's doubts on the supposed suicide.

2. What actions, by the inspector, would you expect to follow in relation to his suspicions about the scene of death?

Case Three: Message Understood

The police in Cornwall had been watching a small group of men for some time, believing that they were carrying out various criminal activities. Investigations sometimes need a little luck to take them forward and the detective squad was fortunate to intercept a radio message between members of the gang. At first the meaning was unclear but after some consideration the police realised that they had valuable information upon which to act.

The message was:

> FY3097 10K 985817 ELGAR DB37 086206 + 20,000

Your Tasks

1. Work out the meaning of the intercepted message.
2. Explain what action you would have taken if you had been in the police squad dealing with the case.

Case Four: Diamonds Are Forever

The police arrived at Marshcott Manor in response to an anguished call from Sir Henry Williams. He and his family had returned home to find that Lady Williams' jewellery box had been rifled. Inspector Prescott conducted a search and carried out interviews. Her investigation threw up some unusual points.

There was no sign of a forced entry. Indeed, it was some minutes before the family realised that anything was amiss. The jewellery box stood opened on the top of the dressing table in which it was normally kept. It lay open but there was no damage to the box or its lock. Nothing else in the room had been disturbed at all.

Two more points interested Inspector Prescott. The family had been away for the weekend to attend the funeral of a well-known relative. Not all the jewellery had been taken. Only the valuable pieces had gone – the cheap and decorative items had been left.

Your Task

Inspector Prescott believed that she had uncovered some vital clues as to the perpetrator(s) of the robbery. Explain how the information above helps to narrow the search for the criminal(s).

Case Five: A Strange Confession

Inspector Dent was confused, very confused. He was investigating the murder of wealthy businessman Julian Battersby, who had been found dead in his study at home, as a result of a violent blow to the head. Suspicion had fallen upon his brother, David Battersby, and David's twin sister Sheila – not least because the will had revealed that the two had been left the huge bulk of the dead man's substantial fortune. The various pieces of evidence pointed to David and Sheila although there were contradictions and gaps.

David Battersby then, out of the blue, confessed to the crime. Inspector Dent, unknown to David, had already secured evidence that a figure had been tentatively identified as David Battersby in the local village at the critical time for the murder. It was a cold day and the figure had been well wrapped up, thus making identification more difficult, but the trilby and overcoat of David Battersby were well known to locals. Inspector Dent had not acquainted David with this information as yet.

Your Task

Inspector Dent could not, for some time, understand why David had made a confession before a case had been made against him, especially given the fact that there were witnesses available to give him an alibi.

Eventually the inspector worked out a possible solution. Can you do the same? What was the purpose of David Battersby's confession? Why was he not informing the police of his whereabouts at the critical time?

Critical Clues

Teaching Notes

Critical Clues has five very different cases to look at. Logical thinking is needed but lateral thinking is also involved as a variety of answers are possible, provided that key elements of the data have not been ignored. Adults who are lovers of detective fiction are more likely to recognise certain themes but children will be placed at the 'frontier of knowledge' and will have to think out answers from base.

Success Criteria

- The answer takes note of the information.
- Imagination is displayed but within realistic possibilities.
- The solution is appropriate for the setting of the case.

Key Elements

- logical thinking
- lateral thinking
- analysis of the data
- deduction and inference
- word play
- an appreciation of genre

Contexts

Critical Clues can be used in a variety of ways:

- as five separate units in normal classroom activity
- as a total piece in normal classroom activity
- as enrichment work for those ahead in standard tasks
- as differentiated homework
- as an activity within an enrichment session, summer school or cluster day
- as an open-access competition.

Some Answers

A number of appropriate answers can be made and therefore the following are only suggestions.

CASE ONE: LADY IN RED

The significance of the woman's appearance is that it is dramatic and eye-catching. She will certainly be remembered. Another important point is that the wide brim of the hat hides the face and therefore the actual person would be difficult to remember, unlike the clothes. The 'showy' behaviour looks like an effort to be noticed. Her luggage did not justify going through the special gate but the woman would imprint herself on the mind of the attendant. Asking the time seemed unnecessary (unless her watch was not working properly) but it would fix the exact time of her arrival at Victoria tube station.

Critical Clues

The clothes were stunning and could have been deliberately chosen to gain attention. They might be very similar to an outfit worn by another woman who is the victim of a crime or who is involved in activities elsewhere. The episode of the watch gives a time when the 'Lady In Red' is alive and well. However the other woman may already be dead or kidnapped so that alibis and movements have been confused and made difficult to validate. The woman at Victoria may well have been a decoy so that an accomplice could carry out a crime elsewhere at a different time and, probably, with the authentic 'Lady In Red' as the victim.

It is the case as a whole, the third element of the tasks, that is likely to have a variety of suggested solutions.

CASE TWO: SUSPECTED SUICIDE

The slip of paper is very odd. Why is it torn and so closely torn at that? This may very well be part of a sentence meaning something very different; for example, '*I can't go on accepting lifts without paying towards the petrol*'. There are a very large number of possibilities.

Graham Digby had been doing the crossword – it was nearly finished. Is this the likely occupation of a man about to kill himself? The revolver lay by the dead man's right hand. However the layout of the desk suggests a left-handed person, as does the ink stain on the forefinger of the left hand.

There are many, many possible routes in terms of the inspector's actions. They include:

- trying to find the rest of the paper from which '*I can't go on ...*' was torn
- checking on whether Graham Digby was right- or left-handed
- checking on the revolver – ownership, fingerprints and so on
- checking the rest of the room for clues – fingerprints, mud, threads and so on
- interviewing family and friends on the state of mind of the dead man, whether he had any enemies, was he wealthy, what would happen to his money, and so on.

CASE THREE: MESSAGE UNDERSTOOD

The author had a very definite scenario in mind but children have made other appropriate responses.

FY3097	This could refer to the registration number of a boat from Fowey in Cornwall. (Note: this is not normally four digits but the author did not want to inadvertently give the registration of a real boat.)
10K	This could mean ten kilometres (thousands or kilograms have been suggested).
985817	Perhaps this is a six-figure grid reference (telephone number is possible).
ELGAR DB37 086206	The most recently issued £20 notes have a picture of Elgar on them. DB37 086206 is an actual serial number. (Pupil suggestions have included nicknames, code-names, a ship's name, docking base 37 and a musician's valuable manuscript.)
+ 20,000	This could be 20,000 £20 notes.

Actions depend upon the interpretation. For the one envisaged above:

- find the owner of boat FY 3097
- trace its movements
- look for 985817 on a map
- try to see how 10 kilometres would fit
- keep a watch of the area
- investigate the serial number of the banknote.

CASE FOUR: DIAMONDS ARE FOREVER
There was no forced entry, and therefore either a key had been used or the criminal was incredibly skilful. The jewellery box had not been damaged and therefore either it had been left unlocked or, again, a key had been used. Nothing else had been disturbed, showing that the criminal knew exactly where to look. Only valuable pieces had been taken, indicating advance knowledge of what was there or very expert knowledge of jewellery. It was a good time to choose with the family being away and therefore the criminal was either lucky or had knowledge of the family's movements.

So much points to this being an 'inside job' – perhaps a servant, a frequent visitor to the house, a member of the family other than those at the funeral (in this case, perhaps for insurance purposes) or a neighbour with a key.

CASE FIVE: A STRANGE CONFESSION
Perhaps the confession by David Battersby was to throw suspicion on himself and invite arrest when he knew that he had an alibi. This would mean that later he would be excluded from further enquiries, perhaps not justifiably. The person who was well wrapped up might not have been David. It could have been somebody wearing his trilby and overcoat while he committed the crime.

Seemingly, David could have cleared his name, but there are several possibilities:

- he genuinely might not have known that somebody else in similar clothing had been spotted – one of the strange coincidences thrown up in life
- as suggested above, reticence about his whereabouts now might later allow him to be cleared and make it less likely that he was re-investigated
- a friend, or his twin sister Sheila, could be dressed in the clothes while he committed the crime
- David might suspect that his twin sister had carried out the crime and he was looking to protect her.

Much rests upon the fact that David and Sheila were brother and sister and were likely to have physical similarities (although they are twins they cannot be identical), and that the figure in the village was wearing distinctive clothing but clothing that hid the person and could have been imitated.

Note
The names and events are fictional and any link to any real people is accidental and coincidental.

Cliffhanger

Devwall Times
March 2001
40p

Local businessman kidnapped!
Police ask for any witnesses to come forward

The Devwall Police Force is at full stretch investigating the kidnapping of a local businessman. They have broadcast messages asking the public to report anything suspicious that might be connected with the case. One evening the constable on duty at the regional headquarters received an anonymous telephone call from a man who did not want to get involved but who believed that he might have witnessed the transfer of the businessman to a house in Babbington.

A transcript of the telephone message

'I think that I might be able to help you with your enquiries into the kidnapping. Earlier this evening I was taking my dog for a walk along the seafront on the top of the cliffs at Babbington. There is a telescope there that is operated with a 10p coin. It was beautifully clear and I put 10p in to look around the bay. My time was nearly up when I swung the telescope to the left and I concentrated for a few moments on the monument on Seaview Hill. I then turned the telescope further to my left. Before I swung the telescope back again my eye was caught by movement in the drive of a large house. Three men seemed to be dragging a fourth man from a large black car into the house. What struck me was that the man struggling was very tall and he towered over the other three. I heard on the radio that the missing businessman is 1.94 m tall.

The house is very large and it stands in extensive grounds. To one side I could see a flash of blue before my money ran out and the shutter closed on the telescope. There was smoke coming out of one of the chimneys. On the left-hand side of the ground floor was a very large window. The right-hand side was partially obscured by two tall trees.

Unfortunately, I only had one 10p coin and I could not take a further look. I do not wish to be involved in the investigation but I hope that this information proves useful.'

Your Tasks

1. Explain whether or not you are going to take the telephone message seriously. Give your reasons.
2. What practical steps do you think that the police could take?
3. Can you identify the house from the information above, the additional advice from the firm who own the telescope, the map of the bay, and the details of properties from a local estate agent?

NOTE
Assume that the houses can all be seen clearly and are not obstructed because the coastline where the telescopes are positioned is higher than the ground where the buildings are located.

Cliffhanger

Information From The Local Estate Agent

(The information is varied in terms of detail and content because of the estate agent's different knowledge of the properties.)

Property number and name	Details known
1 'Bay View'	A medium-sized property noted for its gardens and splendid views. It was built in 1935 and was modernised in the 1950s.
2 'Two Pines'	A large luxurious house with many amenities including a swimming pool. The spacious grounds contain many trees and shrubs. The largest window downstairs belongs to the room housing the snooker table.
3 'Journey's End'	Very little is known about this property.
4 'Casadena'	A medium-sized property belonging to the local doctor. The owner added an additional bedroom and central heating a few years ago.
5 'Cliff Cottage'	A small cottage that dates back to 1732. Its quaint appearance has attracted many potential buyers in the past.
6 'Lamorna'	A large bungalow with very good-sized grounds around it. A swimming pool has been added recently. The tall oak trees date back a long way.
7 'Singing Wind'	A large modern house recently built, fully powered and heated by electricity. The extensive grounds are well kept. Three tall trees to the side of the building have stood there for much longer than the house itself although one was recently cut down after serious storm damage.
8 'Kenilworth'	Very little is known about this medium-sized house with its compact grounds.
9 'Sea Breezes'	An oldish property of great charm. The large house gives panoramic views through its large bow windows. The swimming pool is a fairly recent addition. The considerable grounds contain many trees and shrubs, which have grown to great size over the years.
10 'Way Forward'	A beautifully appointed medium-sized bungalow built specially for the retirement of a solicitor from the North of England.
11 'Channel View'	A fairly small house with wonderful views to the sea.
12 'Apple Blossom'	A large luxury bungalow with adjoining swimming pool and tennis courts. Very little else is known as the only change of ownership in recent years was handled by a different estate agent.
13 'Hawarden'	A large attractive house with beautiful grounds. The owner is very proud of the extensive well-kept lawns that surround the house. To achieve this, some trees were removed so that there would be a clear area for some distance around the house itself. The owner preferred to have a rose garden rather than a recreation area for swimming or tennis.
14 'Redesmere'	A pleasant and fair-sized bungalow with gardens divided between well-kept sections and areas let to go wild to encourage the growth of locally-found flowers.
15 'Coastal Haven'	A one-storey building consisting of three small but luxurious flats owned by retired couples.
16 'Tall Trees'	A large house standing in spacious grounds. Both sides are flanked by pine trees. Owners have shown no interest in modernising their property.

3/3 Cliffhanger

Additional Information From 'Telescopic Vision'

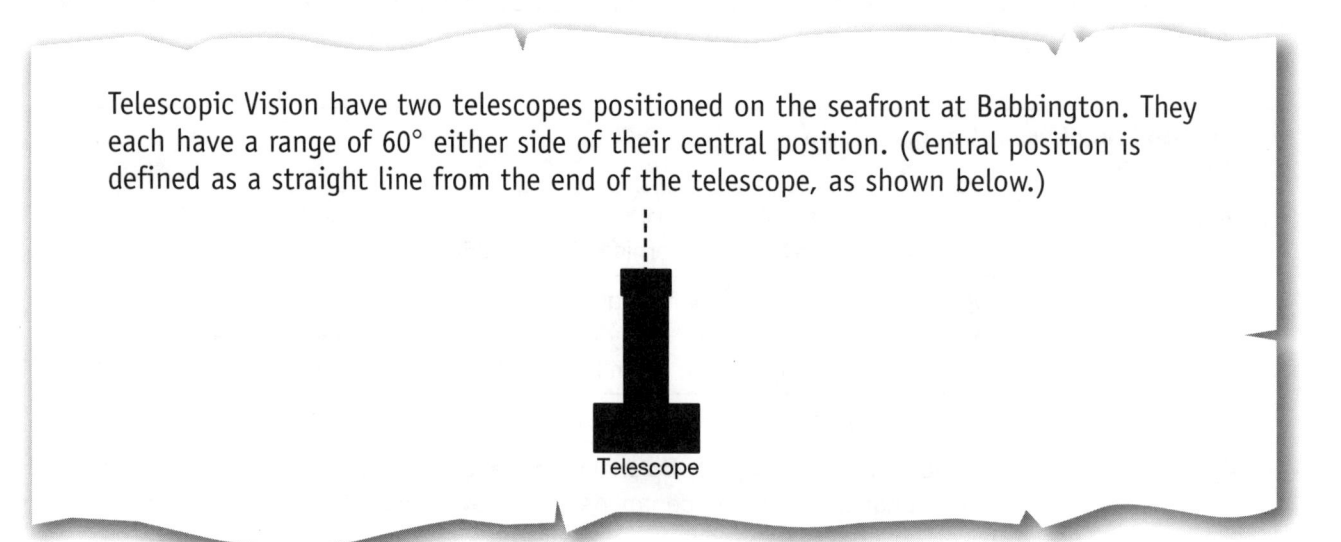

Telescopic Vision have two telescopes positioned on the seafront at Babbington. They each have a range of 60° either side of their central position. (Central position is defined as a straight line from the end of the telescope, as shown below.)

Map of Babbington Bay

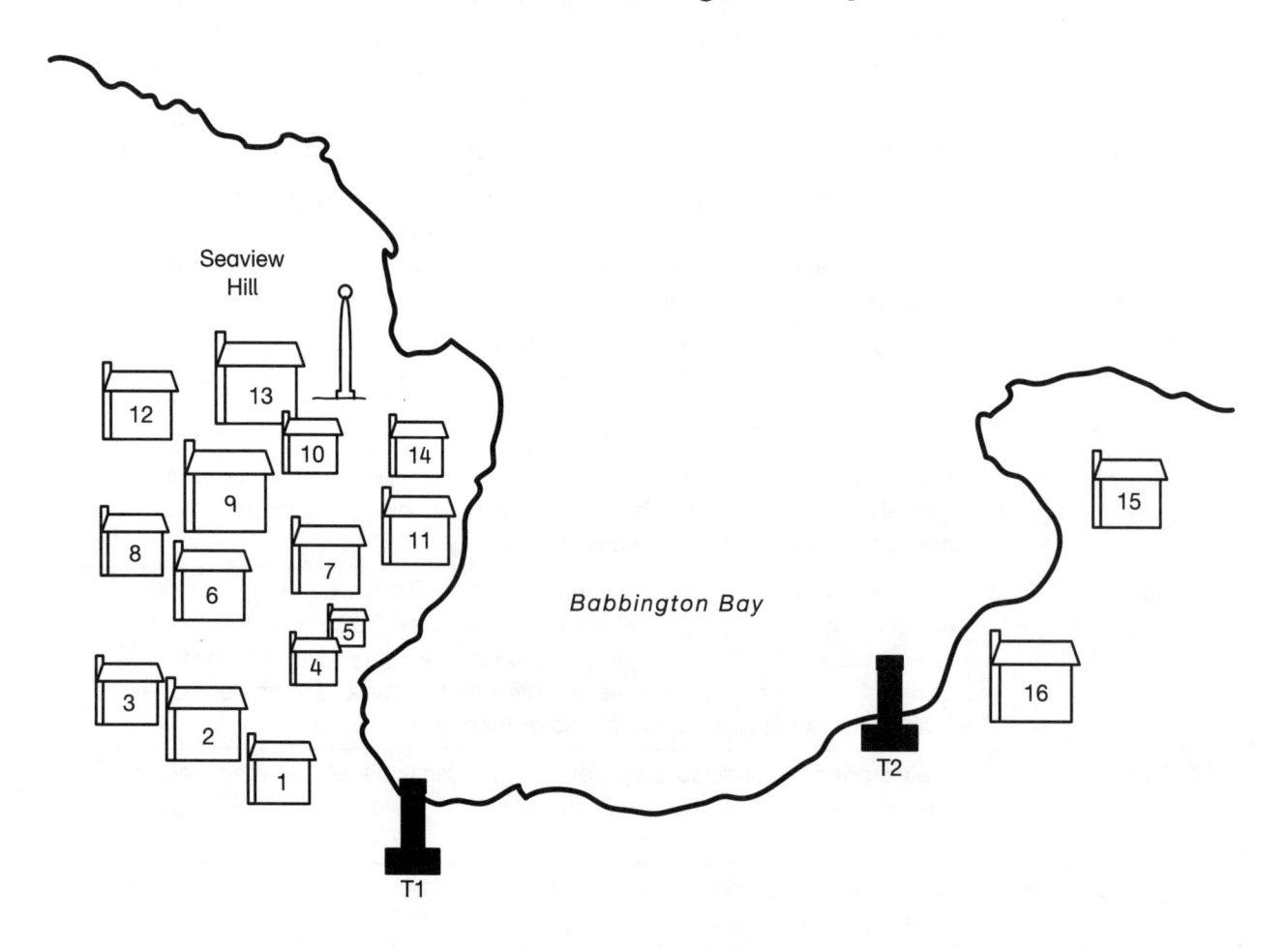

Cliffhanger

Teaching Notes

This piece of work is a combination of information processing and logical thought together with practice in the use of a protractor. Synthesis of different data is needed. The generic thinking skills involved are relevant to many areas of the curriculum.

TASK ONE
It could be argued that in an important case you should take every possible lead seriously. In addition, the message is clear and well explained – it sounds authentic. The details are convincing, even to the height of the man being dragged into the house. The police would be very foolish not to give proper attention to the information.

TASK TWO
1. The police could operate the telescopes on the cliff-top to verify the information.
2. This would immediately narrow the search and therefore the area could be surveyed.
3. All routes out of Babbington could be carefully controlled.
4. Information from estate agents could be used to narrow down the possible houses. At the same time plain clothes men could physically patrol the identified area.

TASK THREE
To add to the drama the teacher could pose as the Chief Constable, needing to rescue the businessman but worried about breaking into the wrong property. The evidence has therefore to be as strong as possible and all the properties have to be considered carefully. The class can be divided into groups as 'crime squads'. They are told that they must move quickly to rescue the businessman but the operation has to be as safe as possible. In this format the teacher can give press conferences as the Chief Constable. The crime squads may be asked to submit a written report for Task three to show they are thinking clearly.

The information about the telescopes cuts down the houses in view. Telescope 2 can only just see Seaview Hill at the limit of its 60° range from the central position and it cannot go any further to the left, as described by the caller. It was therefore Telescope 1 that was used. With this information the following properties can be eliminated:

- 15 and 16 as they are not to the left of Seaview Hill and they are out of range of Telescope 1 anyway.
- 11 and 14 because they are to the right of Seaview Hill.
- 1, 2 and 3 because they are outside the 60° range of Telescope 1.

We are left with properties 4, 5, 6, 7, 8, 9, 10, 12 and 13. This is when the information from the estate agent is needed. A process of elimination now takes place.
- Size further restricts the choice to 6, 7, 9, 12 and 13.
- Numbers 6 and 12 are eliminated because they are bungalows. The caller spoke of a ground floor, implying there was a second floor.
- It cannot be property 7 because the information makes it clear that this particular property is heated and powered by electricity and therefore there would not be any smoke coming out of the chimney.
- Property 13 is unlikely for two reasons:
  1. there is no swimming pool, which is the most obvious explanation of the 'flash of blue' described by the witness
  2. the owner has cleared trees from near the house and the caller's description spoke of the right-hand side being partially obscured by two tall trees.

The evidence leaves us with property 9, 'Sea Breezes'. The information we are given fits the description – large, a swimming pool, extensive grounds, large bow windows. We do not hear specifically of two tall trees but there is reference to the growth of trees and shrubs. Nothing is said about the possibility of smoke from a chimney either positively or negatively. 'Sea Breezes' is the one property where there is not a single eliminating factor even though we have not got positive confirmation of all parts of the caller's description.

Mrs Pascal's Proposition

The children in class 7Y really enjoy their maths lessons, mainly due to the fact that their teacher, Mrs Pascal, is a great enthusiast and is always joking with them. She encourages them to chant 'Maths is Great, Maths is Fun' at the start of the lessons.

On one particular day, Mrs Pascal told 7Y that she would write their homework on the board during break. The children were a little confused when they first saw the homework.

Your Task

Study carefully what Mrs Pascal had written on the board. Then, like 7Y, get over your initial confusion and work out what you have to do. On the strength of this, perhaps you also would like to be taught maths by Mrs Pascal.

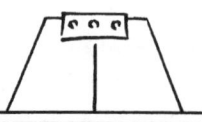

Tonight's Homework

21-34 53-33-45 41-33-142-482-13
398-62-21-41 398-62-13-322-13 21-41
194-33 62-33-29-13-49-33-322-25

But note:
$a = 2x + 3$ where $a = \{1, 3, 5 \ldots 25\}$
$b = x^2 - 2$ where $b = \{2, 4, 6 \ldots 26\}$

and a and b both have to be applied to a word that has a number of letters equivalent to the fourth prime number.

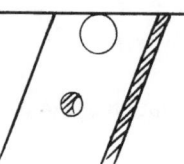

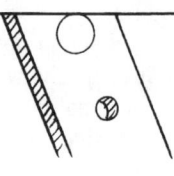

Extension Tasks

1. Use the method in Mrs Pascal's proposition to write other examples.
2. Design a system of your own based upon simple equations.

Mrs Pascal's Proposition

Teaching Notes

Mrs Pascal's Proposition is a number code based upon simple equations. There is here a 'double dose' of abstract, in that codes have one thing standing for another and algebra follows the same principle. Working in the abstract is appreciated by many able children.

$a = \{1, 3, 5 \ldots 25\}$ indicates that a represents the odd numbers from 1 to 25 inclusive.

$b = \{2, 4, 6 \ldots 26\}$ indicates that b represents the even numbers from 2 to 26 inclusive.

The fourth prime is 7 and the word with seven letters accommodating 1 to 26 is 'letters' itself.

Thus, a stands for the odd letters in the alphabet and b stands for the even letters in the alphabet.

We can now construct a table with the letters of the alphabet and their value in this number code, worked out by placing odd numbered letters into $a = 2x + 3$ and by placing even numbered letters into $b = x^2 - 2$.

Letter	A	B	C	D	E	F	G	H	I	J	K	L	M
Position	1	2	3	4	5	6	7	8	9	10	11	12	13
Value	5	2	9	14	13	34	17	62	21	98	25	142	29

Letter	N	O	P	Q	R	S	T	U	V	W	X	Y	Z
Position	14	15	16	17	18	19	20	21	22	23	24	25	26
Value	194	33	254	37	322	41	398	45	482	49	574	53	674

The coded message reads:

> If you solve this there is no homework

No wonder class 7Y like Mrs Pascal!

Extension Tasks

This allows wider use of the method, especially in 2 where any equation can be used. Pupils receive practice without really noticing it.

THE SHAPES

Nigel Short has recently joined the decoding section of his country's Secret Service, at a location that cannot be disclosed. He has been working under the direction of section leader Sarah Hill.

The section has been tense waiting for news from an agent on a very important mission. Just a few days ago Sarah's face broke into a broad smile after she had been studying a piece of paper for some time. She saw that Nigel was interested and, smiling, she gave him the paper. Nigel read it through.

'Is this a joke?' he said.

Sarah explained that it was far from a joke. She asked Nigel if he could work out the reason why. She gave him two pieces of advice.

Your Task

Can you work out what Sarah Hill had learned from the paper? You, like Nigel, might be surprised to see that it is a comic strip called 'The Shapes', apparently aimed at helping young children with their number work.

THE TWO PIECES OF ADVICE

1. Sarah made up a little rhyme:

   My code is very simple,
   You shouldn't get into 'lumber',
   If only you work backwards,
   Once you get my number.

2. She told Nigel to pay particular attention to the weather.

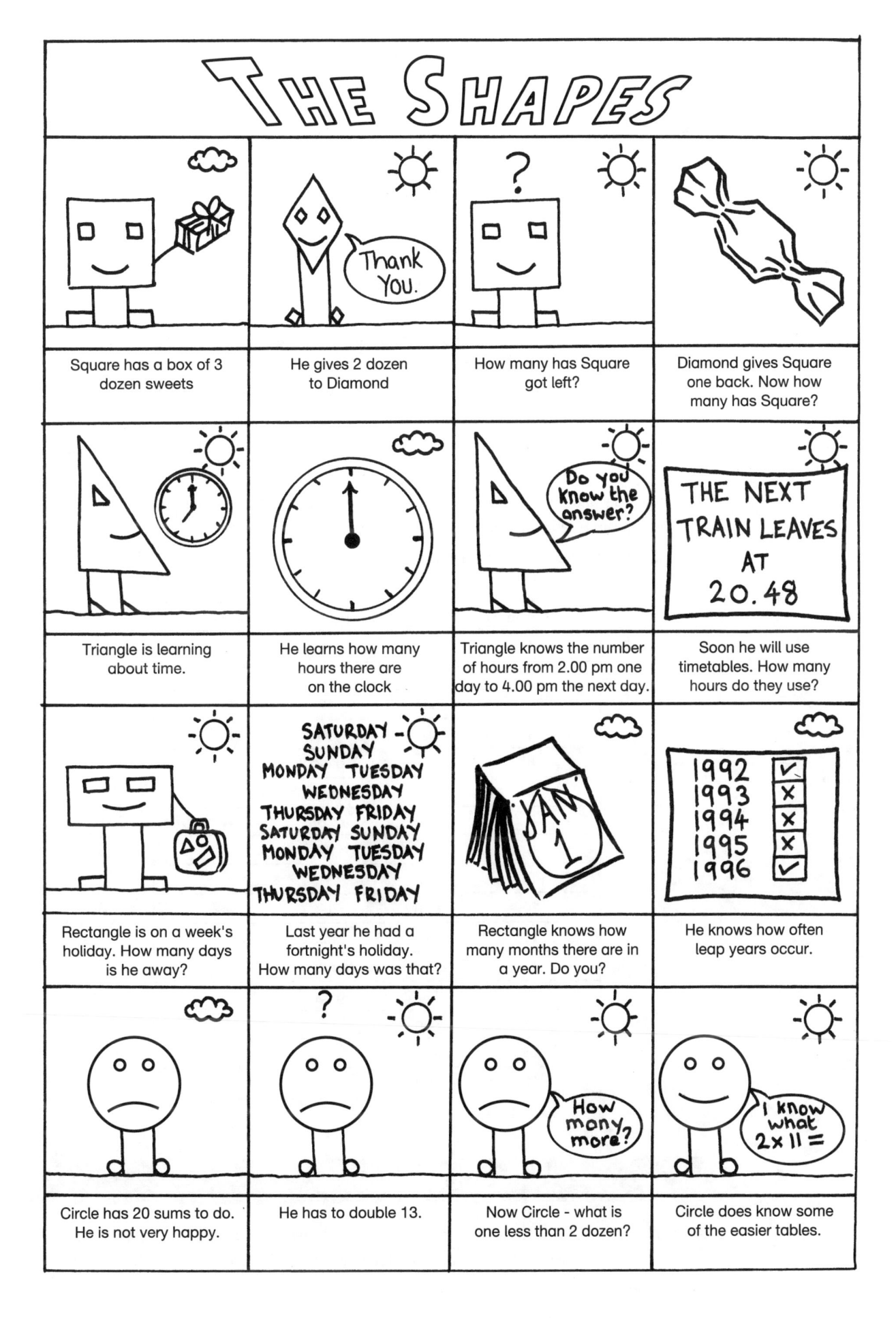

The Shapes

Square has a box of 3 dozen sweets	He gives 2 dozen to Diamond	How many has Square got left?	Diamond gives Square one back. Now how many has Square?
Triangle is learning about time.	He learns how many hours there are on the clock	Triangle knows the number of hours from 2.00 pm one day to 4.00 pm the next day.	Soon he will use timetables. How many hours do they use?
Rectangle is on a week's holiday. How many days is he away?	Last year he had a fortnight's holiday. How many days was that?	Rectangle knows how many months there are in a year. Do you?	He knows how often leap years occur.
Circle has 20 sums to do. He is not very happy.	He has to double 13.	Now Circle - what is one less than 2 dozen?	Circle does know some of the easier tables.

More Effective Resources for Able and Talented Children © Barry Teare (Network Educational Press, 2001)

THE SHAPES

Teaching Notes

The Shapes is a hybrid code in that it relies upon number, interpretation of cryptic information and pictures. The vehicle, a child's comic strip, is likely to attract the attention of children.

A number of sensible routes can be followed even though they do not lead to the solution. Credit should be given for the thinking involved.

1. Pupils should soon come to the conclusion that there is a message hidden in the comic strip. The introduction makes it likely that the agent is involved, and the fact that Sarah Hill is pleased makes it look like good news.

2. Numbers are prominent in 'The Shapes'. Sarah's rhyme is helpful but it still leaves some problems to be solved. The three key points in the rhyme are that the code is simple, it concerns numbers and it works backwards. But what is it that goes backwards – the code itself, the comic strip or the message?

   In fact, the number code is *very* simple – the simplest of all, but backwards. Thus, Z = 1 and A = 26.

3. Sarah's second piece of advice concerns the weather. Each frame has a sun or a cloud in the top right-hand corner. The message only uses the pictures with a sun.

4. The interpretation of the frames is –

Frame	Weather	Result	Letter
1	cloud	ignore	
2	sun	24	C
3	sun	12	O
4	sun	13	N
5	sun	7 o'clock	T
6	cloud	ignore	
7	sun	26	A
8	sun	24	C
9	sun	7	T
10	sun	14	M
11	cloud	ignore	
12	cloud	ignore	
13	cloud	ignore	
14	sun	26	A
15	sun	23	D
16	sun	22	E

Thus the message is:

Contact made

Some pupils may need a little help from the teacher. However, this should not be given too soon. After all, the essence of being a successful code-breaker is trial-and-error. It may take some time for the pupils to find the correct route.

The Hidden Will Of Gresham Grange

A one-time owner of the country house Gresham Grange, Barrington Smith, had a mischievous sense of humour. He decided to have some fun at the expense of his children. Nobody knew what was in his will nor where the will was kept. Barrington Smith did make a will – this was confirmed by the family solicitor – but it was not available simply to be read out on the old man's death.

When the family gathered, Edwin Start, the solicitor, explained that the will was hidden on the instructions of Barrington Smith. He was authorised to pass on information to assist the search. This information consisted of some cryptic messages, details of a shelf of books and a sketch map of part of Gresham Grange.

Your Task

The family had the task of finding the hidden will of Gresham Grange. You are asked to do the same.

The Messages

> My library is normally well indexed but these books are ordered in a very different way.

> Take note of a number of titles and then have regard to the authors.

> Direct directions would be too easy – you have to do some work in terms of interpretation.

The Hidden Will Of Gresham Grange

The Shelf Of Books

The books, in order from left to right, were as follows:

One Corpse Too Many	Ellis Peters
Pictures In The Dark	Gillian Cross
Nerve	Dick Francis
The Three Musketeers	Alexander Dumas
Ordinary Jack	Helen Cresswell
Washington Square	Henry James
The Quiller Memorandum	Adam Hall
The Sign Of Four	Sir Arthur Conan-Doyle
Goodnight Mister Tom	Michelle Magorian
On The Beach	Nevil Shute
The Moonstone	Wilkie Collins
Blott On The Landscape	Tom Sharpe
Redwall	Brian Jacques
Wycliffe And The Four Jacks	W. J. Burley
A Prey To Murder	Ann Cleeves
Carrie's War	Nina Bawden
Cover Her Face	P. D. James
Last Bus To Woodstock	Colin Dexter
One, Two, Buckle My Shoe	Agatha Christie
The Ghost Road	Pat Barker
Dead Before Bedtime	Edgar Box
Three Act Tragedy	Agatha Christie
The Hobbit	J. R. R. Tolkien
Video Rose	Jacqueline Wilson
Deadlocked	Richard Hunt
Emma	Jane Austen
One Across, Two Down	Ruth Rendell
The Tin Drum	Gunter Grass
The Indian In The Cupboard	Lynne Reid Banks
Five Little Pigs	Agatha Christie
Faith	Len Deighton
Caught In The Light	Robert Goddard
Natural Causes	Henry Cecil
Soul Music	Terry Pratchett
I, Claudius	Robert Graves

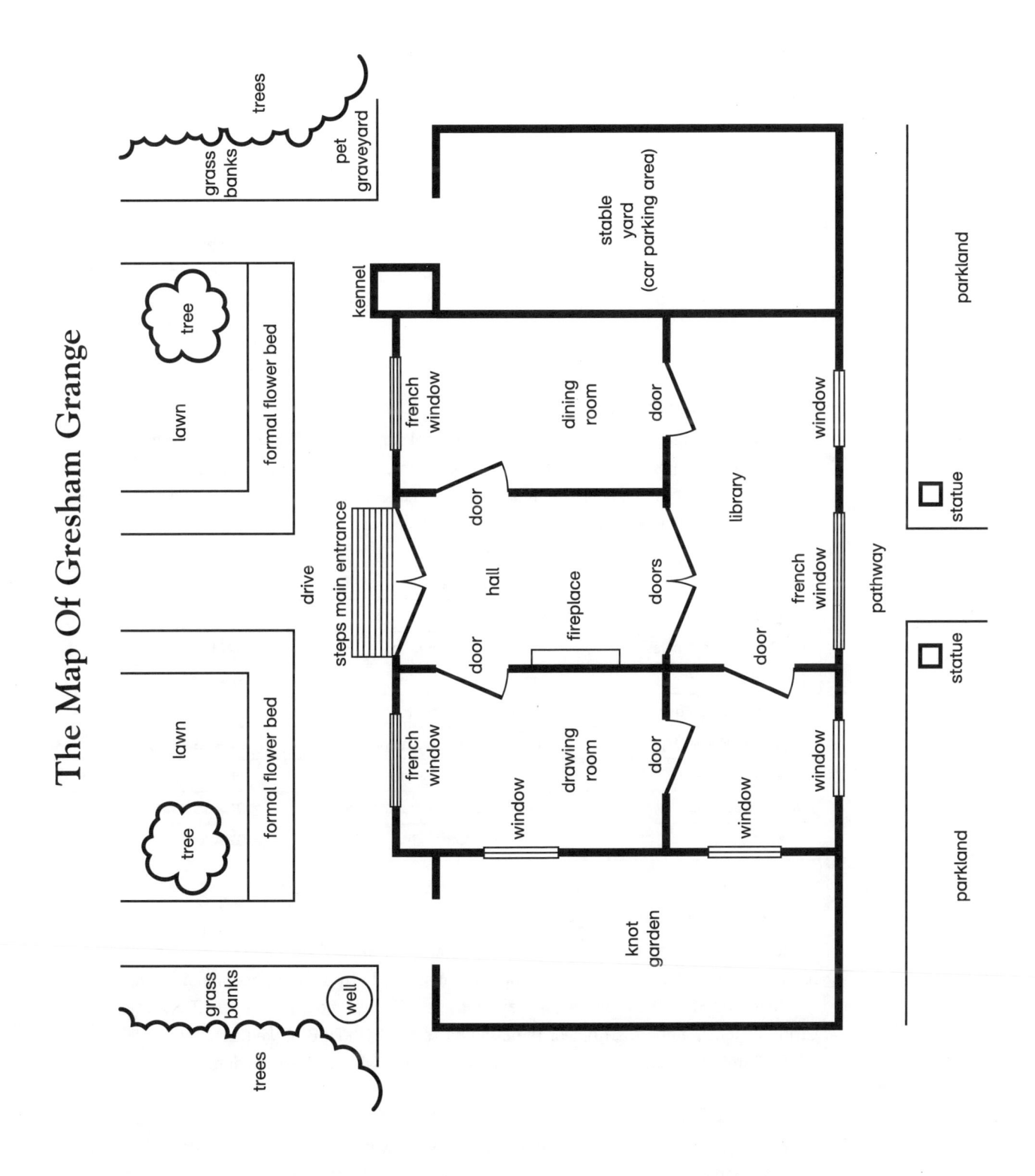

The Hidden Will Of Gresham Grange

The Map Of Gresham Grange

The Hidden Will Of Gresham Grange

Teaching Notes

This is a code that depends upon the interpretation of cryptic messages and their application to a shelf of books and a map of Gresham Grange. Synthesis of the data is necessary. If pupils make little progress it is sensible to add hints at intervals on the board or flipchart, but not before they have worked hard with the original data. Children come up with a number of good ideas even though they may not solve the puzzle. Praise should be given for these methods as it is quality thinking that we are encouraging.

Solution

THE MESSAGES

The first message points out that the order of the bookshelf is important especially as the books are not put together in a logical way of grouping – children's books, detective novels, thrillers, classics and humorous stories are all mixed in together. The second message pinpoints the word 'number' and relates it to the authors. Message three only stresses that the meaning has to be unravelled – it is not given 'straight'.

THE SHELF OF BOOKS

Some children interpret number as the total of books or as an indication that a number code has been used. Eight books actually have numbers in their titles, two of these books having two numbers. If those numbers are related to the surnames of the authors, in the sense of how many you have to move along the shelf, we see words targeted as shown below.

Title	Move indicated	Author name
One Corpse Too Many	move one author to	CROSS
The **Three** Musketeers	move three authors to	HALL
The Sign of **Four**	move four authors to	SHARPE
Wycliffe and the **Four** Jacks	move four authors to	DEXTER
One, **Two**, Buckle My Shoe	move one and two authors to	BARKER BOX
Three Act Tragedy	move three authors to	HUNT
One Across, **Two** Down	move one and two authors to	GRASS BANKS
Five Little Pigs	move five authors to	GRAVES

THE MAP OF GRESHAM GRANGE

If the words obtained from the authors' names are now applied to the map, we find the route to follow. We start where the shelf of books is most likely to be, the library, and go out through the doors to CROSS the HALL to the main entrance. Then we go SHARP(E) DEXTER (which is Latin for right), along the front of the building to the BARKER BOX (kennel). Then HUNT on the GRASS BANKS near the pet GRAVES, which is where the will has been hidden.

Teaching Hints

Pupils will jump to quick conclusions when seeing 'Graves' as one of the authors. They need to be encouraged to show the whole line of working in detail. To strengthen this point, the teacher can take on the role of Edwin Start, the solicitor, insisting that Barrington Smith had specified that only such a full explanation would lead to the terms of the will being carried out.

Searching For Words

The magazine *Mindstretch* is enjoyed by many people who love to work out puzzles, riddles, ciphers and brainteasers. In some issues there are competitions in which readers are invited to submit their own puzzles. The 'Editor's Choice' is published in the magazine and the winner receives a cash prize.

In one competition, contributors were asked to combine a standard feature used on many occasions, such as a crossword, with a second puzzle format. On this occasion the winner was Tanya Zinovitch who used a wordsearch together with a saying of her own and what seemed to be directions about how to get to her home. Her successful competition entry was called 'Searching For Words' and its message pleased the editor.

Your Tasks

1. Study the three complementary parts of Tanya's winning entry:
   a the wordsearch
   b the saying
   c the instructions.
2. Decide upon the puzzle format that Tanya had combined with the wordsearch. In other words – what had she set?
3. Find the solution to the title, 'Searching For Words'. What are the words and how do you find them? This should explain also why the editor was pleased.

The Saying

'Words point the way to meaning.'

The Directions To My House

Visitors who wish a successful conclusion to their trip should take note of the following instructions. 'To start at the beginning, first you go across the road. Then you go down the next way. After that there are two diagonal cuts to take. Then you go up the next street. Finally, look backwards to make sure you have followed the last instructions to the letter. If in doubt at any time because there seems to be more than one possible way even when following the directions, remember to start at the top, keeping to the left before moving the right way.'

The Wordsearch

Find 17 words or phrases associated with detective stories and cases.

X	P	S	U	S	P	E	C	T	P	P	C	R	S	S
F	E	V	I	D	E	N	C	E	U	T	W	Q	Q	C
E	Y	Z	X	Y	Z	G	B	B	S	D	I	S	L	R
V	U	R	E	V	O	L	V	E	R	Z	T	N	F	I
I	P	P	B	Z	N	N	R	O	C	F	N	G	O	M
T	D	A	G	G	E	R	Z	B	B	A	E	C	R	E
O	G	U	L	L	A	Z	H	B	Q	L	S	Q	E	I
M	T	R	Q	G	L	L	B	P	O	I	S	O	N	L
G	G	E	X	Q	C	D	G	K	U	B	E	S	S	V
C	U	D	B	C	F	Q	R	S	M	I	S	Y	I	I
L	L	R	Q	E	X	R	T	T	X	S	G	T	C	C
X	F	U	R	X	Q	S	T	F	E	B	M	C	S	T
D	N	M	E	T	R	O	M	T	S	O	P	G	G	I
P	L	C	B	S	T	A	T	E	M	E	N	T	I	M
D	G	G	B	X	H	V	E	R	D	I	C	T	N	U

Searching For Words

Teaching Notes

The solution to this code involves a wordsearch, the cryptic meaning of a saying and the exact interpretation of the directions. There is great emphasis on precision in following instructions. As always with difficult codes, able pupils should be left to concentrate hard upon the problem themselves before help is given. At intervals the teacher can write additional clues on a board or flipchart but only when a real effort has been made. **Searching For Words** is not easy, deliberately so, and various alternative methods might be tried before success is achieved.

Solution

Tanya had set a coded message through a combination of the three complementary parts of her entry to the magazine.

The first task is to find the 17 words and phrases in the wordsearch that are associated with detective stories and cases. These are shown on the completed wordsearch below.

The saying might provoke several ideas. Clearly the words in the wordsearch indicate letters for the code, but how? 'Point the way to meaning' indicates that it is the letter after the word in the wordsearch that should be used, in the direction needed to spell the word properly.

Now we come to 'The Directions To My House'. This tells us the order in which we take the 17 letters already identified above. Following the paragraph through, first take the letters indicated by words and phrases going across. The last part of the directions paragraph tells us to take these in order from the top, moving left to right across each line. There are seven of them:

1	SUSPECT	pointing to	P
2	EVIDENCE	pointing to	U
3	REVOLVER	pointing to	Z
4	DAGGER	pointing to	Z
5	POISON	pointing to	L
6	STATEMENT	pointing to	I
7	VERDICT	pointing to	N

(These are marked 1 to 7 on the completed wordsearch.)

The next direction is to go down. There are five words or phrases:

8	WITNESSES	pointing to	G	(Note: 'witnesses' is the full word, not 'witness'.)
9	CRIME	pointing to	I	
10	FORENSIC	pointing to	S	
11	ALIBI	pointing to	S	
12	VICTIM	pointing to	U	

(These are marked 8 to 12 on the completed wordsearch.)

Searching for Words

Now we have two diagonal cuts to make:

13	ARREST	pointing to	**C**
14	CLUES	pointing to	**H**

(These are marked 13 and 14 on the completed wordsearch.)

The next instructions take us to the words going up. There are two of them:

15	MOTIVE	pointing to	**F**
16	MURDER	pointing to	**U**

(These are marked 15 and 16 on the completed wordsearch.)

Finally, look backwards for the one word going along a row the wrong way:

17	POST MORTEM	pointing to	**N**

(This is marked 17 on the completed wordsearch.)

The coded message is therefore:

Puzzling is such fun

X	P	S	U	S	P	E	C	T	P^1	P	C^{13}	R	S	S
F^{15}	E	V	I	D	E	N	C	E	U^2	T	W	Q	Q	C
E	Y	Z	X	Y	Z	G	B	B	S	D	I	S	L	R
V	U	R	E	V	O	L	V	E	R	Z^3	T	N	F	I
I	P	P	B	Z	N	N	R	O	C	F	N	G	O	M
T	D	A	G	G	E	R	Z^4	B	B	A	E	C	R	E
O	G	U^{16}	L	L	A	Z	H	B	Q	L	S	Q	E	I^9
M	T	R	Q	G	L	L	B	P	O	I	S	O	N	L^5
G	G	E	X	Q	C	D	G	K	U	B	E	S	S	V
C	U	D	B	C	F	Q	R	S	M	I	S	Y	I	I
L	L	R	Q	E	X	R	T	T	X	S^{11}	G^8	T	C	C
X	F	U	R	X	Q	S	T	F	E	B	M	C	S^{10}	T
D	N^{17}	M	E	T	R	O	M	T	S	O	P	G	G	I
P	L	C	B	S	T	A	T	E	M	E	N	T	I^6	M
D	G	G	B	X	H^{14}	V	E	R	D	I	C	T	N^7	U^{12}

Theme Nine: Lateral Thinking

There are many times when it is necessary to follow a logical progression and to finish with a closed solution. However it is very important for able pupils to be 'freed up' to think laterally. The search for alternative methods and alternative answers is an essential ingredient to stimulate imagination and creativity, which are in too short supply.

The CBI (Confederation of British Industry) has placed the ability to think and to solve problems at the top of its list of desirable qualities in school leavers. Much of the content that we learn at school and at university is not used again but transferable thinking skills are of enormous value. There are some powerful advocates:

> *'Imagination is more important than knowledge.'*
>
> Albert Einstein

> *'If you think there is only one answer, then you will only find one.'*
>
> Scottish Consultative Council On The Curriculum, 1996

> *'The education system should be aware of different ways of thinking and not be restrictive.'*
>
> Professor Sir Harold Kroto

The National Advisory Committee on Creative and Cultural Education, chaired by Professor Ken Robinson, has produced a splendid report, entitled *All Our Futures* (DfEE, 1999). A strong argument is made for teaching creatively and teaching creativity.

Allowing space for individual responses is a very important part of the teacher's role. **One Question, Many Answers** (page 247) carries its message in the title. There are twelve contrasting situations, for the pupil to reach different conclusions from the same data. Logic still plays a part but there is also the need to move sideways, to examine data from various perspectives and to recognise that there is not just one answer.

Eureka (page 253) encourages pupils to revisit the 'frontiers of knowledge' and to find imaginative and creative reasons for a range of discoveries without losing sight of hard fact. The areas of mathematics, science and history are important sources for the piece.

The third item, *Classified Information* (page 255), involves many curriculum areas and visits an important higher order thinking skill – classification. Seeing connections and exceptions is fundamental to many areas of study. For example:

> *'... investigating whether particular cases can be generalised further and understanding the importance of a counter-example.'*
>
> National Curriculum Guidelines on Mathematics (DfEE/QCA, 1999)

ATTENTION

See also the resources suggested below.

Book	Theme or Section	Activity
Elsewhere in this book	Theme Three: Science	The Spider That Loves Mozart
	Theme Eight: Detective Work, Codes	Critical Clues
	Theme Ten: Competitions	Horse Sense
Effective Provision For Able And Talented Children, Network Educational Press, 1997	Section Six	What If?
Effective Resources For Able And Talented Children, Network Educational Press, 1999	Theme Four: Writing	… And That Is The End Of The Story
	Theme Ten: Detective Work	Vital Evidence
	Theme Eleven: Alternative Answers, Imagination …	The Question Is Or Who Am I? Now You See It Just Imagine

One Question, Many Answers

Introduction

Below there are twelve very varied lateral thinking problems. In each case you need to think carefully about the data given. Sometimes there is an answer that fits the facts particularly well but there are nearly always alternative responses, which are equally good. Try to find more than one answer to fit the evidence. Use your imagination but try to avoid totally unrealistic responses.

Look for double meanings of words, 'sleight of hand' and disguise. Be prepared for the unorthodox when tackling **One Question, Many Answers**.

DANGER AWAITS

The situation was tense. One wrong move and who knows what might happen. He looked at their faces anxiously. Quickly assessing the situation, he smiled. All was well – for the moment at least.

? What circumstances explain the man's reactions?

BLACKBIRD

A passer-by overheard a conversation between two women as they sat talking on a park bench. The older woman said to the younger, 'Your granddad could never hear a blackbird without getting upset.'

? What was the origin of this strange statement?

One Question, Many Answers

EDEN DELAYED

Near St. Austell in Cornwall, an exciting development called the Eden Project has been created. Old china clay workings have been turned into an enormous site for indoor and outdoor plants. The development includes huge 'biomes' or conservatories.

During the conversion, there was a period of two months exceptionally heavy rain. The appalling conditions held up the work for six weeks, which caused great concern for the contractors. Turning a two-hundred-feet deep pit with water, waste and sludge in the bottom into one of the great botanical projects of the world was difficult enough without further problems.

Looking back, the chief executive Tim Smit, the engineers and the constructors were delighted about the delay and felt that it was a very good thing that it had taken place.

? Why should they be pleased about a seemingly damaging setback?

BREAKING UP THE HAPPY HOME

The largest offspring in the home was not in fact related to the parents but when this youngster was responsible for the deaths of their children, the adults did not take any action.

? How did the youngster get away with these terrible deeds without punishment?

ROAD SAFETY

On the island of Biwheels most people travel by means of mopeds, scooters and small motorbikes. The politicians in the island's assembly passed a law that all riders of such vehicles should wear a helmet for safety reasons. When reviewing the effects of the law two years later, the politicians found that it had resulted in the hospitals dealing with more casualties than previously.

? Why?

ON THE TABLE

Two students on a train journey challenged each other to a game to pass the time. Each in turn took one word from the title of a newspaper article and asked the other to use that word to form part of 20 new headlines, each covering a different story. One of the words chosen was 'table' or 'tables'.

? Try taking up the challenge and see if you can nominate 20 different headlines involving 'table' or 'tables', each of which would lead to contrasting article content.

THE TWO-MINUTE WAIT

A car pulled up at the kerbside in a typical avenue with houses on either side. The young man at the wheel waited inside the car for two minutes and then drove off again. Nobody got out of the car; nobody got into the car; the driver did not communicate with anybody.

? What is the explanation for the driver's behaviour?

NEIGHBOURS

Two people live next door to each other. They know each other well. The first person is responsible for the second person having a particular job and living in the next-door house but it is the second person who has more control of money than the first.

? Who could the neighbours be?

A LUCKY BRAKE

The famous racing driver approached the bend. Normally he would reduce speed to a degree but this time he braked harder than usual without knowing why. He negotiated the bend, entered the straight and went on to a successful conclusion to his race.

That night he pondered long and hard upon why he had braked more severely than usual. He had a mental picture of the crowd on the bend – they were not watching him approach. That gave him the clue.

? What did the racing driver realise had made him lose more speed than normal and why did it turn out to be 'a lucky brake'?

One Question, Many Answers

THE DISAPPEARING SCULPTURE

The specially prepared sculptures had been commissioned for an exhibition. Security was very tight both before and during the event, yet 24 hours after the official opening the sculptures had disappeared.

? What is the explanation?

A QUESTION OF AUTHORSHIP

Authors jealously guard their writing. There are occasions when a law suit is brought when an author believes that his or her ideas have been copied by another person. Occasionally two people write a book together. For one particular book a publishing company was faced with the fact that no fewer than eight people claimed responsibility for ideas included.

? How could this be, and how could the matter be settled amicably?

DOUBLE PAYMENT

Husband and wife were browsing in a bargain book shop. They each chose a number of items. Some the man kept in a pile of his own, some he handed to his wife. In the same way the woman kept some items in a pile of her own and handed some to her husband. The two then took their piles of books to the counter. Instead of paying for everything together each paid for their own pile of books even though each had chosen some of the items in the other person's pile.

? Why did the couple behave in the way described?

One Question, Many Answers

Teaching Notes

Many pieces of work in the book deal with logical thinking where there is one correct answer. **One Question, Many Answers** allows a variety of responses so long as the data is taken into account properly.

Methods Of Working

A productive way to use items like this is to divide the class into groups of five or six. Each scenario is read out twice and the pupils have one minute brainstorming time to reach one, or more, suitable answers. Responses are then discussed. Pupils in other groups are asked to listen carefully to each suggestion and to say whether the data has been used properly and how strong and realistic each answer is.

Clearly the twelve problems can be answered by individuals in a written method.

Contexts

One Question, Many Answers can be used in the following ways:

- as normal classroom work
- as an enrichment task for those who have completed other work
- as differentiated homework
- as an activity within an enrichment session or cluster day
- as an open-access competition.

Some Answers

In the spirit of the work, many appropriate answers are possible. A few suggestions are given below.

DANGER AWAITS
The man could be playing a board game – perhaps 'Monopoly', where he just misses landing on a hotel owned by another player. The faces might be those on the dice.

BLACKBIRD

- Grandmother's nickname was 'blackbird'. She died young and therefore the Grandfather is sad when he thinks of her.
- Grandfather had gone deaf and when he saw a blackbird calling he thought back to when he could hear.
- Grandfather used to be a gardener and got the sack for patches on a lawn that were caused by blackbirds.
- Grandfather had a blackbird's nest in the garden when he was a boy and the baby blackbirds died.

One Question, Many Answers

EDEN DELAYED
There was so much water from the springs and fissures that the engineers were able to channel them all into a drainage system that would deal with all future rainfall.

BREAKING UP THE HAPPY HOME
The youngster is a cuckoo in the nest of another bird.

ROAD SAFETY
Fewer people died instantly in accidents, and more were therefore treated as casualties in hospital.

ON THE TABLE
Possible headlines might include:

- table a motion
- table wine
- turn the tables
- league table
- antique table
- tax table
- water table
- 'under the table'
- table-turning (spiritualists)
- multiplication table
- table manners
- table talk (small talk)
- table d'hôte menu
- tablespoon
- table football
- table tennis
- table leaf
- tide table
- table licence
- 'at the table' (politics)
- Table Mountain (RSA)
- bus timetable

THE TWO-MINUTE WAIT
The young man and a friend had had a row. Even so, he waited outside the friend's house to take him to a concert, as arranged, but after two minutes he gave up and drove away.

NEIGHBOURS
- Prime Minister and Chancellor of the Exchequer (living at Nos. 10 and 11 Downing Street)
- shopkeeper and bank manager

A LUCKY BRAKE
This is based upon a real-life story about Fangio, the racing driver, who avoided a crash after a bend. He later realised that he had reacted subconsciously to the fact that the crowd were not looking at his approach but rather their heads were turned to view an accident on the track beyond the bend.

THE DISAPPEARING SCULPTURE
As is the case with some exhibitions, the sculptures were made of ice.

A QUESTION OF AUTHORSHIP
There were eight authors who had contributed chapters. This could be non-fiction but some novels have also been written collaboratively such as *Finbar's Hotel* (Irish writers) and *The Floating Admiral* (detective writers).

DOUBLE PAYMENT
One of the final piles consisted of books for pleasure, the other was made up entirely of books for the family business that had to be paid for by a different credit card.

Eureka

A famous story is told about the origin of the Archimedes Principle, which states that when a body is wholly or partly immersed in a liquid, the upthrust on the body is equal to the weight of liquid that would fill the immersed part of the body. It is said that Archimedes thought of the idea as he was getting into a bath filled to the brim. His excitement was so great that he ran home naked from the baths shouting 'Eureka!' (I have found it).

Your Task

Use your imagination but also your knowledge (mathematical, scientific, historical and so on) to write an alternative account of this and other moments of discovery. You may need to research each situation first but don't use the explanation that is normally given. Make up your own version but you should not ignore the relevant principles involved – in other words, your account cannot contravene the mathematics, science or history involved. Consider the following situations and let your imagination flow as to how the 'Eureka' moment was reached!

The Events, Theories And Formulae To Consider

1. The Archimedes Principle (described above).
2. The discovery of penicillin.
3. The idea of using a wheel.
4. Pythagoras' Theorem: in a right-angled triangle, the area of a square drawn on the longest side is equal to the sum of the areas of squares drawn on the two shorter sides.
5. William Harvey's pronouncement that blood circulates around the body.
6. The application of steam power.
7. The Law of Reflection: the angle at which the light from an object hits a mirror (the angle of incidence) is equal to the angle at which the light leaves the mirror (the angle of reflection).
8. Euler's Formula: for networks, nodes + regions = arcs + 2
   for polyhedra, vertices + faces = edges + 2
9. The notion that tea would make a refreshing drink.
10. The discovery of how to make fire.
11. The development of Jethro Tull's seed drill to make sowing fields more economical and efficient.
12. The principle that stringed instruments can be plucked to produce musical notes.
13. The discovery that a mixture of saltpetre, sulphur and charcoal produces explosive results.
14. The Bessemer Converter, which greatly assists the production of steel.
15. The use of ether as an anaesthetic.

Eureka
Teaching Notes

Thinking skills and the ability to solve problems are at the heart of the needs not only of able pupils but of society generally. Being able to find out known information is important but nowhere near as important as thinking for ourselves.

We accept many situations that are now regarded as commonplace but there must have been experimentation that led to that 'Eureka' moment. How, for instance, was it realised that a mixture of saltpetre, sulphur and charcoal would cause an explosion. Using tea leaves to produce a refreshing drink has been a great boon but trying the same thing with yew leaves would have had a very different result.

Some situations have been discovered by accident and the brilliance of the discoverer is to have recognised the significance of that accident. The most famous example is that of penicillin, when Sir Alexander Fleming was growing bacteria in petri dishes. Some mould fell into a dish causing a clear area in the bacteria. Fleming recognised the importance of that happening and developed from it a powerful antibiotic. There are many other examples and a number of them are described in the excellent book *Serendipity* by Royston M. Roberts (John Wiley and Sons, 1989).

The Teacher's Role

The teacher's role here is a tricky one. Pupils will need to carry out a certain amount of research to understand the situation. However, we do not want them just to regurgitate known facts without thinking. We wish to place them at the 'frontier of knowledge' so that they think out an appropriate method for themselves. Imagination and creativity are important elements but within the parameters of sound science, mathematics, history and so on. Again, it is a delicate balance for the teacher to safeguard.

Contexts

Eureka can be used in a number of ways:

- as extension work following particular areas of content
- as differentiated homework
- as enrichment work for those ahead on standard tasks
- as an activity within an enrichment session, summer school or cluster day
- as an open-access competition
- as an activity for relevant extra-curricular clubs in science, history, mathematics and so on.

CLASSIFIED INFORMATION

Classification is the placement of items, animals or people into categories. It requires an important type of thinking, involving seeing connections and exceptions. Classification skills are used in 'odd one out' exercises in which you are required to find a reason to leave one choice out of the group because it does not fit the connection or link between the other choices.

For example, given a list of

| cat | dog | tiger | hamster | budgerigar |

the most obvious 'odd one out' might be 'tiger', as the other four are domestic pets. However, 'budgerigar' could be chosen as the only bird. 'Hamster' is the one rodent in the list. In this way, alternative answers can be found by thinking laterally.

Your Task

Below there are 12 groups.

- Write down which choice in each group is the most obvious 'odd one out'.
- Write down your explanation as to why you have made that particular choice.
- Look for other reasons for that particular choice.
- Look for a second 'odd one out' in the group and give your reason or reasons.
- Try to find more ways of classifying the items to leave out the other items as 'odd ones out'.

THE GROUPS

	a		b		c		d		e	
1	a	9	b	25	c	16	d	17	e	49
2	a	France	b	Spain	c	Switzerland	d	Poland	e	Brazil
3	a	Inspector Morse	b	Lord Peter Wimsey	c	Miss Jane Marple	d	Sherlock Holmes	e	Hercule Poirot
4	a	Ann	b	Ian	c	Owen	d	Una	e	Ron
5	a	Monopoly	b	Snakes and Ladders	c	Rummy	d	Trivial Pursuits	e	Cluedo
6	a	Tennis	b	Ice Hockey	c	Cricket	d	Rugby	e	Baseball
7	a	Bicycle	b	Train	c	Car	d	Taxi	e	Motorcycle
8	a	Oak	b	Yew	c	Horse Chestnut	d	Birch	e	Alder
9	a	Liverpool	b	Manchester United	c	Arsenal	d	Barnsley	e	Everton
10	a	Monet	b	Van Gogh	c	Degas	d	Picasso	e	Constable
11	a	Kestrel	b	Owl	c	Fox	d	Cuckoo	e	Eagle

More Effective Resources for Able and Talented Children © Barry Teare (Network Educational Press, 2001)

CLASSIFIED INFORMATION

Teaching Notes

Classification is a higher order thinking skill. Finding connections and recognising exceptions involves important thinking processes. Many experts agree that more sophisticated classification is one of the general characteristics of many able children. Indeed, Anita Straker in *Mathematics for Gifted Pupils* (Schools Council/Longman, 1983) included 'use of sophisticated criteria for sorting and classification' as one of the pointers to early mathematical ability in pre-school or infant children.

Doing exercises of this sort is very worthwhile to encourage lateral thinking and alternative answers. The danger lies in their use with a rigid mark scheme especially when the choice of items does not have to be explained. In such situations able pupils using sophisticated classification finish up penalised and receiving less credit than children giving very standard responses. The fact that such questions are still included in entrance examinations for some schools does cause concern about the narrowness and limitations of the marking scheme.

Some Solutions

It must be stressed that any suggestions are only for guidance. The key point is that many answers can be suggested, which work for a whole range of explanations. It is vitally important that we know the reasoning behind the choice.

Examples

GROUP ONE

- c   16 – the only even number
- d   17 – the only number that is not a square number, or the only prime number
- a   9 – the only single-digit number

GROUP EIGHT

- a   Oak – the only one with lobed leaves
- b   Yew – the only conifer of the five
- c   Horse Chestnut – the only one with hand-shaped leaves
- d   Birch – the only one with silver-white bark
- e   Alder – the only one producing cones or the one of the five to flourish in waterlogged conditions

Extension

Pupils can be asked to create their own groups so that at least three of the five can be the odd one out for different reasons.

Theme Ten: Competitions

The most important materials are those that are used in normal lessons as that time constitutes the huge majority of teaching time that any child experiences. However, it is valuable to build up a richness and variety of provision through extra-curricular activities, enrichment sessions, summer schools, cluster activities and open-access competitions. The last named can be run for enjoyment and to make pupils feel that it is 'cool' to be a geographer, or a writer, or a historian, and so on. Fun and enjoyment tend to be in short supply in our education system and that is a great pity for both pupils and teachers. Open-access competitions produce pleasant surprises with really good entries from pupils who may not have been identified as particularly able.

Enjoyment is a good enough reason on its own, for learning should be fun and education should be an exciting and challenging experience. *Games Teasers* (page 259) is a very light piece but it does contain an element of word play. Serious purposes can be achieved at the same time as enjoyment. It is often reported that children know very little of the locations of places even in their own country. *The People Of Britain* (page 261) is entertaining and has produced very good results but it does contain elements of geography and word play.

The Mathematics Guidelines in the National Curriculum (DfEE/QCA, 1999) include the aim:

> *'... communicate mathematically, including the use of precise mathematical language.'*

Snakes And Races, Squares And Quotients (page 263) provides an unusual vehicle for mathematics language and operations. It takes pupils across the mathematics curriculum in one piece of work.

The Scottish 5–14 Guidelines on Environmental Studies encourage:

> *'... considering the meaning of heritage.'*

The programme of study for the 1999 version of the National Curriculum for History includes:

> *'Pupils should be taught to select from their knowledge of history and communicate it in a variety of ways.'*

The Millennium Sampler Competition (page 265) requires a good deal of analysis and evaluation in selecting from huge content. The method of presentation is certainly rather different.

All English curriculum guidelines promote a variety of ways of exploring vocabulary. This is certainly true of the Literacy Framework where we find encouragement to:

> *'... invent words using known roots, prefixes and suffixes.'*
>
> *'... practise and extend vocabulary; e.g. through inventing word games such as puns, riddles, crosswords.'*
>
> *'... experiment with language.'*

Horse Sense (page 267) plays to the above elements while also using organisational skills and logical thinking.

The pieces in this section can be used as 'straight' activities or as competitions. If they are used for competitions some details need to be added in terms of dates, target group and conditions of entry.

ATTENTION

See also the resources suggested below.

Book	Theme or Section	Activity
Effective Provision For Able And Talented Children, Network Educational Press, 1997	Section Seven	The Geography Person Goldilocks

Games Teasers

You may be familiar with sets of questions in which items are described by just numbers and initials. This technique has been applied here to games and to games equipment.

For example, '**52C and 2J in a P**'

could stand for '**52 cards and 2 jokers in a pack**'.

To make the clues below manageable, 'in a game of' has been shortened to 'in'.

For example, '**in M**'

could be '**in a game of Mancala**'.

Section A

Can you unravel the fifteen teasers below?

(**Note:** Just one refers to an outside game.)

1	3 T in a P in MJ	6	15 R in S	11	4 C in a HF
2	2 U in M	7	18 H in G	12	4 S in a P of C
3	64 S in C	8	20 N on a DB	13	5 D in Y
4	6 S in C	9	13 T in W	14	90 N in B
5	6 S on a D	10	9 S in N and C	15	6 W in TP

Section B

Add ten more clues of your own, using different examples.

More Effective Resources for Able and Talented Children © Barry Teare (Network Educational Press, 2001)

Games Teasers

Teaching Notes

Answers

1   3 tiles in a pung in Mah Jong
2   2 utilities in Monopoly
3   64 squares in Chess
4   6 suspects in Cluedo
5   6 sides on a dice
6   15 reds in snooker
7   18 holes in golf
8   20 numbers on a dart board
9   13 tricks in Whist
10 9 squares/spaces in Noughts and Crosses
11 4 cards in a Happy Family
12 4 suits in a pack of cards
13 5 dice in Yahtzee
14 90 numbers in Bingo
15 6 wedges in Trivial Pursuits

The People Of Britain

What You Have To Do

Consider places that you know, but also study maps or atlases.

Draw up a list of people who live in appropriate places in Great Britain. Use your imagination and sense of humour to create suitable pairings in this piece of geographical word play.

Your answers can be of two types:

1 'The _____ people of _____.'

   For example, 'The **relaxed** people of **Ambleside**'.

2 'The _____ of _____.'

   For example, 'The **horse-riders** of **Canterbury**'.

Criteria

Your list will be judged not just in terms of length but also the quality and originality of the responses.

The People Of Britain

Teaching Notes

Key Elements

- research into suitable places in Great Britain
- use of maps and atlases
- word play
- a sense of humour

Contexts

Here **The People Of Britain** has been included in the competitions section. It could be used in other ways:

- differentiated homework
- a normal but unusual piece of classwork
- as an enrichment item for those who have finished other work
- as part of an enrichment activity
- as an activity for the Geography Club or Society.

Judging

The number of entries does have to be taken into consideration, clearly, but many could be of poor quality. Success can only be judged upon a combination of quantity and quality but there is no exact formula to determine the relative importance.

Snakes And Races, Squares And Quotients

Mathematics covers many diverse areas including opportunities to use your imagination and have fun.

Here is a chance for you to be creative mathematically. You are encouraged to use a variety of mathematical ideas and language in an enjoyable context.

Board games were popular many years ago, and, after a decline, they are again gaining popularity. One standard format is to have a number of spaces arranged in a circle, a square or a rectangle over which the players have to move, encountering hazards and rewards along the way. These spaces are numbered consecutively. This is where the 'Snakes And Races' comes in.

What You Have To Do

Draw out a board containing 100 spaces in whatever shape you wish. Arrange these spaces in such a way that there is a clear route from 1 to 100.

Do not number the spaces as usual. Instead, use mathematical definitions, instructions and ideas to produce the numbers 1 to 100 in correct order.

Some can include calculations but try to use as many different themes as possible. Keep the number of 'straight sums' to a minimum as this is an easy but rather unimaginative way of labelling the spaces.

You can include shapes, cubes, square roots, equations, fractions, formulae, definitions, mathematical terms, alternative number systems and a host of other ideas. Remember that you are trying to make your board as mathematically varied as possible. This is why 'Squares And Quotients' is also part of the title.

Try to be creative and imaginative. Do not repeat yourself any more than you can help.

NOTE
- You may find it useful to consult a mathematical dictionary.

SNAKES AND RACES, SQUARES AND QUOTIENTS

Teaching Notes

Key Elements

- mathematical language
- a variety of mathematical operations
- shape
- open-endedness
- going across the mathematics curriculum all at the same time
- design features

Contexts

This mathematical item has been set as a competition but it can be used in other ways:

- as normal but unusual classwork
- as normal but unusual homework
- as enrichment work for pupils well ahead of others
- as differentiated homework
- as part of an enrichment session
- as an activity for the Mathematics or Pythagoras Club.

Practical Points

The teacher has to decide how much introduction is needed for different pupils. Too much guidance at the start is likely to pre-condition children's ideas so that they do not think sufficiently for themselves. Too little advice might result in rather dull, repetitive answers that do not range far and wide enough. The teacher may feel it is worthwhile to do some preliminary work on mathematical language and operations.

The exercise can be undertaken by children of different ages but the level of sophistication and knowledge in the answers will obviously vary. For younger children the board could be restricted to far fewer spaces.

The open-ended nature of the work should produce interesting, varied and unpredictable results. One of the main tasks of the teacher is to encourage the attitude of mind that will lead to creative and imaginative responses.

Extension

A possible extension of this exercise is to create a game to utilise the board that has been produced.

The Millennium Sampler Competition

People in many walks of life celebrated the millennium in a variety of ways. Those who enjoy embroidery were able to purchase so-called 'millennium samplers' where a number of scenes were depicted to represent the most important events and developments in contrasting areas – exploration, medicine, science, and so on – over the previous 1000 years. Not surprisingly, this led to lively discussion about what should have been included in the limited number of spaces.

What You Have To Do

Draw up a five-by-five square chart and indicate in the 25 spaces the people and events that *you* consider most deserve inclusion on a millennium sampler. Complete your entry by a written statement supporting your choices.

You can choose from three possible versions:

- ▲ British
- ▲ European
- ▲ World.

Of course, even if you go for the World version, you can still include British and European entries.

Criteria

Evaluating choices will be difficult as a degree of subjectivity is inevitable. However the following criteria will be taken into account:

1. the suitable coverage of various facets of human endeavour
2. the sensible use of such a limited number of spaces
3. the quality of the written statement to support the choices in the suggested millennium sampler.

The Millennium Sampler Competition

Teaching Notes

Contexts

This item has been set as a competition but **The Millennium Sampler Competition** could be used in a variety of ways:

- as the basis for classroom discussion
- as the basis for a formal debate
- as a piece of enrichment work for pupils well ahead
- as an extension piece leading on from consideration of significant moments
- as part of an enrichment activity
- as differentiated homework
- as an activity for the History Club or Society.

Practical Points

1. If used as a school competition, entry details including target audience, closing date and so on need to be added.

2. The chart can be produced in a number of ways from simply writing in entries, to producing an individually illustrated sheet, to insisting on the use of computer graphics.

3. The teacher can restrict or extend the versions on offer to fit with other objectives; for example, African, American, musical, technological and so on.

4. Judging in competition terms is bound to be subjective but the suggested criteria on the pupil sheet (page 265) define important areas. These can of course be added to or changed depending upon the particular aims the teacher has in mind.

5. The teacher may wish to demonstrate a particular set of choices to 'get the discussion going' or to give a starting point.

Horse Sense

Racehorses are named in a number of ways. Some are called after famous people or places. Others are given a name that results from the names of the sire and dam – their parents. Thus, the famous 'Golden Miller' had parents called 'Miller's Pride' and 'Goldcourt'. Currently there is a horse in training called 'Chief Mouse' where the sire and dam are 'Be My Chief' and 'Top Mouse'. Naming horses in this way involves a particular form of word play.

See if you can use 'horse sense' to complete both tasks in this competition.

Task One

Below are 36 names of horses. Sort them into twelve groups of three such that each group represents firstly the two parents and secondly the 'neatly-named' foal. Each of the 36 must be used once. Most have cryptic solutions.

1	Blue Riband	13	Dress Sense	25	Burned Toast
2	Ocean Blue	14	Gone To Sea	26	Sailing Away
3	Beanstalk	15	Demonstrate	27	Celebration Blues
4	Variety Show	16	Air Commander	28	Breakfast Time
5	Red Coral	17	Alphabet	29	Everlasting Wood
6	Grass Snake	18	Pine Lodge	30	Confidential
7	Tight Lines	19	Birthday Girl	31	Monarchy
8	Ball Gown	20	Fitting The Occasion	32	The Vicar
9	Spice Of Life	21	The Summit	33	Sea Serpent
10	Staying Power	22	Parson's Reef	34	Flying Orders
11	Top Secret	23	Jobs Of The Day	35	Jack's Adventure
12	Plant Growth	24	Kingfisher	36	Diversion

Task Two

For each of the 10 pairs of parents' names below, give your suggestion for an appropriately-named foal.

a	The Queen Of Hearts	Bank Loan
b	One, Two Three, Go	The Shepherd
c	Crimson Lake	Will Scarlet
d	Mount Everest	Seven Days
e	Toy Cupboard	Small World
f	Honeypot	Catchy Tune
g	Sunny Day	Sharp Showers
h	Going Down	Mad March
i	A Spoonful Of Sugar	Flying High
j	Ajar	Golden Opportunity

Criteria

The winner will be the person who not only sorts out Task One in a logical manner but who also devises imaginative and creative responses to Task Two.

Horse Sense

Teaching Notes

This piece has been included in the competition section but it could be used as classwork or homework for English or Literacy. The word play involved answers a phrase from the new National Curriculum document: *'how language is used in imaginative, original and diverse ways'*. If used as a competition, **Horse Sense** needs details adding in terms of target group, dates and so on.

Possible Solutions

TASK ONE

1	Blue Riband	+	19	Birthday Girl	→	27	Celebration Blues
10	Staying Power	+	18	Pine Lodge	→	29	Everlasting Wood
21	The Summit	+	30	Confidential	→	11	Top Secret
6	Grass Snake	+	2	Ocean Blue	→	33	Sea Serpent
5	Red Coral	+	32	The Vicar	→	22	Parson's Reef
16	Air Commander	+	23	Jobs of the Day	→	34	Flying Orders
35	Jack's Adventure	+	12	Plant Growth	→	3	Beanstalk
28	Breakfast Time	+	36	Diversion	→	25	Burned Toast
31	Monarchy	+	7	Tight Lines	→	24	Kingfisher
8	Ball Gown	+	20	Fitting The Occasion	→	13	Dress Sense
17	Alphabet	+	26	Sailing Away	→	14	Gone To Sea
9	Spice Of Life	+	15	Demonstrate	→	4	Variety Show

NOTES

- This combination uses all 36 names appropriately. Individual variations are possible, even to fitting all 36 horses. Which are the parents and which the foals may also be a debating point.
- Pupils may use different working methods, including writing the names on 36 separate slips. Let them make their own minds up.

TASK TWO

One or two possibilities only are given. Many more good answers will be suggested.

a	The Queen Of Hearts + Bank Loan	→	Credit Card/In The Red
b	One, Two, Three, Go + The Shepherd	→	Counting Sheep
c	Crimson Lake + Will Scarlet	→	Shades Of Red
d	Mount Everest + Seven Days	→	High Time/A Week At The Top
e	Toy Cupboard + Small World	→	Doll's House
f	Honeypot + Catchy Tune	→	Sweet Melody
g	Sunny Day + Sharp Showers	→	Rainbow/Weather Forecast
h	Going Down + Mad March	→	Haircut
i	A Spoonful Of Sugar + Flying High	→	Bird Table/Mary Poppins
j	Ajar + Golden Opportunity	→	Open Door

Also available from Network Educational Press

Effective Resources for Able and Talented Children **by Barry Teare**
- Contains a wealth of practical photocopiable activities designed to inspire, motivate, challenge and stretch able children in both the Primary and Secondary sectors, encouraging them to enjoy their true potential.
- Resources are organised into National Curriculum areas, such as Literacy, Science and Humanities, each preceded by a commentary outlining key principles and giving general guidance for teachers.

Imagine That... **by Stephen Bowkett**
- Hands-on, user-friendly manual for stimulating creative thinking, talking and writing in the classroom.
- Provides over 100 practical and immediately useable classroom activities and games that can be used in isolation, or in combination, to help meet the requirements and standards of the National Curriculum.

Self-Intelligence **by Stephen Bowkett**
- Helps explore and develop emotional resourcefulness in teachers and their pupils.
- Aims to help teachers and pupils develop the high-esteem that underpins success in education.

School Effectiveness Series

Series Editor: Professor Tim Brighouse

The School Effectiveness Series focuses on issues of whole-school improvement through enhanced teaching and learning, and offers straightforward, practical solutions that can make life more rewarding both for teachers and for those they teach.

Book 1: *Accelerated Learning in the Classroom* **by Alistair Smith**
- The first book in the UK to apply new knowledge about the brain to classroom practice.
- Offers practical solutions on improving performance, motivation and understanding.

Book 2: *Effective Learning Activities* **by Chris Dickinson**
- An essential teaching guide, which focuses on practical activities to improve learning, raise achievement, deepen understanding, promote self-esteem and improve motivation.
- Includes activities suitable for GCSE, National Curriculum, Highers, GSVQ and GNVQ, designed to promote differentiation and understanding.

Book 3: *Effective Heads of Department* **by Phil Jones and Nick Sparks**
- Contains a range of practical systems and approaches, designed to develop practice in line with OFSTED expectations and DfEE thinking by monitoring and improving quality.
- Addresses issues such as managing resources, leadership, learning, departmental planning and making assessment valuable.

Book 4: *Lessons are for Learning* **by Mike Hughes**
- Brings together the theory of learning with the realities of the classroom environment.
- Offers practical suggestions for activities that bridge the gap between recent developments in the theory of learning and the constraints in classroom teaching.

Book 5: *Effective Learning in Science* **by Paul Denley and Keith Bishop**
- Encourages discussion about the aims and purposes in teaching science and the role of subject knowledge in effective teaching.
- Tackles issues such as planning for effective learning, the use of resources and other relevant management issues.

Book 6: Raising Boys' Achievement by Jon Pickering
- Addresses the causes of boys' under-achievement and offers practical, 'real' solutions, along with tried-and-tested training suggestions.
- Looks at examples of good practice in schools to help guide the planning and implementation of strategies to raise achievement.

Book 7: *Effective Provision for Able and Talented Children* **by Barry Teare**
- Describes methods of identifying the able and talented, addresses concerns about achievement, and suggests appropriate strategies to raise achievement.
- Suggests practical enrichment activities and appropriate resources.

Book 8: *Effective Careers Education and Guidance* **by Andrew Edwards and Anthony Barnes**
- Discusses the strategic planning of the careers programme as part of the wider curriculum and aspects of guidance and counselling involved in helping students to understand their own capabilities and form career plans.
- Provides practical activities for reflection and personal learning, and describes case studies where such activities have been used.

Book 9: *Best behaviour* **by Peter Relf, Rod Hirst, Jan Richardson and Georgina Youdell**
- Provides support for teachers and managers who seek starting points for effective behaviour management.
- Focuses on practical and useful ideas for individual schools and teachers.

Best behaviour FIRST AID (pack of 5 booklets) **by Peter Relf, Rod Hirst, Jan Richardson and Georgina Youdell**
- Provides strategies to cope with aggression, defiance and disturbance
- Suggests straightforward action points for self-esteem.

Book 10: *The Effective School Governor* **(including audio tape) by David Marriott**
- Straightforward guidance and practical support on how to fulfil a governor's role and responsibilities.
- Develops your personal effectiveness as an individual governor.

Book 11: *Improving Personal Effectiveness for Managers in Schools* **by James Johnson**
- An invaluable resource for new and experienced teachers, in both Primary and Secondary schools, containing practical strategies for improving leadership and management skills.
- Focuses on self-management skills, managing difficult situations, working under pressure, developing confidence, creating a team ethos and communicating effectively.

Book 12: *Making Pupil Data Powerful* **by Maggie Pringle and Tony Cobb**
- Shows teachers in Primary, Middle and Secondary schools how to interpret pupils' performance data and how to use it to enhance teaching and learning.
- Provides practical advice on analysing performance and learning behaviours, measuring progress, predicting future attainment, setting targets and ensuring continuity and progression.

Book 13: *Closing the Learning Gap* **by Mike Hughes**
- Helps teachers, departments and schools to close the 'learning gap' between what we know about effective learning and what actually goes on in the classroom.
- Encourages teachers to reflect on the ways in which they teach, and to identify and implement strategies for improving their practice.

Book 14: *Getting Started* **by Henry Leibling**
- Provides invaluable advice for Newly Qualified Teachers (NQTs) during the three-term induction period that comprises their first year of teaching.
- Advice includes strategies on how to get to know the school and the new pupils, how to work with induction tutors, and when to ask for help.

Book 15: *Leading the Learning School* **by Colin Weatherley**
- Shows how effective leadership of true 'learning schools' involves applying the principles of learning to all levels of educational management and development planning.
- Describes thirteen key principles of learning, derived from up-to-the-minute research on how our brains learn, and explains how the American Critical Skills Programme has incorporated these key principles into a comprehensive, practical and outstandingly effective teaching programme.

Book 16: *Adventures in Learning* **by Mike Tilling**
- Offers a framework in which the intuitions of individual teachers have been synthesised into a broader understanding of how learning happens.
- Uses the metaphorical notion of the Learner's Journey, to discuss how learning happens over time.

Book 17: *Strategies for Closing the Learning Gap* **by Mikes Hughes with Andy Vass**
- Highlights and simplifies key issues emerging from the latest discoveries about how the human brain learns.
- Offers proven, practical strategies and suggestions as to how to apply this new research in the classroom, to improve students' learning and help them achieve their full potential.

Book 18: *Classroom Management* **by Philip Waterhouse and Chris Dickinson**
- Classic best-selling text by Philip Waterhouse, set in the current context by Chris Dickinson, which is full of practical ideas to help teachers find ways of integrating Key Skills and Thinking Skills into an already overcrowded curriculum.
- Covers topics including whole-class presentation, dialogue and interactive teaching; teacher-led small group work; classroom layout; interpersonal relationships in the classroom; and collaborative teamwork.

Accelerated Learning Series
General Editor: Alistair Smith

Accelerated Learning in Practice **by Alistair Smith**
- Structured to help readers access and retain the information necessary to begin to accelerate their own learning and that of the students they teach.
- Includes over 100 learning tools, case studies from 36 schools, nine principles of learning based on Nobel Prize winning brain research, and the author's seven-stage Accelerated Learning Cycle.

The ALPS Approach: Accelerated Learning in Primary Schools **by Alistair Smith and Nicola Call**
- Professional, practical and exhilarating resource that gives readers the opportunity to develop the ALPS approach for themselves and for the children in their care.
- Provides practical and accessible examples of strategies used by highly experienced Primary teacher Nicola Call, at a school where the SATs results shot up as a consequence.

MapWise **by Oliver Caviglioli and Ian Harris**
- Provides informed access to the most powerful accelerated learning technique around – Model Mapping.
- Shows how mapping can be used to address National Curriculum thinking skills requirements for students of any preferred learning style by infusing thinking into subject teaching.

The ALPS Resource Book **by Alistair Smith and Nicola Call**
- Follow-up to the authors' best-selling book *The ALPS Approach*, structured carefully to extend the theoretical and practical advice given in that publication.
- Provides a wealth of photocopiable, 'hands-on' resources for teachers to use in, and outside, the classroom.

Education Personnel Management Series

These new Education Personnel management handbooks will help headteachers, senior managers and governors to manage a broad range of personnel issues.

- *The Well Teacher – management strategies for beating stress, promoting staff health and reducing absence* by Maureen Cooper
- *Managing Challenging People – dealing with staff conduct* by Bev Curtis and Maureen Cooper
- *Managing Poor Performance – handling staff capability issues* by Bev Curtis and Maureen Cooper
- *Managing Allegations Against Staff – personnel and child protection issues in schools* by Maureen Cooper
- *Managing Recruitment and Selection – appointing the best staff* by Maureen Cooper and Bev Curtis
- *Managing Redundancies – dealing with reduction and reorganisation of staff* by Maureen Cooper and Bev Curtis

Vision of Education Series

The Unfinished Revolution by John Abbott and Terry Ryan

- Draws on evidence from the past to show how shifting attitudes in society and politics have shaped Western education systems.
- Describes a vision of an education system based on current research into how our brains work, and designed to encourage the autonomous and inventive thinkers and learners that the 21st century demands.

The Literacy Collection

Helping With Reading by Anne Butterworth and Angela White

- Provides clear, practical and easily implemented activities that directly relate to the National Curriculum and 'Literacy Hour' group work, including sections on 'Hearing Children Read', 'Word Recognition' and 'Phonics'. Ideas and activities can also be incorporated into Individual Education Plans.

Class Talk by Rosemary Sage

- Looks at teacher–student communication and reflects on what is happening in the classroom.
- Discusses and reflects on practical strategies to improve the quality of talking, teaching and learning.